DATE DUE

Adult Supervision Required

Families in Focus

Series Editors

Anita Ilta Garey, University of Connecticut
Naomi R. Gerstel, University of Massachusetts, Amherst
Karen V. Hansen, Brandeis University
Rosanna Hertz, Wellesley College
Margaret K. Nelson, Middlebury College

Anita Ilta Garey and Karen V. Hansen, eds., *At the Heart of Work and Family: Engaging the Ideas of Arlie Hochschild*

Adult Supervision Required

Private Freedom and Public Constraints for Parents and Children

Markella B. Rutherford

Rutgers University Press
New Brunswick, New Jersey, and London

LIBRARY OF CONGRESS CATALOGING-IN-PUBLICATION DATA

Rutherford, Markella B., 1973–
    Adult supervision required : private freedom and public constraints for parents and children / Markella B. Rutherford.
        p. cm. — (Families in focus)
    Includes bibliographical references and index.
    ISBN 978-0-8135-5149-4 (hardcover : alk. paper)
    1. Parenting—Social aspects—United States.   2. Child rearing—United States.   3. Parent and child—United States.   4. Mass media and families—United States.   I. Title.
    HQ755.8.R88   2011
    649'.109730904—dc22

                                                            2011001041

A British Cataloging-in-Publication record for this book is available from the British Library.

Visit our Web site: http://rutgerspress.rutgers.edu

Manufactured in the United States of America

For Jason, Annabelle, and Daniel

CONTENTS

ACKNOWLEDGMENTS

I AM GRATEFUL FOR THE MANY FRIENDS, colleagues, family members, and students who expressed an interest in my ideas and encouraged me in this work during the past few years. First and foremost, I thank all the parents who allowed me to interview them and who so generously shared with me their perspectives on the struggles and triumphs of parenting. Liz Hart transcribed the interviews and shared her own experiences with parenting, as well.

Financial support for this project was provided by Wellesley College's awards for faculty scholarship. Because of Wellesley's financial support, I was privileged to have the assistance of several undergraduate students at various points in this process. I especially thank Sanja Jagesic, Rebekah Rosenfeld, Danielle Boudrow, and Katy Walline for their capable assistance and good cheer. I received both financial and intellectual support for this work from the Newhouse Center for the Humanities at Wellesley College. My cohort of Newhouse fellows provided an engaging and stimulating interdisciplinary backdrop for thinking through this project. It was an honor to share ideas with Margaret Burnham, John Carson, Cathleen Cummings, Lidwien Kapteijns, Tim Peltason, Carol Oja, Maria San Filippo, Bryan Turner, Daniel Ussishkin, Heidi Voskuhl, and Ellen Widmer. In particular, my heartfelt thanks go to Ann Velenchik and Vini Datta for careful attention to my half-formed ideas and for providing much-needed moral support and reassurance that the pieces would come together in their own time. I am grateful to my colleagues in the sociology department—Lee Cuba, Tom Cushman, Jonathan Imber, Peggy Levitt, Smitha Radhakrishnan, and Joe Swingle—for their support and especially for stepping in to help when I experienced a sudden illness at the end of the project. Without their help covering classes, meeting with students, and even providing dinner for my family, I could not have finished revisions on time while I was recovering from surgery. Thanks are also due a million times over to Adriana Mihal, who makes my life easier in countless ways. Others at Wellesley who have served as key reminders to me that the scholar's life need not be solitary include Donna Patterson, Sally Theran, Don Elmore, Barbara Beatty, Ken Hawes, and Nancy Genero.

I am indebted to all those who offered helpful comments and feedback on earlier versions of my research and this manuscript. This is a better work because of the responses and suggestions I received from Barbara Beatty, Garry Breland, Mary Beth Breland, Tom Cushman, Anita Garey, Julia Grant, Ken Hawes, Rosanna Hertz, Jonathan Imber, Annette Lareau, Peter Mickulas, Murray Milner, Peggy Nelson, Jason Rutherford, Felicia Song, Bryan Turner, and Marlie Wasserman. I am especially grateful to the editors at Rutgers University Press, the series editors who shepherded this work, and copy editor Lisa Jerry for her careful attention to detail. Any remaining errors, of course, are my own.

Parts of this argument were previously published in December 2009 in *Qualitative Sociology*. They are used here with permission.

Finally, I could not have completed this book without the inspiration and support of my family. My own parents taught me most of what I know about good parenting. My extraordinary children, Annabelle and Daniel, are teaching me the rest. Although they deserve a mother who spends more time doing parenting than writing about parenting, they have never complained about the mother they have. I am proud of the many ways they contribute to our family and community, and I hope that what I have learned in this process will benefit them as they continue to grow into responsible and independent members of our society. My husband, Jason, has my undying admiration and utmost appreciation for cheerfully doing the thankless chores, for patiently nurturing our kids, for encouraging me to believe in my ideas, and for sustaining me with his unfailing love.

Adult Supervision Required

Introduction

IT'S A COOL AND RAINY SUMMER MORNING, and I'm
sitting in Michelle's living room with Michelle and Nadine, while their
children are having a play date.[1] Their seven-, five-, and four-year olds
are upstairs in a bedroom playing a game, and a toddler, playing with the
toys scattered around the living room, is especially fascinated by several
that make electronic noises. A younger baby is napping in the next room.
Michelle and Nadine are hoping that the weather will clear up before
lunch so that they can all go for a picnic and swim at the beach. In the
meantime, they've agreed to talk to me about parenting. Both women
are white, middle-class, stay-at-home moms, and parenting is a topic
with which they are obviously comfortable and discuss regularly with
each other, as they allude frequently to other discussions they've had.
I ask a few questions, but mostly I sit and listen to their conversation.

Eventually—inevitably—the conversation about parenting turns
toward rules. Speaking of *other* parents, Michelle says: "I feel like people
kind of let kids go. I see it just in terms of the way people behave with
their children in public places and the things they expect of them there.
I kind of translate that to what must happen at home, if that is what they
are allowing in other places." When I ask what kinds of behavior she has
in mind, she describes two very different scenarios. First, she speaks
generally about parents who watch their kids make a mess and do not
make them pick up afterward. Next, she describes a specific incident in
which she observed children climbing on a second-story railing at a
museum; she felt the activity was dangerous and insisted that she would
never allow her own children to do that sort of thing. At that point,
Nadine, jumping into the conversation, says: "We actually have something that comes out of my mouth all the time—too often for my own
liking. 'I am sorry, different rules for different families. Sorry.' [My daughter]

will see children doing things in restaurants or she will see children doing things that are inappropriate for public places. 'But so and so was doing it.' I cannot explain it any other way. We don't do that." After explaining her oft-used phrase, "different rules for different families," Nadine goes on to say: "We don't all have to live by the same rules, but I think there are some basic things."

This is a book about the cultural messages American moms and dads encounter about parenting, especially regarding such decisions as setting rules, establishing boundaries, and encouraging children's independence. It is a book about supervision, freedom, and constraints for both parents and children. Throughout the course of the twentieth century, there were important changes in our cultural understandings of authority and autonomy. In this book, I explore how these changes are reflected in popular depictions of the relationship between parents and children by analyzing the advice given to parents in popular magazines between 1910 and 2009.

Parenting advice is an intriguing place to look at how freedom and constraints are understood and shaped for both adults and children. The very nature of the parent-child relationship raises constant questions of dependence, independence, and interdependence, and the balance between these is perpetually shifting and changing. Anyone who has children knows full well that children's ability and right to make their own choices is a site of constant negotiation. Not only do parents find it challenging to set firm boundaries, but some choices and actions disallowed today may be renegotiated next month or next year because children grow up—and, typically, a growing measure of autonomy is an integral part of what growing up means.

To the extent that childhood is understood as a formative period of socialization, parenting is culturally constructed as important for shaping children to become independent, productive members of society. Furthermore, socialization does not end after childhood. Parents, too, undergo a process of socialization in which they are supervised, and their own autonomy as parents is negotiated in their relationships with others, such as extended family, local communities, expert systems, popular media, commercial entities, and the state. Thus, in making decisions about what they will permit for their children—through either explicit rules or more implicit patterns of parenting behavior—parents are often aware that their own freedom has limits.

DIFFERENT RULES FOR DIFFERENT FAMILIES

The establishment, negotiation, bending, and defending of "different rules for different families" is necessary in the twenty-first century because the growing diversity of American families means that one-size-fits-all prescriptions and models for childrearing have become outdated. In general, today's parents feel freer than past generations to experiment with a variety of parenting practices and to individualize their practices to suit their particular family's social location and lifestyle.[2] Greater cultural diversity, the normalization of dual-earner parenting, and the increasing social acceptance of family forms other than the two-parent nuclear family have resulted in advice to parents to tailor childrearing to their individual circumstances and values, rather than expecting a single, shared model of parenting to work for all families. In Nadine's words, "we don't all have to live by the same rules." In some ways, parents have gained more freedom to select from and experiment with varied styles of family structure and childrearing techniques. There is much to celebrate in this greater acceptance of diverse and varied family styles. Women, especially, have been the beneficiaries of expanded opportunities for equal treatment and self-fulfillment as their roles within families have become less narrowly prescribed.

However, the lack of an overarching cultural model for parenting means that parents seeking advice receive many conflicting and ambiguous messages about social expectations for childrearing. Within a culture that idealizes, even sanctifies, notions of individual autonomy and choice,[3] American parents today must weigh questions of freedom and boundaries on two distinct fronts: they must navigate questions of both how much autonomy they themselves have as parents in making childrearing decisions and how to balance their authority as parents with children's autonomy. In other words, parents grapple with issues of freedom and boundaries in trying to both be the right kind of parents and form the right kind of child. Parents turn to many sources of information when making these parenting decisions, including family members, friends, neighbors, doctors, teachers, counselors, and other parents, as well as broadcast media, online communities, childrearing advice books, and parenting magazines. Given the exponential increase in the sheer amount of parenting information and advice, it is challenging for parents to discern and agree about the "basic things" to which Nadine alluded.

To chart a course in an age of competing and contradictory models, parents must continually make individual decisions about parenting. Although many experts acknowledge that parents must tailor their practices to their own children and situation, they still often provide highly specific prescriptions. Thus parents are caught on the horns of dilemmas such as whether to "Ferberize" their infants (that is, insist that they sleep alone) or to embrace the family bed. They are told that it is vital to build and protect their children's self-esteem, but they are also cautioned against giving kids an overinflated sense of self-importance. They are advised that they must boost their children's chances of long-term success with rigorous academics and structured enrichment activities but also that kids need ample free time for imaginative play and creativity. Advocates for "helicopter parenting" and "free-range kids" are equally loud and insistent. While many parents are glad to have varied options and styles to choose from, they sometimes feel anxious about their ability to discern which option is right for them and their children.

In constructing their own models of family life and childrearing, many parents feel a lack of societal support for the everyday work of parenting. With increased geographic mobility, urbanization and sub-urbanization, the disappearance of neighborhood schools, and declining participation in religious communities, parents today may feel as though they are lacking community involvement in and support for child-rearing. Compared to past generations, fewer parents today are aided by the active involvement and participation of informal, community-level networks of concerned adults in their children's socialization. However, even though parents often feel isolated, many also feel a pervasive sense of social scrutiny. They are often keenly aware of the pressures presented by diffuse cultural expectations for parents, and they frequently engage in direct comparisons between themselves and other parents. State and government agencies are more involved than ever before in this social scrutiny of parents: parents today are subject to an ever-increasing number of legal constraints that dictate the acceptable boundaries of child protection and discipline. Thus, parenting practices have become increasingly reliant on the individualized and privatized authority of parents at home at the same time that they are circumscribed by the authority of the state and the publicly institutionalized knowledge of child development experts. In sociological terms, the weakened influence of civil society, combined with increased state supervision and intervention, results in a bifurcation of authority between the macrosociological institution of the state and the microsociological institution of the individual nuclear family.

Examining Advice

In this book, I analyze the public portrayal of the parent-child relationship by examining the advice given to parents in popular magazines and the concerns of parents who encounter and interpret various forms of parenting advice. The study includes qualitative and historical-comparative content analysis of parenting advice in popular magazines, in-depth interviews with parents and other informants, and observation at parent support group meetings.

For the textual content analysis, I systematically sampled 565 articles and advice columns about childrearing that appeared in popular magazines between 1910 and 2009.[4] Several recent histories have documented the growing reliance upon expert advice and the role of childrearing manuals during the nineteenth and twentieth centuries.[5] In this study I turn to popular magazines, rather than book-length childrearing manuals, for several reasons. First, because magazines publish articles by a wide variety of authors, they portray the prevailing contours of cultural attitudes toward children and parenting in a way that is not dependent upon the dominant personalities of the relatively few childrearing experts who cornered the market on parenting advice for much of the twentieth-century. Second, magazines have historically reached a wider, more ethnically diverse and less class-bound audience than books. Literary scholar Nancy Walker, for example, found that, although the advertising in mid-twentieth-century women's magazines almost uniformly depicted white, middle-class families, the content of the magazines assumed a more socioeconomically and racially diverse readership.[6] In the early twentieth century, magazines were important sources of information for populations who had more limited access to books. Historian Julia Grant reports that a 1930 study found

79.4 percent of white parents of the highest socioeconomic status had read at least one book on child rearing in the previous year, in contrast to 26.7 percent of parents from the lowest socioeconomic group. Among African-American parents, 71 percent from the higher socioeconomic group had read at least one book on child rearing and 46.1 percent from the lower group (interestingly, a higher percentage than among lower-class whites). More members of all groups read newspaper and magazine articles on child rearing than read books, however, with 88.2 percent of the white population and 78.1 percent of the African-American population claiming to have read at least one article.[7]

Therefore, magazines have played an important historical role in disseminating and popularizing academic research and scientific knowledge about children and childrearing. Third, magazines have served as a forum in which medical and academic advice mingles with the lay advice proffered by parents and readers. It is important to remember that the lay advice included in magazines is ultimately subject to editorial control and therefore may not be representative of all readers' opinions. However, the inclusion of readers' letters, tips, and suggestions, as well as the incorporation of articles written by parents, means that magazines offer a better sense of the interaction between expert advice and lay opinion than manuals written solely by professional childrearing experts.

Although magazine articles and advice columns cannot tell us what parents actually believe or do in their everyday childrearing practices, they do reflect general trends over time in widely recognized cultural ideals of family life and parenting and may even help to shape cultural changes from one generation to the next.[8] That is, parenting advice reflects cultural values, even if it sometimes distorts cultural reality. According to Eva Illouz, a noted scholar of popular culture, the importance of advice literature has been insufficiently acknowledged. As she writes, "much of contemporary cultural material comes to us in the form of advice, admonition, and how-to recipes, and given that in many social sites the modern self is self-made—drawing upon various cultural repertoires to decide on a course of action—advice literature is likely to have played an important role in shaping the vocabularies through which the self understands itself."[9]

To situate popular advice texts within a context of contemporary parents' actual childrearing concerns, exposure to advice, and use of childrearing advice, I conducted intensive, open-ended interviews with thirty parents.[10] These interview respondents are not a representative sample of the American population of parents, but they do include parents who represent a variety of perspectives on parenting, including mothers and fathers, middle- and working-class parents, stay-at-home mothers and those who are employed outside the home, and parents from different racial and ethnic groups.[11] In addition to one-on-one parent interviews, I also observed several meetings of two parents' support groups in which the parents have primary-school aged children and conducted twelve additional interviews with a variety of professionals who work with children and families, including teachers, social workers, preschool and after-school program directors, and therapists.

SOCIOLOGICAL UNDERSTANDINGS OF FREEDOM AND CONSTRAINT

This study of how freedom and constraint are depicted in popular parenting advice is grounded in a sociological concern about contemporary expressions of authority, autonomy, and agency. Fundamentally, authority refers to the ability to impose one's will on others: to give commands and to have those commands carried out. Autonomy refers to the ability to exercise one's own free will and to be controlled by self rather than controlled by another. Since its beginnings, the discipline of sociology has taken questions about the nature of authority and autonomy as some of its core concerns. The nature of freedom and constraint were among the key conceptual issues addressed by European scholars in the nineteenth and early twentieth centuries as they sought to understand the massive social changes that marked the emergence of the modern era— for example, the industrial revolution, rapid urbanization, declining religious authority, and the rise of democratic forms of government. Max Weber outlined different forms of authority and theorized why they are regarded as legitimate and obeyed.[12] Ferdinand Tönnies and Georg Simmel examined which societal conditions allow for the greatest expression of individuality and the exercise of free will.[13] Emile Durkheim asked how social cooperation and solidarity could be sustained while allowing for the fullest development of the individual.[14] These questions about authority and autonomy are tied to the understandings of human nature, the nature of society, and the relationship between individuals and societies that undergird a great deal of the sociological perspective.

In contemporary sociological theory, questions of the relationship between individuals and societies have often been conceptualized through debates about *structure* and *agency*. Social structures refer to those aspects of social life that are patterned, durable, and confront individuals as external realities; these include culture, social institutions, and patterns of social stratification. To recognize social structure is to apprehend that both the conditions of our social existence and the strategies available for responding within those conditions are not entirely of our own making. Agency, in an essentialist sense, refers to the human capacity for meaningful action; to acknowledge agency is to assert that human behavior is not strictly predetermined and that social realities are created, recreated, and transformed by human action. Of course, both social structure and agency are necessary for any adequate sociological account, but sociologists differ in the extent to which they regard human individuals as either shaped by social structures or acting with intention to change social reality. Although some strains of sociological theorizing have implicitly associated social structure with boundaries and agency with freedom, it is important to remember that social structures enable as well as constrain.[15] Likewise, although some free range of choice represents a key component of how agency is conceptualized, actions need not transform the world anew in order to entail agency: even highly habituated actions can be conceived of as entailing agency when we consider that the individual could have chosen to behave otherwise.[16]

The fact that individuals have agency is a fundamental assumption of contemporary Western culture. In a constructivist sense, however, we can treat agency as a property that may, or may not, be ascribed to different categories of individuals.[17] By conceptualizing agency from a constructivist stance, we are able to ask empirical questions about the degree to which parents and children have historically been ascribed agency and the ways in which their autonomy and agency have been understood and experienced. Parenting advice is a cultural product that offers clues to the ideas, values, and norms that work alongside institutional arrangements to structure parenting. The very nature of advice is such that parents are expected to interpret the advice and choose a course of action, ultimately rejecting, adapting, or implementing the advice in their actions; thus, advice-givers typically ascribe some measure of agency to advice-recipients. As I show, however, the degree to which these cultural texts point toward cultural assumptions of autonomy and agency for parents varies over time and across contexts.

Similarly, the degree to which children are culturally depicted in advice as having autonomy varies. Until recently, in fact, children were conceptualized by sociological theory as the objects of socialization in such a way that their agency as social actors was largely denied. As a result, children were all but ignored by sociology. Since the 1990s, a number of sociologists have begun intentionally carving out a subfield on the sociology of children and childhood and arguing for a new paradigm of research that takes children's agency seriously.[18] To study children's social relationships and the ways in which children actively construct their own social lives, much of the work done in this area is ethnographic and designed so as to make children active participants in the research process and the production of sociological data.[19] A few examples of this new paradigm in action include Barrie Thorne's ethnography of children's negotiation of gender through their play at school, William Corsaro's explorations of nursery school peer relationships, Marjorie Orellana's account of the ways that young immigrants contribute to their families and schools, and Allison Pugh's analysis of the meanings children construct from consumer culture.[20] In psychological research on socialization, there has been a similar move toward regarding children as agents in a bilateral model of socialization in which parents and children engage in a relationship of interdependence and causality is bidirectional.[21]

Although my research makes inquiries about childhood through popular media representations that are produced and consumed by adults, I incorporate the insights of the new paradigm in sociology of childhood by treating childhood as a social construction rather than a natural or biological process and by seeking to understand the ways by which children are culturally regarded not just as passive objects of socialization but as active agents. By focusing on children as competent social actors ("beings" instead of "becomings"), Allison James and Alan Prout argue that we might learn more about the perennial sociological problem of the relationship between structure and agency—that is, "the ways in which 'society' and 'social structure' shape social experience and are themselves produced and refashioned through the social action of members."[22] Indeed, the parents and educators I interviewed in the course of this study talked at length about the necessity of appropriate disciplinary structure and family routines in shaping children to be and become independent members of society. Thus the parent-child relationship forms a microcosm for thinking about the central and abiding sociological puzzle of structure and agency.

PRIVATE FREEDOMS AND PUBLIC CONSTRAINTS

Adult Supervision Required argues that there has been a historical trade-off between the private and public forms of autonomy experienced by parents and children in American culture. Both parenthood and childhood have increasingly been constructed around private freedoms at the same time that they have entailed growing public constraints. It is no coincidence that when the conversation I described at the beginning of this introduction turned toward rules, Michelle and Nadine immediately raised questions of appropriateness *at home* and *in public*. Like Michelle, we may attempt to "translate" between public and private behaviors, but the boundaries between the public and the private are shifting and contested terrain, even as these two spheres shape and create one another. While today's parents are striving to interpret conflicting advice from experts and create their own models of childrearing, they are often the most concerned about decisions regarding how to balance their own authority as parents against the desire to cultivate the right kinds of autonomy for their children. I contend that we need to consider the ways that our culture understands parents and children as inhabiting public and private social roles in order to better understand the various sites of negotiation over parents' authority and children's autonomy.

I first examine the public-private trade-off regarding the degree to which parents experience autonomy over childrearing decisions. Popular advice has contributed to two modern beliefs: parents must depend on expert knowledge, and many decisions about how to implement such knowledge presume individual responses. The weakening of older cultural models of family life and parenting as well as their growing autonomy vis-à-vis experts have given parents greater freedom to pursue their own self-fulfillment and to tailor their parenting practices to their particular needs and social location. With this privatization, though, parents have increasingly become regarded as an interest group that speaks for a relatively small segment of the population rather than as a group that fills a public role or acts in the interests of the society as a whole. At the same time, certain parenting decisions have become subject to increased supervision by the power of the state and child welfare agencies, introducing new public constraints on parental autonomy and authority.

A historical trade-off has also occurred in popular depictions of children's autonomy: ideals of children's autonomy have increasingly focused on private forms of self-expression, while public forms of autonomy for children have dramatically decreased. Parents have increasingly been encouraged to allow and foster children's independence in a variety of matters of daily life, and advice has increasingly emphasized children's autonomy over their own developmental needs and emotional expressions. However, both a decline of community-level solidarity and greater involvement of state agencies in child welfare have contributed to a heightened sense of children's vulnerability that constrains parents' decisions about how much public independence to allow their children and what kinds of responsibilities to expect of them. Therefore, contemporary standards of safety have resulted in parents keeping a much tighter leash on their children—restricting their freedom of movement, supervising them closely, providing structure to their activities, and intervening more in children's interactions with their peers.

The trade-off between public and private experiences of autonomy has been shaped foremost by a therapeutic cultural ethos that arose during the twentieth century and came into prominence after the 1960s. This therapeutic ethos grounds its understanding of personhood in psychological models of development and privileges emotional expression as a key form of personal freedom. The overwhelming focus on privatized and individualized freedom of emotional expression has tended to obscure cultural recognition of the public dimensions of both parenthood and childhood. The therapeutic ethos is primarily shaped by the cultural ascendancy of psychological knowledge, but it is also reinforced by its strong affinities with contemporary capitalism and other cultural changes that shape the social context of parenting and childhood.

Organization of the Book

In chapter 1, I first examine the relationship between parents and parenting experts and summarize the nature of advice-giving and advice-taking by examining the historical development of parents' autonomy and agency over childrearing decisions. Chapters 2 through 4 then explore twentieth-century depictions of children's autonomy in some primary situations about which advice is sought and given. Chapter 2 describes the growing emphasis on children's freedom at home as seen in advice about many daily activities of life and basic strategies of discipline—that is, topics such as getting children to eat, sleep, and behave appropriately. In chapters 3 and 4, I contrast children's autonomy in private with the growing constraints on children's experience of more public forms of autonomy. In chapter 3, I detail the increased demands to closely supervise children and limit their independent movements in public spaces. Chapter 4 examines contemporary ambivalence and mixed messages regarding children's opportunities for gaining and exhibiting meaningful social responsibility in the arenas of home, school, and community. Chapter 5 explains the source of these changes in the rise of a therapeutic ethos that has emphasized children's emotional well-being, self-esteem, and social competence and has privatized our cultural conceptions of self and agency. In the conclusion, I summarize the demographic, cultural, and economic changes during the twentieth century that shaped the trade-off between public and private autonomy for families and argue that the intensified privatization of the family as a social institution indicates a deeper cultural shift in the ways that we conceive of the self and its agency in the private and public arenas of social life.

CHAPTER 1

Take It with a Grain of Salt

How Parents Encounter Experts and Advice

Everybody wants to give you advice on the new baby. My advice to new moms when they have baby showers [is] "Listen, but take it with a grain of salt. Weed out what you want and what you don't want and go from there. Everything has to work for you and there is no formula that works the right way." —Jill

It is great to read and to have any other input, but you also have to do it yourself. . . . I mean, I think the pediatricians can obviously know a great amount about children but every child is different and they see a lot of different children as patients. They have an incredible amount of knowledge but they don't know what is always best for your child. —Doug

I make it up as I go along. I probably should read more but everybody says something different, . . . everything has its own philosophy. You really have to be able to trust your own instincts. Even when people are telling you different things, well it makes sense for me and my family. —Denise

During the twentieth century, parents relied heavily on professional advice for scientific knowledge about children and the best childrearing practices. A constant undercurrent of tension, however, regarded the scope of such professional authority. Although tension between professional authority and parental autonomy has been evident throughout the modern era, by the 1970s there was a subtle but noticeable shift in the balance as experts became less authoritative. In the earlier part of the century, professional advice-givers were more likely to be regarded (and position themselves) as *authorities* about childrearing, but by century's end it was more common for such professionals to be regarded (and position themselves) as *experts*. Both authorities and experts, sources of specialized scientific or technical knowledge, are recognized as legitimately sharing such information based on their education, training, accomplishments, or credentials. The difference between the two lies in neither the nature of their training nor the content of information presented but in the way that information is offered by the professional and regarded by the lay person. To regard those with specialized or technical knowledge as authorities means that one holds their prescriptions as having authority over the individual in the Weberian sense: the probability exists that commands will be obeyed.[1] Authorities offer not just opinions but legitimated commands that ought to be followed. The knowledge and advice of the expert is no less scientific and no less sought-after; contemporary expert advice, however, is more likely to be regarded as an individual (informed) opinion with less authority to dictate a right or correct way to parent.

Today's experts may describe a better way of parenting or may even opine upon the best way to parent, but they no longer tell readers how they *ought* or *must* rear their children. To use Zygmunt Bauman's terms, contemporary experts are more likely to be interpreters instead of legislators.[2] Legislators, Bauman explains, make "authoritative statements which arbitrate in controversies of opinions and which select those opinions which, having been selected, become correct and binding."[3] Interpreters, he contends, play a different role as intellectuals, translating statements between competing systems of expert knowledge. As Bauman points out, no clear line in the twentieth century divides these two types of intellectuals; both types can be intermixed, just as modern and postmodern orientations coexist. The tone of parenting advice offered in popular magazines clearly and discernibly shifted the balance between authorities and experts beginning in the 1970s; thus, parents have gained considerable autonomy over many parenting decisions that were once governed more substantially by widespread cultural norms. As illustrated by the epigraphs, the parents I interviewed all professed that there is no one right way to parent and that they follow their intuitions in discerning and deciding what works best for themselves, their families, and their children. Even though they all rely upon information and advice from a variety of sources—including advice books and articles authored by professionals—these contemporary parents exhibit the attitude toward professional advice-givers as experts that became increasingly typical after the 1970s.

Although professional advice-givers—as public intellectuals—are less likely to make authoritative or binding statements in advice offered directly to parents, some professionals have gained indirect authority through institutionalization and the power of the state. For example, doctors, psychologists, and social workers influence the legal boundaries within which parents make decisions regarding such wide-ranging issues as disciplinary methods, transportation practices, and vaccination. Therefore, although parents today experience individualization of many parenting decisions, they also encounter increased state supervision over certain parenting practices, especially those involving safety and education.

CHILDREARING AUTHORITIES
IN THE TWENTIETH CENTURY

As the twentieth century dawned, childrearing, like many other social concerns in the Western world, was swept up in an enthusiasm for science and a confidence that scientific approaches could provide answers to social problems. In this progressive era, organized campaigns sought "scientific" approaches to everything, including medicine, management, public administration, housekeeping, childrearing, and social work.[4] Middle-class mothers, in particular, joined their new social role as domestic guardians with the enthusiasm for scientifically guided practices and sought evidence of the best childrearing patterns in order to perfect themselves and their children.[5] During the first two decades of the twentieth century, mothers were instrumental in the child study movement, as they banded together to form mother's movements that advocated for scientific study of children and childrearing methods and organized lectures by new childrearing experts, such as G. Stanley Hall.[6] Faced with the transformations brought on by industrialization, urbanization, rapid technological change, and cultural shifts in the maternal role, modern mothers felt that the information handed down by more traditional female networks was "insufficient to cope with the realities of modern life."[7] Mothers instead turned to the authority of science to provide answers to their questions. Although the idea of using a book to rear a child was sometimes ridiculed in the earliest years of the twentieth century, by the 1920s parental education had become much more widespread and popular. In the years following the First World War, childrearing advice also gained popularity among working-class mothers.[8]

The medicalization of childbirth and the growing practice of hospitalized birth subjected childbearing to medical and scientific authority and played a large role in advancing "medicalized mothering" and the precepts of scientific child care.[9] In 1900, less than 5 percent of American mothers gave birth in a hospital; by 1940, half of U.S. births occurred in hospitals, with nearly 75 percent of urban women birthing in hospitals.[10] In the early 1900s, the American Medical Association—founded in 1847 as an organized campaign to secure the authority and professional dominance of physicians over lay healers, midwives, and homeopaths—launched a rhetorical campaign against midwifery that characterized midwives as unsanitary, ignorant, incompetent, and an impediment to the assimilation of immigrants.[11] By the 1930s, this campaign was largely successful: midwifery had been outlawed in many states, and fewer than 15 percent of births were attended by midwives.[12] By asserting that medically trained and credentialed physicians were the safer and more scientific professionals attending childbirths, the medicalization of birth also laid a foundation for the growing authority of physicians over childrearing practices. Even today, hospitalized birth remains an important source of the earliest guidance in infant care and safety that most parents receive.[13]

Through the newly formed American Pediatric Society and the Pediatrics Section of the American Medical Association, physicians also maneuvered to position themselves as authorities on scientific childrearing. Medical authority over child care was further institutionalized and legitimated through the widely circulated U.S. Children's Bureau pamphlets, *Infant Care* and *The Care of the Child*. Originally published in 1914, the Children's Bureau's *Infant Care* was for most of the twentieth century the most popular and widely distributed of all federal publications.[14] The 1914 edition of *Infant Care* was written by Mary Mills West, the mother of five children, who combined medical and nutritional advice drawn from medical manuals, such as Dr. Luther Emmet Holt's *The Care and Feeding of Children*, with her own maternal experience, time-saving tips, and implicit calls for progressive reform. In subsequent revisions of the pamphlet, however, West's credentials were questioned because her motherly, lay expertise was deemed insufficiently scientific, and by 1929 the booklet was authored by a panel of physicians, which signaled the solidification of professional medical authority over child-rearing practices.[15]

In early twentieth-century scientific advice literature, mothers were regarded as consumers of child development expertise, rather than producers of formal expertise. Physicians often assumed that the traditional practices handed down among women were backward and harmful; the tone of much advice was condescending, and physicians often expected mothers to look to them for exact prescriptions to be enacted verbatim.[16] Much of this advice concerned the routine physical care of healthy children—feeding, bathing, and exercising—as well as instructions for caring for sick children. Indeed, improvements in medical knowledge, sanitation, and nutrition were crucially important in eradicating many childhood diseases and lowering infant and child mortality rates in early 1900s. The nineteenth-century establishment of the laboratory science of bacteriology had by 1900 established physicians as public health authorities and raised their status considerably.[17] According to Rima Apple, the decline in mortality rates for children under one year of age from 162.4 in 1900 to 21.4 in 1970 was correlated with not only medical breakthroughs, such as antibiotics and vaccines, but also increases in literacy rates, the production of child-care literature, and the adoption by women of "scientific motherhood," which included a reverence for scientific and medical authority.[18]

In addition to physicians, child scientists from an array of disciplinary backgrounds vied for professional "turf" in childrearing advice. As child mortality rates dropped during the first half of the twentieth century and children's physical survival became more certain, child psychologists sought professionalization by claiming equal expertise with physicians. Psychology, eventually emerging as the dominant paradigm for understanding children, gained an edge over medicine, sociology, and social work.[19] Increasingly, parenting advice began to center more on children's mental, emotional, and social development than on their basic physical needs.[20] Thus, in addition to medical advice about nutrition and hygiene, the science of childrearing during the 1920s and 1930s included ample advice about how parents should discipline children's behavior.

Although child psychology has never been a unified field, the dominant school of thought in psychology at the start of the twentieth century was known as behaviorism.[21] This approach, expounded by such medical experts as Dr. Winfield Hall, Dr. Luther Emmett Holt, and Dr. John B. Watson, viewed children as needing training and strict routines to socialize them into full humanity.[22] Ehrenreich and English argue that the dominance of the behaviorist childrearing method in the early twentieth century reflected the necessity of regularity for industrial workers. Even though child development psychology emerged alongside a social movement for the liberation of children from industrial life, the behaviorist science of childrearing also produced a sense that a child's development could be controlled so as to shape him early into a member of industrial society. "The goal was industrial man—disciplined, efficient, precise—whether it was his lot to be an industrial laborer, a corporate leader, or another expert himself. The key to producing such a man was regularity."[23] Behaviorist advice, though, disciplined parents as much as it disciplined children; in particular, it frequently warned mothers to curb their desires to show tenderness or affection for their children. Behaviorist advice was highly prescriptive and discouraged parents from exercising their own decision-making over which behaviors were desirable and undesirable in children.

Despite the prescriptive tone of scientific advice, early twentieth-century mothers were not always just passive accepters of professional instruction. Instead, they determined—given their own constraints and through their own agency—how expert prescriptions would be put into practice. As Grant reports, the detailed records left by mothers' groups and child-study clubs reveal that they formed "interpretive communities," actively negotiating between traditional child-rearing practices and professional advice by evaluating prescriptive texts against local norms, expectations, and practices.[24] Correspondence to the Children's Bureau leaves further evidence that, although mothers were eager to know the latest scientific advice, they did not uniformly or unquestioningly accept the recommendations of either the Children's Bureau or modern medicine.[25] Nonetheless, in popular magazines, which were instrumental in popularizing the new scientific advice in the early twentieth century, both the tone of professional advice and the letters submitted by readers indicate that parents in the early twentieth century largely regarded professional advice as authoritative.

As the economic importance of disciplined industrial producers gave way midcentury to the centrality of consumers, the science of child-rearing shifted as well toward both more permissive recommendations and more concern with children's developing psyches. After a series of skirmishes, by the late 1950s developmental psychology had succeeded in supplanting behaviorism as the dominant school of thought in academic psychology.[26] Influenced by Piaget's theory of cognitive development, popular experts such as T. Berry Brazelton and Penelope Leach discarded the previous image of children as unformed creatures in need of training and substituted a model of children as intuitive and exploratory beings whose impulses and wants were indicative of their developmental needs and critical to fulfilling their future potential.[27] Not only was this developmental advice more permissive toward children (as I discuss in more detail in chapter 3), but it also began to encourage parents to exercise greater autonomy in their childrearing decisions.

Dr. Benjamin Spock was a leading childrearing expert in the post-war era. Spock, who blended medical knowledge with discipline and behavioral advice, was an early harbinger of the growing autonomy of parents vis-à-vis experts; he told them to "Trust yourself. You know more than you think."[28] Despite his encouraging tone, parents of the era regarded Spock as an authority figure, referring, for example, to his book, *The Common Sense Book of Baby and Child Care*, as their "Bible" and exhibiting dependence on his medical and behavioral advice.[29] A 1956 *Parents* article about generational differences in childrearing reveals this orientation to authority in its description of "Marion Rogers, [who] considers herself a truly modern parent. She told me with satisfaction that her mother hadn't been allowed to come near the baby until she had read Drs. Spock and Gesell from cover to cover and been quizzed on them."[30] Mothers, fathers, and even other doctors wrote to Spock in search of his guidance on particular issues of concern to them and often expressed their admiration and loyalty to his prescriptions.[31]

Regardless of professional turf wars and changing schools of thought, professionals who offered childrearing advice were primarily regarded as authorities well into the 1960s. Evidence from parents' letters to popular magazines indicates that parents acknowledged the authority of doctors and other child-training specialists and strove to enact their recommendations as well as they could, given their particular constraints. In fact, some tips they offered one another through magazines included ways to make it more practical to follow the exact prescriptive recommendations of authorities—as in the case of this mother, who wrote in 1946 about a trick she had discovered for folding diapers: "I found folding diapers a time-consuming job, so as soon as my baby was old enough to wear the standard fold for oblong gauze diapers, as recommended in the U. S. Government booklet 'Infant Care,' I folded each diaper accurately with a yardstick and stitched it across the top and bottom with the longest stitch on my sewing machine. This proved to be a real time and energy saver. The diapers were easier to handle in washing and hanging, and took less space on the line: They took a bit longer to dry, but then they were ready to use immediately. When I need the diapers in another size, it will be easy to rip out the large stitches.—Mrs. C. M. Z., Missouri."[32] Other letters included casual references to the fact that parents generally looked to the advice offered in childrearing manuals and parenting magazines as necessary and useful: "How I dreaded it, that first trip to the barber. Then one day I read an article, probably in *Parents*, since that is my baby encyclopedia, explaining that we parents were at fault for the screams so often heard in a children's barber shop. We taught the baby to connect 'hurt' with scissors, and then wondered why, when he saw a man coming at his head with a pair, he screamed. . . . —Mrs. W. S. E. Pennsylvania."[33] Not only did this mother's letter reveal that she regarded *Parents* as an "encyclopedia" of facts, but it also evidences the fact that she was receptive to the philosophy of parenting on offer: parents are at fault for the ways they shape children's behavior. Indeed, despite shifts over time between stricter and more permissive recommendations, *Parents* articles typically regarded parents themselves as the ultimate cause of children's behavioral problems. In 1931 one psychologist bluntly chided parents: "If you had followed certain modern theories, you would not now have your problem."[34] This attitude was echoed, though sometimes in a more muted tone, by other popular magazines of the era.

Whether all readers in the early twentieth century thoroughly imbibed the underlying philosophy of popular advice, it is evident that many parents relied heavily upon various forms of printed advice and took seriously both exact prescriptions and the philosophy offered by the professionals and specialists they regarded as authorities. Furthermore, the fact that such advice was widely regarded as having authority meant that there was more general cultural consensus about what constituted accepted practice—that is, there was a recognized normative model of parenting, regardless of whether all parents conformed to it. Even when they were unable to carry out authorities' instructions, parents were self-conscious of the gap between their practices and the modern, scientific, and right methods for childrearing. As several historians document, much of the correspondence received by the Children's Bureau was written by mothers who were not only eager to receive printed, scientific instructions to follow in caring for their infants and children but also struggling to find the best solutions when their situations prevented accurate and full implementation of those directives.[35] Often, this gap between recommendations and reality arose because printed advice typically assumed a middle-class audience and standard of living. Many working-class parents were eager to conform yet lacked the resources necessary to carry out the authorities' instructions exactly. One of the most frequent and specific instructions offered in popular advice (then and now) is for parents to consult a doctor when they have additional questions. Letters to the Children's Bureau during the first half of the twentieth century evince that barriers of access and affordability were major concerns for less affluent parents eager to implement modern medical advice.[36]

Even when the recommendations were about situations and conditions that were clearly not life-threatening, parents struggled to enact them as well as they could: "Certain child-training authorities said, 'Have your child pick up his toys every evening, helping if possible.' Ann's mother tried, but the picking-up ritual was beyond Ann's understanding, and the little girl had a sturdy resistance to boredom. Her mother soon decided that a pleasant relationship was more important than a routine of neatness. She changed her technique to 'Oh, what a messy room. Can you help me put the toys away?' Sometimes Ann could, and did. Mother wrangled as much help as possible, but kept the occasion light and the responsibility for neatness in her own capable hands."[37] In this example, even though having the child pick up her toys herself was not working for the mother who had to change her approach, she still regarded the child-training authorities as authoritative. She could have decided that the experts overvalued neatness and that the toys did not really need to be put away at all. Instead, even though following the "rules" was not working very well for her and her daughter, she still accepted the prescriptions of the authorities as binding and struggled to conform to them as closely as possible.

Perhaps, though, the clearest evidence in popular magazines that specialists and professionals were to be regarded as figures of authority is the ways that professional advice was explicitly distinguished from that offered by lay people—that is, the parents who submitted articles, letters, and helpful hints. While the words of professional advice-givers (recognized by their scientific credentials) stood on their own merits, lay advice carried editorial disclaimers. For example, a regular feature of *Parents* magazine for most of its history has been the reader advice column in which parents share letters describing how they solved their own problems.[38] In the era of the childrearing authority, these lay advice columns ran with prominent disclaimers, such as: "Below, printed in italics, are problems which every parent is apt to meet in bringing up children. The solutions described by readers are not presented as magic formulas that will always succeed. But we do feel that they contain suggestions of value which may be used or adapted to fit the individual case.—The Editors."[39] These disclaimers that preceded the columns of readers' advice indicate the authority that the magazine had (or thought it had) over readers. Advice given by specialists carried no such disclaimer. The fact that the editors felt it necessary to explicitly distinguish lay from professional advice, anecdotes from science, is a sign that they considered professional advice to be scientific, trustworthy, and authoritative.

THE AGE OF THE EXPERT

By the 1970s, featured authors such as doctors, psychologists, and other child development professionals had been transformed from childrearing authorities into childrearing experts. The transformations in lay advice columns mark this subtle but noticeable historical shift that narrowed the gap between specialists' authority and parents' authority. Unlike the disclaimers offered in earlier years, by the 1970s, lay advice letters ran with the simpler explanation: "Readers tell how they handle problems of children and teenagers."[40] Beginning in the 1990s, lay advice columns carried the upbeat announcement: "'It worked for me!' Parents share their tried-and-true tips and wise advice."[41] Expert advice now sometimes carries a disclaimer, explaining that there are differing opinions among experts, that no solution is right for everyone, and that parents may need to adapt advice to fit their particular needs.

Following the transformation of authorities into experts, middle-class parents still actively sought expert advice, but because the advice was no longer seen as authoritatively binding, parents gained a measure of individual autonomy in determining the best course for parenting their children as individuals. As a 1956 article about intergenerational conflicts over parenting advised: "It may be true that [your mother's] way of doing things would be as practical as yours. But yours is the best for you—just because it is your own."[42] This understanding, however, that parenting decisions could be liberated from traditional patterns and personalized to fit the individual soon included recognition of parents' autonomy from childrearing authorities as well.

In articles and advice from the early decades of the twentieth century, parents are depicted as following the exact prescriptions of childrearing authorities; parents refer, for example, to Dr. Spock's book and the U.S. Government Booklet *Infant Care* as exact specifications on how to care for children. By the 1970s, parents were more apt to regard expert advice as suggested practice, rather than law. That is, they had begun to adopt the attitude that the parents quoted at the beginning of chapter 1 share. Tatiana, a white middle-class mother and professional, exemplified this attitude when she said: "I admire the confidence of the people who wrote the books have, but [in real life] it is not always that way. Especially for every family—every family is different and every authority is going to be different." This attitude is often reflected now in popular advice itself. As one expert cautioned parents in a 1991 question-and-answer column: "Books can help you gain information and perspective, but they are tools, not inflexible authorities."[43]

Because mothers have typically been assumed to be primary parents for the last century, this newer reflexive, critical stance toward child-rearing experts is in part linked with changing gender roles. As women steadily gained higher levels of education and greater economic independence, they became less likely to passively accept advice offered in the prescriptive, condescending, and paternalistic tone that was typical of childrearing authorities at the start of the twentieth century. An early site of gendered resistance to medical authority was mid-twentieth-century objections to some procedures of medicalized childbirth. For example, between 1955 and 1956, the *Ladies Home Journal* carried a continuous op-ed discussion of "modern" childbirth procedures, with both mothers and maternity nurses writing to describe and object to traumatic birth experiences.[44] The public discourse about paternalistic control by doctors and degrading birth experiences eventually grew into the natural birth movement, which in the 1960s and 1970s began to advocate in a more organized way for a model of partnership between women and their doctors.[45] Contestations over childbirth also had ramifications for mothers' responses to doctors' expert prescriptions for childrearing: mothers were less likely to accept doctors' orders as unbending law. Furthermore, changing gender roles in families have meant that, since the 1980s, popular advice has acknowledged that individual families make their own choices about issues of family structure and roles. Although most popular magazines still present the two-parent, heterosexual family as the unquestioned ideal, they acknowledge that within and even outside these parameters a range of options inform decisions regarding employment, care for children, and household work. Because of these variations in families, expert advice is no longer assumed to be one-size-fits-all.

The more critical stance toward experts, though, extends well beyond changing gender roles. As Anthony Giddens describes, the simultaneous dependence upon and skepticism toward expert systems is a prominent feature of late modernity, and such reliance places the burden of choice upon the individual:

> Our relationship to science and technology today is different from that characteristic of earlier times. In Western society, for some two centuries, science functioned as a sort of tradition. Scientific knowledge was supposed to overcome tradition, but actually in a way became one in its own right. It was something that most people respected, but was external to their activities. Lay people 'took' opinions from the experts. The more science and technology intrude into our lives, and do so on a more global level, the less this perspective holds. Most of us . . . have, and have to have, a much

more active or engaged relationship with science and technology than used to be the case. We cannot simply 'accept' the findings which scientists produce, if only because scientists so frequently disagree with one another, particularly in situations of manufactured risk. And everyone now recognizes the essentially mobile character of science. Whenever someone decides what to eat, what to have for breakfast, whether to drink decaffeinated or ordinary coffee, that person takes a decision in the context of conflicting and changeable scientific and technological information.[46]

Sometimes the contradictory nature of expert advice is acknowledged in popular advice itself. One expert, for example, addressed this directly in 1998: "As one exasperated mother put it: 'You experts are always changing your opinions about the best way to bring up children.' As a parent, I can relate to this frustration. But as a child psychologist, I believe that there is surprising consensus among experts, bolstered by a wealth of research that has followed children and families over long periods of time."[47] In fact, as authors have attempted to lend greater credibility and weight to their words in the era of the expert, the phrase "experts agree . . ." has become commonplace in contemporary magazine articles as an attempt to bolster the authority of recommendations. Despite claims of professional consensus, contemporary readers are typically assumed to exercise a significant measure of autonomy in considering various expert opinions and selecting from among them. For parents, this means that the responsibility of making many childrearing choices is increasingly privatized; the parents in each family must individually evaluate and select among the overlapping, competing, or disparate options offered by local or traditional customs on the one hand and by abstract expert systems on the other.

DISCIPLINE AND OVERSIGHT

Although readers of popular advice are typically assumed to be the final arbiters of what will work for their families and many parenting decisions have been increasingly privatized during the past hundred years, this does not mean that ultimate authority over all childrearing decisions has come to rest solely with parents. At the same time that parents have gained greater autonomy to choose among diverse familial arrangements, parenting styles, and practices, the state has also claimed more specific authority over children's lives in certain areas—most notably, in setting limits regarding child safety. The state's oversight of parents parallels the contemporary advice offered to parents: set certain firm boundaries around matters of safety and values of great importance but offer a lot of choices for other things.[48]

The state has exerted increasing authority over child safety and protection during the last hundred years.[49] Increased family intervention by state-sponsored agencies, coupled with changing social norms and practices, are among the most likely explanations for recent declines in statistical rates of child maltreatment and victimization.[50] The state's assertion of authority over child safety means, among other things, that although parents still have a wide range of choices over discipline techniques, they are officially disallowed to use those disciplinary measures that are defined by the state as abusive (a definition that is contested). Although no U.S. state currently outlaws spanking, parents who prefer to use any form of corporal punishment are often aware of the state's authority to investigate and determine the boundaries of appropriate child discipline. It is important to note, however, that the supervisory presence of the state is not felt equally by all groups. A number of researchers have observed that African American parents and parents at lower socio-economic levels tend to emphasize respect and obedience, use stricter "no-nonsense" approaches to discipline, and favor physical over psychological forms of discipline. Attitudes toward corporal punishment also vary by age and gender of parent, age and gender of child, religion, and region of residence.[51] Many groups of culturally marginalized parents are more likely to engage in parenting practices that, though legal, are more likely to warrant state investigation and adjudication. These parents often find themselves very precariously positioned: they may feel the need to engage in stricter forms of discipline to keep their children safe and out of trouble in a society that discriminates against them, yet they are more likely to attract state attention for harsher forms of discipline simply because they belong to a marginalized group.

Among the parents I interviewed, white, middle-class parents were the most likely to tell me that they feel free to parent in the way that seems best to them. They describe a sense of freedom to find what works best for their families and seem largely unaware of public rules that constrain their decisions. Because the official rules governing parents closely match—and indeed are shaped by—their "mainstream" preferences, these parents rarely feel constrained by rules. Although middle-class parents feel a sense of competitiveness among parents and an impossible challenge to be perfect, they do not typically have concerns about government intrusions into their family life. In contrast, working-class parents and parents of color were more keenly aware that they are outside the mainstream and that public scrutiny of parenting practices could quickly turn from neighborly judgment into official action.[52] Even the middle-class parents of color I talked with were more likely to raise issues of legality regarding child discipline. Norma, for example, mentioned corporal punishment when I asked about whether there were clear rules for parenting: "the spanking and all that, the physical abuse stuff as far as corporal punishment, I think there are definitely rules there."

Most of the working-class parents with whom I talked worried about government intervention in their disciplinary choices. Marcos, for example, a working-class Hispanic dad, said that the biggest challenge facing parents is:

> Not being able to be a parent. There are a lot of organizations, schools meddling in the way you are rearing a child. Again, they are looking for their well-being but sometimes it is a little bit too much. Sometimes it is overbearing also and that conflicts with how you want to raise your child. . . . I mean, in school a kid has a scratch on his back and DSS [Department of Social Services] is breathing down your neck . . . even the government. They are the ones who make the rules. Sometimes they get a little bit over zealous, maybe a little too much into the business. . . . It could be a neighbor. They think the way they are raising their family is better than most people or the way you are raising your family. That is a challenge that makes it tough for you trying to raise children. It is a lot of stress having to have somebody tell you how to do your job. It's the last thing you want to hear.

These working-class parents were more likely to approve of spanking or other corporal punishments than middle-class parents were; however, they were aware that their preferred methods of discipline were at odds with the mainstream culture.[53] A white working-class mother described one of her greatest worries about parenting when she was expecting the birth of her first child: if she disciplined the child in public, she feared that someone would call DSS. Social workers, of course, deal with parents in situations where parental authority over discipline is often contested by the state. A social worker described to me the frequent occurrence of parents with lower socioeconomic status "feeling like their hands are cut off where they cannot do anything," describing the violence not only of bad parenting but the state's violence felt by decent parents who have a "fear of DSS taking your children away." Katina, a black working-class mother, described the consequence as a limitation on parents' ability to effectively discipline their children, which results in the kids getting out of hand: "Parents are afraid to be parents. Kids know. To me I believe they know they have the upper hand in the situation. When they say, 'Oh yeah, my dad will freak out all he want but he better not touch me because I'll call 911.' It's too much."

The state's authority over child safety extends beyond questions of discipline and corporal punishment to other parenting practices. For example, seat belt, child safety seat, and helmet laws dictate specific requirements to which parents are legally obligated. The state adjudicates the boundaries between self-care and neglect and influences when parents are able to leave children and adolescents home alone. And the state has become increasingly active regarding decisions about children's health, from requiring vaccinations to sometimes insisting on medical interventions for children despite parental objections.[54]

WHERE PARENTS SEEK ADVICE

Throughout the last hundred years, the authority of experts to dictate correct practices has weakened; however, this does not mean that experts have become obsolete. On the contrary, extremely expert-guided contemporary parenting has contributed to the general intensification of the work of parenting, along with the increased demands of time, expense, and emotional involvement faced by contemporary parents.[55] Today's parents are expected to consult experts, read advice books, compare and evaluate contradictory advice—what one dad referred to as "shopping around"—and ultimately devise their own solutions and strategies that incorporate a uniquely chosen selection of elements from expert advice. The parents I interviewed for this study give us some indications of the range of advice available to parents today and the variety of ways in which parents interact with that advice when charting the course of their parenting.

Taken all together, these thirty parents rely most heavily on interpersonal advice received from family, friends, and coworkers. Many of them turn first to their personal networks when they have questions or are facing a new parenting challenge. This personal advice is also the kind of advice that most parents claim to find the most helpful. However, these parents are also very expert-guided: they use a wide variety of printed and multimedia sources of advice and information and consult with doctors, therapists, and educators. Where respondents turn for help and information when they have questions varies by how much social support they feel they have for parenting. Respondents with dense interpersonal networks tend to rely more on family and friends and less on impersonal forms of advice, such as books, magazines, and the Internet. Respondents whose personal networks are less dense—for example, those without family support or who have experienced more geographic mobility—tend to use more printed and professional advice.[56] Often parents filter impersonal expert advice through interpersonal networks: several respondents described using word-of-mouth recommendations to direct their reading, preferring to read advice books that had been recommended by either a trusted friend or a doctor or therapist. Although they seek these various forms of lay and expert advice, they all profess to "take it with a grain of salt," as they believe that any advice must be critically evaluated and adapted to their own family. As Cassandra put it: "I have found there is not one-size-fits-all. . . . Every situation is unique." Many parents claim that they never believed there was "one right way" to parent; those who did start with this belief say that they eventually discarded it.

Almost all of the parents I interviewed say that they have used some form of printed advice literature, and those who do not use printed advice seek out parenting advice and answers to questions on the Internet. Those who reject advice literature say it is because they have tried using it in the past and found it either too general or too prescriptive to be helpful. In lamenting the generality of advice, they describe ways that advice literature often assumes too much uniformity among families and children; they talk about not only the uniqueness of each family but also the individuality of each child. Parents with more than one child often describe finding that they need different strategies for each child. They do turn to advice literature for help on these strategies, but in so doing they are deciding what will work not only for their family but also for each child with that family. Their use of advice literature varies, however, beyond their personal preferences and what works for their families to more categorical differences like stage of the family life cycle, social class, and gender.

On the whole, these parents all describe relying most heavily on generalized expert advice literature when their children were young. While their children were infants, most of these parents read at least one of several widely popular contemporary books—those most frequently mentioned were the *What to Expect* series and the books in the Sears parenting library.[57] They describe these books as having been particularly helpful when they were new parents feeling unsure of how to care for an infant.

> When they were really young, or babies, I would look at certain books. When they are newborns you are like, "Oh my God, what does this mean." You are sort of overwhelmed and you buy these books about parenting or sleep or that kind of stuff. I did a lot of that when they were babies. . . . I have read the *What To Expect* . . . the first one. I have read *The Baby Whisperer*. I actually found that helpful and then, in retrospect, I was like, are you kidding? This infant was two weeks old. In retrospect it seems silly but, at the time, it was really helpful when you are up nights and are not sure you are doing the right thing. I liked that. . . . But as they have grown up I don't do that. Part of it is a time thing. It is like there were so many different issues I don't have time to read five books about adjustment to kindergarten (Denise).

When I asked parents what would prompt them to seek advice about young children, the single most frequently mentioned issue was sleep. As parents of young children, many of these respondents were desperate to find solutions to their children's problematic sleeping patterns. Stan, a white middle-class father, said that he read a lot of parenting advice "in the beginning, definitely. Especially about trying to get them to sleep more." Madeleine, a white middle-class single mother, described: "When he was little it was things like how do you get him to sleep more than two hours in a row? He did not sleep more than two hours in a row for two and a half years. I was beside myself with sleep deprivation. The book *Sleep Habits & the Healthy Child* or something like that . . . It had some really good concrete things to say. I sort of took that and incorporated it, made my own little plan up and executed on it." Other issues that prompted advice-seeking for parents of young children were eating and nutrition, health concerns, and developmental milestones.

Many mothers also describe having subscribed to or regularly read a parenting magazine while their children were infants and toddlers. The titles they mention most frequently are *Parents*, *Parenting*, and *Family Fun*. Most found that as they gained greater confidence as parents they relied less on parenting books and gradually let magazine subscriptions subside. Naomi, a black middle-class mother explained: "You know, when I was a new mother I read them. But right now I find some of the things sort of comical. You know, common sense says you are not going to do this, this. I don't find them as interesting, I don't read them as much as I used to." Some mothers expressed a sense of disappointment that there was too little helpful advice about older children in magazines and general parenting guide books. They also found that as their first child got older and many of them had second children, they simply had less free time to read.

During the middle years of parenting, when children were in grade school, parents tend to rely mostly on their friends and other parents for advice. Respondents described seeking out their own friends and parents of their children's friends who shared similar values, parenting styles, and philosophies to compare notes with. "I kind of have become friends with people that share more similar parenting skills. But it is nice to be able to pick and choose" (Kimberly). In the parenting groups I observed, it was apparent that parents had a clear desire to talk with other parents about how they deal with children's "annoying behaviors," such as not listening, talking back to parents, and being loud, rowdy, or messy. For some parents, these relationships with other parents of similar-aged children are a welcome reassurance that their parenting style is working and that their children are developing normally. For example, Nadine, a white middle-class stay-at-home-mom explained: "To hear that your child, so-and-so's children are doing this, and my other friends' children are doing this, in the mall or in the car or whatever, makes me just feel better about the fact that I cannot fix that my daughter is doing this. Other children are doing exactly the same thing. Okay, I cannot fix it but they are doing it too and it's fine. Somebody else is tearing their hair out because of it. I won't tear my hair out." Parenting groups were also eager to share their concerns about children's social development, such as how to help children get along well with their peers, make friends, and avoid being teased or bullied. Nearly all of the respondents with children this age said that they especially valued the information they received from friends whose children were a couple of years older than their own. Unless there were particular difficulties with a child, advice-seeking at this stage of parenting was more a matter of reassuring themselves that their children are normal and being prepared for what was coming up next in terms of children's development. Some mothers continued to read parenting magazines in this stage of life, but others said that they either found that there was too little advice about older children or that by the time their children were this age, the advice in magazines had become repetitive. In these middle years, parents who were most likely to read a lot of parenting literature were those with a child who had some kind of a "special needs" issue. These parents sought specific information about handling learning disabilities or problematic behavioral issues from both books and professionals. Teachers and school counselors—often the key points of contact when children have special needs—offered advice, reading recommendations, and referrals to other professionals.

For parents of teenage children, questions about the transitions of puberty, teenage sexuality, and weathering the storms of adolescence had sent some parents looking for new advice books and sometimes prompted them to seek personalized advice from family therapists. Several lamented the lack of good advice about teens in magazines. For example, Deborah, a white working-class mother said, "I always look at magazines and look at different articles but, you know, there really is not much written on teenagers. There is an article a friend of mine referred to me about the teenage brain." A few parents sought out books about puberty and parenting teenagers. Others turned increasingly to online searches to deal with issues confronting adolescents today: "I don't find many articles about teenagers or older kids now-a-days. That is why

I catch them online. Basically, it is talking about self-etiquette, computer etiquette, things like that. It is geared to the older children" (Naomi).

In addition to sources of parenting advice varying by stage of the family life cycle, parents' social class and level of education made a difference in where they turned for advice and how they thought about that advice. Middle-class and highly educated respondents relied more upon parenting books than their working-class and less educated counterparts, but they are also highly critical of many of the books they have read. Among highly educated respondents, quite a few say they dislike or are skeptical of advice literature; nonetheless, they still seek it out and read it, especially when they are facing a new challenge or looking for new information. In fact, some parents who were the most avid readers of advice books were also the most critical of them. For example, Madeleine, a highly educated professional, explained both her passion and disdain for advice books:

> I have read a lot of books. . . . I am extremely opinionated about the fact that books tend to fall into one of two categories. They are either, "Oh my God, how fucked up are you as a parent? How could you possibly not do this the right way?" That makes you feel bad but there are some that have some practical, concrete suggestions. Or books that are like soothing and comforting and like, "It's really going to be okay. You cannot really fuck this up unless you are beating them. Here are some concrete suggestions." So mostly what I do is I look for practical things I can do to address whatever the underlying problem is. I usually will triangulate off of things my friends have tried and things the books suggest. It is a little hit-or-miss. . . . A lot of the books [are] patronizing to the grownups because they assume that we are screwing up and they, the expert, will help us figure it out. It also, I think, implicitly (*What to Expect When You are Expecting* in particular, which I despise—the whole series), sort of assumes too much power on the part of the grownups to affect little kids.

In evaluating Madeleine's stance, Bauman's words about the shift from legislators to interpreters are particularly apt: "There is hardly any way left leading from this self-propelling, self-perpetuating, self-divisive, autonomous and self-sufficient mechanism of expert knowledge, back to the kind of generalized expertise entailed by the traditional role of the legislators."[58] Middle-class parents not only conform to the expectations that ideal parenting is intensive and expert-guided, but they are also highly likely to regard the authors of professional advice as experts, rather than authorities. Like Bauman's interpreters, these experts cannot make binding statements about what is correct; they can only facilitate communication between autonomous participants. Another middle-class stay-at-home-mother explained: "I did read the books. Finally, I came to a point where I would read them, take something from them and then put them down and just kind of go with what seems to be working. Maybe look at another book that had conflicting advice. I would try to find one that worked for me." Even when parents are looking for books that will give them concrete methods to follow, they cannot regard any single expert as authoritative, in part because they know that so many other experts will disagree. Though several parents expressed frustration with the contradictory nature of expert advice, they have come to expect these contradictions as normal.

Most working-class parents I interviewed also read parenting books, but in general they listed fewer books and were somewhat less likely to continue to seek out parenting books after their children were no longer infants. More working-class parents instead described parenting as something you have to learn by doing and not something you can learn from a book. Doug, a white working-class father, described his feelings: "I feel like as a parent this is something you have to learn. I mean, it is a growing experience. It is great to have . . . it is great to read, and to have any other input but you also have to do it yourself. You have to learn." Catherine, a middle-class mother who made a point to describe her family of origin as working class expressed a similar understanding that parenting is not learned from a book: "My mother had one baby book. She told me she would listen to Dr. Spock. Everybody had it but it was only one book. . . . Yeah, there is too much now. . . . I had friends who if it was not in the baby book they did not know what to do. If a problem came up and the baby book did not give them an answer they just did not know what to do. I was like, 'Use your human instincts. You are a mother.'"

However, three working-class mothers I interviewed (who are, as far as I know, unacquainted with one another) told me that they use the Bible or other religious books as a parenting guide. Belinda, a single mother who works part-time as a hair stylist, said: "The Bible to me is my parenting advice book. . . . Having God in the center of our relationship as you parent a child is very important. I have tried it all different ways. I tried reading magazines, I've tried reading parenting advice books and I am not saying they definitely don't work. Those also help me along the way." Miriam, a working-class stay-at-home-mother, also said she uses both the Bible and other books by religious authors as parenting guides: "I think I read every book that is out there; every Christian-authored book. I did not like secular authors but I have read a lot of self-help, Dr. Dobson and those kinds of things. You know, a lot of times when I would read them I would end up feeling like, 'I cannot do this . . . I'm such a failure.' But, bits and pieces of books I would take. . . . I felt inadequate by reading the books. But, again, like I said, there were some things I would take out of there."

Working-class parents also expressed more general appreciation for popular forms of mass media advice. As with middle-class respondents, working-class consumption of magazines varied by personal preference; nonetheless, working-class mothers who said they read parenting magazines were more likely than middle-class mothers to say that they learned new and helpful information from magazines. In addition, a few working-class parents also mentioned gaining useful ideas from television shows like Super Nanny and Dr. Phil. Although I am reluctant to make broad generalizations based on these few interviews, there is some indication that, when compared to middle-class parents, working-class parents may both look to a slightly different set of experts for guidance and be more likely to regard those experts as authoritative.

Finally, gender presents another categorical difference in how parents use different forms of advice. Although most fathers I interviewed say they have read at least one parenting book, on average, women were more likely than men to name long lists of books they have read and to recount frequently consulting parenting advice books. Although some fathers I interviewed are full and equal participants in a range of parenting decisions, several men said that they can rely upon their wives to relay information that they have read or to suggest reading material. When directly seeking advice about parenting on their own, men rely more exclusively upon family members, friends, coworkers, and doctors. No father whom I interviewed read any parenting magazines. Despite editorial content that purportedly appeals to men, the magazines' advertising content confirms that these magazines are primarily targeted at women. (However, a few of the mothers I spoke with claimed that their husbands do read parenting magazines.) Instead, many of these dads, given their slight preference for the Internet as a source of information and advice, appreciate the fact that Internet searches can target specific questions.

POPULAR MAGAZINES AS CULTURAL BAROMETERS

How do parents think about and use popular magazines as sources of parenting advice? Among the parents I interviewed, only mothers say they read magazines targeted specifically at parents. About half of the mothers I spoke with said that they read parenting magazines somewhat regularly; the other half said either that they used to read parenting magazines when their children were quite young (for example, they might have received a free subscription for the year following a child's birth) or that they might pick one up occasionally (while waiting in the doctor's office, for example), but this half doesn't read them with any real frequency. A few mothers said that they do not like and do not read parenting magazines. However, all of the mothers and a couple of the fathers expressed at least a passing familiarity with parenting magazines. That is, even those who disdain parenting magazines consider themselves familiar with the genre and its content.

Those parents who expressed dislike for parenting magazines offered various reasons, including a dislike of magazines in general and a sense, particularly for the men I interviewed, that parenting magazines simply were not for them. They were also critical of parenting magazines because they find them either too generalized or too idealized to be helpful. Katina, a black working-class mother, said: "I don't find it that you can learn from the books and magazines. It's a hands-on thing. Some of the advice they give is a little bit ridiculous to me. I just don't bother." Melissa, a white stay-at-home-mom who subscribes to several parenting magazines and finds them helpful in some ways, was also critical of how idealized they are: "I feel like the general advice tends to be terribly preachy. It tends to be terribly idealized. I don't know which generic child they are referring to for a lot of that stuff but I just feel like it's not always applicable." In fact, whether mothers said they liked magazines, they described them as the most general form of mediated advice and therefore not very helpful for specific problems and dilemmas. In such critiques of magazines, these parents exemplify the contemporary attitude toward experts as offering opinions to be evaluated rather than rules to be obeyed.

Despite the fact that many of these parents are critical of magazines as a source of parenting advice, those who do read magazines use them as a parenting aid in several concrete ways. Most describe them as helpful for learning about developmental stages and milestones when children are young. They also find that they are good sources for tips and practical ideas that are easy to implement, such as chore charts and kid-friendly recipes. Magazines are also valued as practical sources of ideas for entertaining kids, like crafts, games, activities, and outings. For some, they are simply appreciated for their entertainment value: "Magazines are my thing. I love magazines. They are fun, quick" (Belinda).

Beyond these concrete uses, however, many mothers describe magazines as a kind of touch point to confirm that they are in the mainstream. As Deborah, a white working-class mother said, she reads parenting magazines "Just in case there could be something I'm missing." For many parents magazines seem to serve as a kind of general "barometer" of trends. Kimberly, a white middle-class mother, saw magazines as reflecting and helping to form prevailing cultural trends: "I nursed my kids for a year and that had nothing to do with my mother. That definitely has to do with *Parenting* magazine and the culture that I was living in at the time. I think those two, and the science and it just felt right and it worked for us. Other women that I was around really supported me in that choice." By reading parenting magazines mothers are keeping an eye out to see if they should be aware of a new idea or a new way of doing things. Jill, a white middle-class mother and professional, explained:

> I think I look at it to see what the trend of thinking is. I definitely get ideas from [magazines] as far as . . . we are toilet training my daughter right now. I have been sort of looking at what they are saying, what rewards work, what does not work. I don't take it as solid, this is what it is. I understand where this information is coming from and it is really just somebody decided to write an article about it. So, I think it is helpful but I don't necessarily think it is "the word." . . . I would probably say I am more inclined to look at magazines

because it is short, quick and to the point. . . . When it comes time for temper tantrums or behavioral plans and reinforcements, I like to see what the trend is and go with that. I think it is important as well, because, if you are doing something that is completely off base and nobody else understands what you are doing, nobody is going to help you follow through with it anyway.

Michelle, a middle-class stay-at-home-mom, similarly stated:

I get input from here, here, and here and somehow I make sense of it all in some way that I'm not really aware of. . . . There was an article in one of the parenting magazines the other day that was, "Are you too strict with your kids?" or something. Like, it had scenarios and you were supposed to say what you would do. They would tell you where you would fall on the spectrum. Are you going too much over the top? There were quite a few things that I was probably going too over the top and over-reacting on. Like, I came back from that going, "You know, I probably could stand to chill out on a few things." That would be okay. . . . That was kind of useful. That was one of the most useful things I got from those magazines in a long time.

These parents describe looking at magazines to see if they are generally in line with current trends, missing something they should know, overlooking something to try with their children, or forgetting something for which they may need a reminder. For them, the parenting advice in popular magazines serves as a useful cultural barometer, signaling trends and changes over time. The parenting advice contained in popular magazines is useful to the sociological and historical researcher in much the same way that it is useful to contemporary parents—not as a direct measure of the exact and specific realities of parenting practices, but as a generalized measure of cultural ideas about and attitudes toward parents and children. Indeed, the fact that these parents describe using magazine advice to affirm their general alignment with others confirms their belief that magazines accurately reflect general cultural trends, even if they reflect these trends in highly idealized and unrealistically homogenous ways. Therefore, popular magazines provide a useful historical indicator of widespread cultural assumptions about the nature of parents' and children's autonomy.

SUMMARY

Throughout the twentieth century, there was tension over the degree of authority held by childrearing experts and the autonomy exercised by individual parents in meeting particular parental challenges. In the first half of the century, professional advice-givers were more likely to be recognized and responded to as authorities whose words and prescriptions carried normative weight for parents. By the 1970s, a shifting balance of authority began to recognize parents more consistently as the final arbiters of advice. Contemporary parents, though expert guided, often assume a skeptical stance toward the advice offered by professionals and in the media; parents screen and selectively implement ideas that they judge appropriate for their families and children. At the same time, however, that they enjoy increased autonomy vis-à-vis experts, contemporary parents are increasingly supervised by the state in certain parenting practices. By institutionalizing their knowledge through the state's authority, physicians, psychologists, and other experts have legislated the boundaries of acceptable practice regarding matters such as discipline, safety, education, and parents' financial obligations.

Despite the more critical, postmodern standpoint of contemporary parents, many are anxious to keep abreast of mainstream trends and practices. Therefore, they often find that the advice they receive from friends, other parents, and in books and magazines is a useful barometer of cultural values, ideals, and currents. These cultural ideals guide and constrain parents as they make a wide range of decisions about the many practices that constitute their parenting. In particular, even as parents negotiate their own autonomy and authority over parenting decisions, they also face numerous decisions that help to define the boundaries of their children's autonomy. Like other parenting decisions, choices that affect children's autonomy are made after assessing a variety of advice, from family members, friends, teachers, community leaders, books, and magazines. In the following chapters, I consider what popular parenting advice reveals about historical changes in the forms of autonomy and agency experienced by children.

CHAPTER 2

Seen and Heard

CHILDREN'S GROWING FREEDOM AT HOME

> The way I was raised it was children were seen and
> not heard. These days children are heard, seen, and
> everything else. It is so different. . . . There is no
> authority figure in some of these homes other than
> the child.
> —Katina

WHEN DISCUSSING DISCIPLINE, the parents I inter-
viewed often noted the increasing outspokenness of children and the
decreasing sense of both boundaries and parental authority at home
(usually, though, in reference to *other* families' homes). Though such
assertions were typically anecdotal, these parents' sense that something
has changed is corroborated by historical changes in popular advice. In
many activities of daily living—especially diet, sleep schedules, elimination,
grooming, and dress—the twentieth century saw children come to be
regarded as the best experts about their own needs while a more child-
centered approach displaced behaviorism in parenting advice. Popular
advice also recommended greater autonomy for children over their
behavior and general comportment at home, especially in relation to their
parents, as more democratic models of family began to be favored over
those based on positional authority. Additionally, the current widespread
disapproval of corporal punishment underscores children's rights over
their own bodies. These changes represent not only a transformation of
childrearing recommendations aimed at parents, but they also represent
children's increased autonomy over their own bodies and behavior at home.

At the beginning of the twentieth century, in popular advice experts
expressed the dominant view that children should be trained to respond

obediently to parents. By the 1930s, however, a new strain of advice appeared that began to view the child as the expert on her own developmental needs. By the late 1940s, the challenge to behaviorist tendencies had become common in expert advice in magazines, and during the latter half of the twentieth century recommendations remained consistent that parents should follow their children's lead in such matters as eating habits, toileting, and personal appearance. Furthermore, parents in the second half of the twentieth century were advised to be largely tolerant when children challenged their authority, were contrary, or expressed disagreement about many routines of daily family life. The portrayal of children's greater autonomy over activities of daily living, however, should not be characterized as disappearing discipline. Instead, recommendations about discipline issues shifted from regulating activities of daily living toward regulation of interpersonal relationships; more rules focused on getting along well with others.

BEHAVIORIST CHILD TRAINING—STRICT ROUTINES AND FIRM DISCIPLINE

In the earliest years of the twentieth century, a recognizably behaviorist approach is evident in popular parenting advice: children were often described as requiring training, routines, and strict schedules. Daily activities such as feeding, diapering, and bathing of infants were proclaimed to establish the basis upon which childhood and adolescent discipline were founded. A 1911 article explained:

> "The training of the child should begin on the day of his birth," says a thoughtful mother. This is unquestionably a correct statement of the case, for the child doubtless begins at once to receive impressions from the big, wide world into which he has come. The seemingly mechanical acts of moving the little body about for the purpose of providing nourishment and comfort, at once begin to impress the unscarred nervous system and to leave their forms. So the little life should at once begin a rhythmical movement. To give the infant his nourishment at exact and measured periods and to provide for his sleep, his bath, and the like, in the same careful way, is to impart his first lessons of obedience.[1]

Another clear summary of the behaviorist approach appears in a 1929 article, "How to Get Obedience": "By discipline we mean the reasonable regulation and supervision of the fundamental habits of a child throughout all stages of his development and a consistent plan for having him obey simple rules such as regular meal-times, regular bed-times, training in elimination, eating what is placed before him, wearing the clothes that are provided, observing certain proprieties of conduct."[2] Activities of daily living such as eating, toileting, dressing, and sleep were presented as disciplinary challenges, and any difficulties presented by children in such matters were understood as disobedience. In popular advice literature, children were allowed little room for individuality, self-expression, or autonomy over these basic daily activities. Even for newborns and infants, failure to conform to strict routines and schedules was understood to lay the foundation for future disobedience and behavioral problems.

It is clear that this behaviorist advice in the 1910s and 1920s sought to discipline mothers just as much as children. Without sticking to "scientifically-informed" routines, mothers were assumed to coddle and spoil their children. Mothers were told that they needed to seek out expert guidance and modern information to train their children: "The mother who takes great pains to learn all she can about the proper care and feeding of her child, and who counts no sacrifice too great if it helps to develop in that child the best possible health habits, is laying a foundation for a wholesome, likable personality."[3] Advice included cautionary tales of mothers whose children had become unruly and difficult because they had indulged them in infancy instead of requiring obedience to authority. Instead of feminine affection and indulgence, which would spoil them, children were declared to need strict training: "The beginning of wisdom in training the child to obey is to exact regular and punctual habits of sleep and diet and to avoid all excesses. Mere petting and tenderly caring for the child will not inculcate obedience. The child so treated may grow into a monster of selfishness and disobedience. The practice of obedience should be early trained into the child until such conduct becomes a matter of habit."[4] Tightly constraining children's daily behavior at home was understood to be a necessary means of constituting proper human selfhood. By means of such training parents brought about children's "gradual change from little animalish things into human beings who in a constantly increasing range of experience can reason and act on their impulses."[5]

Proper training required adult constraints on children's daily activities and firm discipline, including the consistent use of punishments when needed. As a 1911 *Good Housekeeping* article advised: "Many parents adhere firmly to the view that physical punishment of children is never necessary, but I wish to take issue with such persons. . . . I take the view that in every promising and wholesome young life there are 'sins' of both commission and omission, which require rigid discipline in order to bring the learner gradually to a true sense of duty and to the practice of performance."[6] In establishing rigid discipline, parents were warned against allowing their children excessive autonomy in matters of daily life. For example, in 1929 one author cautioned that giving children too many choices was a disservice: "There is no dishonesty worse than a steadfast 'What-would-you-like-to-do?' system. . . . In standing between the child and the harsher contacts we should not nourish impulse at the expense of will. Free expression is a fine thing, but will commands."[7] Thus, parental decisions about how and when these routines of daily life would be carried out constrained children's daily experiences.

Although no experts advocated the frequent or capricious use of corporal punishments, several popular advice-givers in the early twentieth century admitted the occasional necessity of "a good spanking."[8] Those who demurred corporal punishments in this era objected to them primarily on grounds of effectiveness. For example, one expert in the 1920s explained that the trouble with corporal (and other punishments) was that they may be impractical to administer in the moment: "When children do not recognize clearly the probability of actual punishment, they do not control their behavior in any marked degree as a result of a threat. Threats are effective in controlling the behavior of children only when the parent is willing to put words into action—and that immediately."[9] Several disciplinary experts explained that the objective of modern child training, properly implemented, was to avoid the need for harsh punishments by instituting strict enough routines that problematic behaviors would not have a chance to take root. Another expert wrote in 1929: "Implicit obedience used to be the end-all and be-all of child training. If you couldn't get it any other way, you whipped them. Whipping,

I dare say, may be necessary sometimes for a child who has been started wrong. But on the whole, it is a miserable confession of failure and lack of imagination."[10]

As a scientific practice, behaviorist childrearing was often broken down into a rationalized series of steps: for example, a 1931 article about punishment prescribes "10 steps for training children's behavior."[11] Following such orderly scientific principles, problem behaviors (such as crying, thumb-sucking, finicky eating, rowdiness, loudness, or messiness) could be trained out of children. For example, a 1936 article states that "the well-fed and comfortably routinized baby will not cry regularly during his first six months unless he has learned the habit of crying."[12] Because of their basis in behavioral science, these modern principles of discipline over daily activities were not assumed to be obvious to parents (primarily mothers), and therefore expert guidance was advisable. For those parents who were not able to solve such behavioral problems on their own, a new and burgeoning group of specialized experts was ready and waiting to help: "Be big enough and broad-minded enough to admit that you—like every other parent—make mistakes in child training and that seeking advice from persons (like psychiatrists) whose business it is to have technical knowledge of this subject is no stigma on your ability as a parent, nor does it lay you open to blame."[13] (Indeed, it would seem that blame was unnecessary when seeking personalized psychiatric advice; it was doled out so freely in popular magazines that there could hardly be need of any more!)

It is important to note that early twentieth-century discussions of child discipline began with routine physical care and saw implications for children's obedience and social adjustment in how they ate, slept, dressed, and toileted. In these crucial matters, children could not be left to their own designs; rather, their behaviors needed the loving constraint of an informed and knowledgeable parent. Experts viewed the routinization of activities of daily living as crucial to both physical health and social well-being. One expert emphasized the importance of routines to physical health in his 1931 warning against insisting on manners as the proper realm of discipline: "The common argument in favor of teaching social forms at an early age is that these habits, like habits of eating and sleeping, should be formed early in life when the child is most impressionable. . . . We must remember, however, that in teaching manners we are teaching habits that are not at all essential to health as is the case with habits of eating and sleeping."[14] However, Maryland State Commissioner of Mental Hygiene G. H. Preston, a medical doctor, advised that such early childhood training was crucial not only to health but also to future happiness: "whether a person will be successful and happy in life is determined to a great extent by his early training." He advised not only that children's behavior problems were primarily the result of improper training in their earliest years but also that lifelong problems of social adjustment, including those of "chronic fighters, the chronic quitters, the chronic complainers, the nervous invalids, the misfits of society," resulted from lack of authority of parents (usually mothers) over their children in such matters as learning "to eat and sleep in conforming ways."[15] Another expert similarly cautioned that failure to adhere to a strict feeding schedule for infants could lay "the foundation for derangement of the physical health, for abnormalities of appetite, for irregularities of mature life, and possibly for a criminal career."[16] (So much for parents not being subjected to blame!)

The seeming abundance of cautionary tales and woeful parents pleading for advice about their own unruly children might indicate that in actual practice behaviorist child training was neither as widespread or firmly rooted as it appeared to be in popular magazines nor as effective in preventing discipline problems as promised. Judging by their letters, however, I found that at least some parents took behaviorist child training principles to heart. For example, one mother described her family's problem and the solution she and her husband devised: "Two-year-old Alice went to bed smiling but screamed the minute we shut her door or started downstairs. She crawled out of bed, opened the door and came downstairs still screaming." Then she described the careful sequence of steps by which they solved the problem:

> After Alice's supper Daddy gave her ten minutes time for talking or a story while Mother made certain that everything customary was in readiness for bed and sleep. Alice was put to bed and when she got up she was put back in bed, gently but firmly. When she got out the second time we put her to bed saying, "You can stay . . . sleep now." The third time we put her back saying, "Mother will help you stay." Alice lay on a light-weight cotton blanket. This we folded over her

and pinned securely so that she was forced to relax. The first time she struggled but soon fell asleep and was un-pinned and the blanket thrown off her. The second night we went through exactly the same procedure. The third night after her story she was put to bed but pinned in the first time she got out of bed. Mother quietly said, "Mother will help you stay in bed—sleep now." The next night (fourth) when she went to bed she said, "Not help me—Alice sleep by self." And she did.—Mrs. B. E., New York.[17]

Dr. Watson, a leading proponent of behaviorism, surely would have approved of such thoughtful training. Another mother described a similarly sequenced and routinized procedure for training her daughter to eat more quickly: "Dorothy always dawdled over her meals. She had so many late marks at school that the teacher complained, and she wasn't getting sufficient nourishment. Finally we decided to have her eat alone with the understanding that when, for three consecutive meals, she had eaten the food that was placed before her and done it within a reasonable time, she was to be permitted to eat with the family again. It was hard at first, but now it is working. She is proud of herself when she is allowed to come back to the table, and the periods when she has to retire to solitude in the kitchen are becoming fewer."[18]

These examples illustrate parental implementation of recommended behaviorist disciplinary advice. Although letters requesting advice showed parental concern with behavioral issues such as children's manners, orderliness, tidiness, and compliance with requests and instructions, a great deal of the concrete suggestions offered by experts focused primarily on the importance of shaping children's patterns of sleeping and eating through routine step-by-step training. Experts advised that children's obedience in other matters was first established by bringing about children's compliance in the routine activities of daily living, over which parents should exert authority in setting and enforcing strict standards of acceptable behavior.

By the 1930s, a more permissive, developmental view began to appear and be intermixed with strict behaviorist advice. A 1931 article authored by a psychologist indicates that although parents were still thinking about how best to train their children, "modern" psychology wanted to show a better way: "'Talk to us about anything you choose, but be sure to tell us how to punish our children.' The program committee of the Mothers' Club is engaging the efforts of a child psychologist. The remark is characteristic. Parents who so hopefully approach scientific psychology seem to feel certain typical needs and desires, and the desire for better modes of punishment is one very frequently expressed. . . . The modern psychologist believes that what parents need to discover is, not a better technique of punishment, but better means of preventing situations where punishment seems necessary."[19] This psychologist's recommendations for preventing punishment situations involved not behaviorist child training, but the need for better understanding children's "natural mental development," including their eagerness and inquisitiveness. In her estimation, a mother who punished her child for displaying these natural qualities was "blameworthy, rude, destructive . . . paving a veritable path of punishments for her child."[20] This new strain of advice began to encourage mothers to learn from new understandings of children's development and to tolerate certain childlike behaviors that were previously discouraged, but there were still cautions that discipline must remain firm. Although some experts were beginning to question the value of traditional punishments, others still advocated the judicious application of spanking and other forms of corporal discipline.

A NEW WAY—TRUSTING CHILDREN'S NATURAL APPETITES

By the 1940s, the developmental view of children's behavior had become more prevalent, and magazines began to include increasing depictions of children's growing autonomy over daily activities that were previously constrained by behaviorist routines. The strict routines and imposing discipline of earlier decades were discarded, and parents were advised instead to recognize the individuality of each child and to follow the child's lead to respond to her developmental readiness. A good early example of this kind of advice is a 1941 article in Parents, "New Ways for Mothers," which rejects the older view of prescribed routines of infant and toddler feeding, toilet training, and discipline:

> Perhaps the most important as well as the most helpful advice that can be given to the parents of small children is: Don't push too hard; don't rush the child into accepting something new before he himself

shows readiness. This principle should be followed as soon as the baby is born. Never mind if the book or the doctor says eight ounces and the baby takes only five at a feeding, or if solids are rejected in favor of milk and milk only, or if the child wants his vegetables pureed instead of chopped. . . . Parents should help the child to take the next step forward, but should be able also to accept the child's own indications of readiness. Offer him a new food or a new way of doing something. Be ready to abandon it if his behavior bespeaks a clear no, and try again in a few weeks. A contented infant, unharried by rigid schedules, is nine-tenths of the battle for mental health.[21]

Evidence of the clear shift toward granting children—even infants—greater autonomy over certain daily necessities is perhaps most clearly exemplified by the contrast between older advice about feeding and the new advice about eating. In the 1940s and 1950s, articles—such as "Fussy Eaters," "Don't Make Your Child a Fussy Eater," and "The Problem Eater"—considered the potential problems with children's diets, but they also showed a shift away from children as the passive recipients of feeding toward children as active agents who are eating.[22] Remarkably, the insistence on strict feeding schedules and rigid infant training in the 1910s and 1920s was matched by equally strong insistence from experts a generation later that infants and young children should dictate their own food needs without the strictures of a standardized schedule. By the 1940s, mothers who insisted on schedules and forced food on their children were described as creating, rather than preventing, problems: "What does an unwise mother do about a fussy eater? She shows anxiety, becomes tense, pretends to feed a doll and then unexpectedly stuffs food into the child's mouth. She tries force. Because she's stronger, she gets some food down. By then, what should be a peaceful meal is a turmoil."[23] Instead of a parent-determined and strictly enforced feeding regime, midcentury experts in magazines advised allowing children's own appetites to govern what, when, and how much they would eat. Although "few problems are more distressing to a mother than that of the child who won't eat,"[24] midcentury mothers were advised to: "Let the baby be the judge of when he should be fed. He can tell you whether the interval should be three or four hours. . . . Assume that when he is hungry he will eat."[25] "By and large a baby's appetite is an excellent guide to the amount of food he needs. It's a better guide than any standard feeding schedule, which may meet the need of the average child but not necessarily your child. . . . You can trust his appetite to regulate the quantity of food he needs."[26]

This encouragement to follow children's lead on feeding continued beyond infancy and throughout childhood. Parents were now advised to allow toddlers and older children a growing measure of autonomy over their own diets. In a reversal of the earlier insistence on routine and discipline, advice-givers now explained that allowing children to make choices about what they ate was the basis for creating "good eaters": "Children who are good eaters like food because meals are relaxed and pleasant. Mealtime should be a happy time with no nagging or scolding about food at the table. The meals, of course, should be served at regular hours and the food should be both appealing to the eye and satisfying to the palate. But most important, the child should be allowed to eat the amount of food he wants and to have some choice about what he eats."[27] Even though most advice was directed toward mothers who seemed to be concerned about possible undernourishment, similar instructions to recognize children's own inclination and willingness were also invoked when dealing with problems of overweight children: "Perhaps the most important consideration in controlling obesity is the child's own willingness and desire to be thinner: without this he is defeated at the start."[28]

We can see from their letters that parents adopted the idea that it was bad to force children to eat. In 1971, one mother admitted her own shortcoming in "What I Learned From My First Child": "I used to stand over him at every meal, making him clean up his plate regardless of his likes and dislikes and whether or not he was hungry. Poor Tony!"[29] In another mother's letter in 1981, mealtime woes were symbolic of her more general conclusion that "My Husband Was a Terrible Father": "From the time the children started eating at the table with us, mealtimes were a nightmare. Small as the kids were, he ordered them to 'eat every bite on your plate' in a drill sergeant's tone. It was a rare meal that didn't end with at least one of the children bursting into tears."[30] Although parents I interviewed are still concerned about getting children to eat vegetables and meeting proper nutritional requirements, they corroborate that this advice has taken root. Several of them echo the advice, unwavering since the 1950s, that children's appetites can be trusted. Connie, a Hispanic middle-class mother, explained:

> It should just be whatever works. I think moms will stress out. Like when you have a newborn how much should they eat? Eight to ten times a day? Nurse for twenty minutes? You are stressing out because they are eating more, eating less or you don't know how much they are taking. . . . The baby needs to eat. But I also think that *sometimes we have to let the baby do what they need to do.* If they are gaining and growing then that's okay. . . . There have been questions on the [online parenting] forums on nutrition and what kids are eating or not eating. Kids get to be one or two they get to be picky eaters, they don't want to eat or they want to eat the same thing for every meal. People will go on and say, "My kid will only eat mac and cheese, what are you doing?" You get reassurance that it is okay. A lot of kids go through it. They don't eat a lot between the first and second year. They slow down in their eating but they are fine. *They live, they eat what they need, but it's okay.*

According to both popular depictions and parents' descriptions, children are now generally allowed more freedom over not only what, but also how, they eat. Several parents, for example, described their sense that strict rules such as eating only in certain rooms or using formal table manners matter a lot less to them now than would have been true in earlier generations.

What this shift in advice about children's eating habits represents is not a matter of changing nutritional guidelines, but a new depiction of children as rightly exercising personal autonomy over certain basic matters of their daily life and physical existence. Eating stands as an example of children's increased autonomy, but this new realm of choice is also reflected in the recommendations regarding other activities of daily life at home. For the most part, parents were also advised in the latter twentieth century to allow children autonomy not only in matters of diet but also in toilet training, dressing, grooming, and physical exertion. Rather than portraying children as the objects of training and routines determined by adults who knew what was best, the advice of the mid-twentieth-century and later assumed that "children know better" regarding basic physical needs and requirements.[31] The wise parent was in tune with children's expressions of those needs and followed children's natural inclinations, even when these contradicted previous notions of what children "must" do. In these matters of daily home life, children were being portrayed as autonomous individuals who could assert their rights. One article about dealing with fussy eaters asserted: "At any age he has as much right to refuse a meal as you have. Respect this right. No harm will come from missing a meal occasionally."[32] The message was implicit: refusing to eat was no longer regarded as an act of disobedience; rather, it simply expressed a child's natural, healthy appetites. A fussy eater was developmentally normal, not undisciplined or "bad." Young children's finicky eating habits, reluctance to potty-train, or insistence on wearing the same red shirt every day were no longer assumed to foreshadow discipline problems later in life; such behaviors were simply normal and necessary aspects of child development. (Gary Cross points out that this general shift toward a more permissive philosophy was encouraged by not only doctors and developmental experts but also advertisers, who cleverly nudged parents to trust children's "natural" inclinations and appetites, which, of course, included desires for consumer goods.)[33]

By the last quarter of the twentieth century, children's rights to autonomy over basic activities of daily living had become so well established in the popular mind that their assertion of individual choice in such matters was regarded as critical to their healthy formation of self. Again, food is both exemplary and symbolic in a 1976 article, "The Many Meanings of Food": "Even in early childhood, children are already developing strong likes and dislikes in foods. This assertion of individual taste is really an assertion of self, of individual identity. By expressing his own tastes and distastes the child says, in effect, I am myself—an independent, separate, self-determining person. Thus the child's basic identity is helped to develop through the experience of eating and making choices."[34] In chapter 5, I describe in more detail the therapeutic view of selfhood that had become fully established by the 1970s and undergirded insistence that children's choices were critical to their self-development. This individualized, psychological, and therapeutic view of selfhood has had substantial consequences for parental advice about matters of discipline. Increasingly, parents have been both instructed to view children's defiance around activities of daily living as a necessary form of children's self-agency and advised to tolerate various behaviors that challenge parental authority.

RESPONDING TO DEFIANCE

The increasingly developmental emphasis in late twentieth-century popular advice redefined children's and adolescents' challenges to parental authority, especially when they disagreed about activities of daily living, such as eating, toileting, dressing, and general comportment at home. Parents in the late twentieth and early twenty-first centuries have been increasingly advised that children's and teenagers' defiance and rebelliousness surrounding the daily activities of life at home represent normal developmental milestones and should be constructively tolerated. Although parents are frequently counseled to provide clear limits for children, they are also prompted to interpret rebellion and defiance as cues that children are ready for increased independence and autonomy. Such advice has become especially prevalent in addressing toddlers' behavior problems: "It is to be expected that a healthy baby of this age would begin to exert his will-power by letting his mother know what he likes and dislikes. Babies 'come in their own' toward the end of the first year of life. They begin to realize that they are human beings with the ability to say 'yes' and 'no,' if not in words, in actions."[35] The usual advice recommends some greater measure of autonomy, within clear limits:

According to Matthew Schiff, M.D., a child and adolescent psychiatrist in private practice in Long Branch, New Jersey, your son's behavior is probably just a sign of healthy emotional development. . . . The fact that he freely expresses his anger and rebelliousness shows he has a positive relationship with you and is secure enough to know that you won't reject him. Since your son has been good-natured until now, he has most likely reached a new stage in which he is discovering his will and autonomy, explains Schiff. To assert his new-found independence and his desire to be more separate from you, he becomes contrary—even fresh and defiant— when he doesn't get his way or is being disciplined. Schiff suggests that, instead of trying to stop your son's outbursts, you help him shape his new independence in ways that are more acceptable . . . teach him the language to use to express his dislikes and disagreements instead of his current emotional eruptions. . . . You'll also need to set limits on his behavior, such as not allowing him to hit, kick, or curse.[36]

While children are by no means given free rein to behave however they wish at home, the advice given to parents has increasingly recommended allowing children to express themselves freely, even when this means defying and arguing with parents. Middle-class families, in particular, are likely to tolerate and even encourage children's verbal challenges to parents' directions or opinions. As described in chapter 1, the "mainstream," middle-class approach to discipline has increasingly frowned upon the use of spanking and other corporal punishments and favored instead a more verbal style. This is part of middle-class parents' general approach to childrearing, which includes a pattern of reasoning with children and accommodating their preferences.[37] A great deal of contemporary popular childrearing advice is consistent with this approach wherein parents are advised not only to tolerate children's autonomous expressions of defiance but also to respond to them by offering more choices and independence. A 2006 *Parents* article, for example, tells how to "Tame Preschool Anger":

> Provide choices. First, let your child know you understand why she's angry . . . then, give her some control by letting her make a decision—for example, playing in the tub for five more minutes or getting out and hearing a story. Allow for independence. Let your child do some things on her own, such as dressing herself or trying new food combinations. Given the opportunity to express herself, she'll be less likely to pick fights. This technique helped Michael Berger, of Washington, D.C., avoid many sleepless nights. When his daughter, Naomi, was 4, she decided she wanted to wear shoes to bed. "At first I refused, and bedtime became a nightmare," recalls the dad. "But then I realized it wasn't that big a deal if she slept with her shoes on, so I let her. Indulging this whim ended the bedtime battles."[38]

In this approach to parenting, even reprimands are often phrased in ways that sound as if they are encouraging independent choice in general while they simultaneously deny the particular choice a child has made ("It's not okay; make a different choice").[39]

Advice-givers reassure parents that allowing children to negotiate some rules does not mean that parents are simple pushovers; instead, these negotiations can teach children valuable lessons. "Relaxing rules about finishing all the food on a dinner plate or taking a bath every night, for example, doesn't mean that you're backing down or spoiling your children. It teaches them that there are alternative ways of solving problems and that you can learn from your mistakes."[40] In fact, the overarching message of this advice is that many activities of daily living have been so effectively recast as issues of child *development* that they are no longer regarded as issues of child *discipline*. Young children who insist on wearing shoes to bed, refuse to eat all their food, or balk at taking a bath are no longer regarded as disobedient; they are just expressing their growing sense of self-autonomy in developmentally appropriate ways.

The advice to recognize growing independence and allow greater choice is not just aimed at parents of toddlers, but such advice is also prevalent in addressing attitude and behavioral problems of older children and teenagers. One specific arena of struggle between parents and older children is matters of clothing, grooming, and personal appearance. The typical advice is to respond to disagreements by allowing children greater latitude in making their own choices. In 1991 psychologist David Elkind told parents: "Just as they need to be free to experiment with other facets of their identities, young people need to be free to experiment with clothing."[41] Parents are cautioned against "ruling from on high," simply making pronouncements about what kids should do or relying on "because I said so" reasoning. Instead, parents are advised that it is both more beneficial to children and more effective as a disciplinary strategy to involve kids in decisions about their own behavior: "'Tell anyone what he's not allowed to do, and he's going to want to do it,' says Alan E. Kazdin, Ph.D., a professor of psychology at Yale University. 'That's just human nature.' This is particularly true of preteens, who are trying to assert their independence. At this age, it's better to explain why you think a particular behavior is unwise and to ask your child if she agrees or disagrees. . . . 'When you tell kids what to do and why to do it, you're not preparing them to deal with the world on their own,' Dr. Shure explains. 'It's better to encourage them to find their own solutions for problems.'"[42] Experts inform parents that by "discussing" behavioral rules they help their children develop problem-solving skills and self-confidence, both of which are rewarded by the middle-class social institutions in which many parents want to help their children be successful.[43]

The prioritization of problem-solving skills over obedience is consistent with the middle-class "concerted cultivation" approach to childrearing identified by sociologist Annette Lareau.[44] However, its prevalence in popular magazines not only reflects the cultural capital of middle-class audiences but may also facilitate the growth of this parenting style among working-class parents, who have been observed to value obedience over verbal reasoning and to show more favorable attitudes than middle-class parents toward the use of corporal punishment.[45] For example, Belinda, a single working-class mother, told me that, although she did not read parenting books, she did read magazines and found a lot of helpful advice in them. She described a recent parenting article that had helped her with her ten-year-old daughter:

> This article explained about how to talk without overdoing it with children in general and how to say things that manipulate your words in a way that make her feel like you are not burdening her. That really helped me a lot. For instance, I know in the article it said you saw that John was teasing another little boy. You so badly wanted to say, "Stop, you cannot do that. It's not right. It's wrong." But then there was a way of talking to him to make him feel like you were not overly parenting and just being mean. Bringing it up that, "Maybe so and so did not like to be talked to like that. Would that hurt your feelings if he talked to you like that?" . . . It was the way you talk to them and how to make it seem like you are not overpowering the conversation to be controlling. That is a big help for me. I took that into consideration. . . . I definitely turned to this parenting advice.

One way to characterize what Belinda "took away" from this article is to say that she learned to refrain from issuing directives and adopt a more discussion-heavy disciplinary approach with her preteen daughter. In other words, she learned to draw more heavily on middle-class parenting strategies of reasoning than may have been present in her own class-based cultural repertoire, which relies more on directives.

BEHAVIORAL BOUNDARIES

Both the flexibility of rules and increased tolerance of children's boldness in disagreeing with or even defying parents were often characterized by my interview respondents as a lack of "boundaries" or "structure." Even though I did not use either of these words in my questions to parents, several respondents relied heavily upon these terms when talking about childrearing "then" and "now." A particularly evocative example came from Sarah, a recently retired elementary school teacher and grandmother, who reflected on changes in childhood that she had observed in her thirty-eight-year professional career and her personal multigenerational family. After describing children's need for "structure," she summed up:

SARAH: In terms of structure and freedom and stuff, we had play pens. There are no play pens now.

MARKELLA: What does that mean?

SARAH: Well, when I was home and the kids were somewhat mobile, and I had something to do or I wanted time that I could not be right near them, they had boundaries of a play pen. We don't have that now so . . .

MARKELLA: What does it mean "we don't have play pens"?

SARAH: Well, the alternatives . . . they did not go to the bottom of the stairs before you knew it . . . Now, I think kids just disappear. They don't have any boundaries within the house.

In fact, I must point out that in several homes where I conducted interviews there were safety gates installed to prevent toddlers from wandering too freely or falling down stairs. However, as a figurative image, the example of the play pen is significant. Although she began with the literal physical boundaries of the play pen, Sarah quickly expanded to include figurative behavioral boundaries that were taught at home and carried into public spaces: "I think there are less boundaries with modern-day parents. . . . And I would say, in restaurants. In terms of behavior. I think that kind of thing in the home went outside. Then when we said certain things in restaurants and certain things in public places, supermarkets, anywhere, those boundaries were invisible but they have been implanted. You don't go there. An invisible kind of credibility in our words." As Sarah saw it, parents today do not have the same authority—that "invisible kind of credibility in our words"—to constrain their children's day-to-day activities at home, and this lack of authority carries over to what she observes in children's freedom through their public behavior. Interestingly enough, Sarah was not the only respondent to invoke the image of the play pen as a way of symbolizing generational changes in constraints on children's behavior at home; two other respondents made similar observations about play pens. Although I am not suggesting that these anecdotal observations present a necessarily accurate representation of the actual variations in parental authority today, I do suggest that the image of the "disappearing" play pen signifies a fairly common cultural perception that children have more freedom over their behavior at home than in the past.

Another version of the sentiment that children lack behavioral boundaries at home came from several respondents who said that parents now offer their children too many choices or negotiate too freely with them. Several parents described children talking to parents in ways that they said would have been unacceptable in the past. A school social worker echoed this in telling me: "Yeah, I think many parents do not know how to handle behavior . . . you know, compliance, they get into power struggles a lot. They just do not have good kinds of strategies. . . . I think the pendulum has switched. It has shifted from punitive, 'Do what I say, not what I do,' to a permissiveness and sometimes lack of boundaries." Whether these sentiments accurately capture the nature of parental authority today, they do correspond to an image of parents and children that is widely reflected in the parenting advice of popular magazines. Children today are portrayed as having greater say over their day-to-day lives than was portrayed in past generations, when, for example, Dr. Spock told parents that "it's crucial that parents always require politeness and consideration for themselves from their children."[46] According to the contemporary popular images of negotiation, argument, and defiance, children have gained greater freedom over their behavior at home than was evident in past.

Children's greater autonomy over many daily activities and enlarged freedom to express themselves—even challenging authority—should not be mistaken to mean that contemporary homes do not have rules. Instead, the focus of discipline, as reflected by both mainstream advice and interview respondents, has shifted from emphasizing obedience to parental authority over the mundane matters of daily existence to emphasizing relational skills and getting along well with others. When I asked about discipline, the parents I interviewed were much more likely to describe relational concerns and rules to help kids to get along with others than to be concerned with unbending routines for the activities of daily life or enforcing unquestioning obedience to parental directives. In general, they regard many aspects of daily routines and care as negotiable, rather than subject to inflexible rules. For example, Stephanie, a white middle-class mother, admitted: "I am not very good at being logical and methodical about rules. I tend to be, I don't care if they eat dinner in this room. I don't care if they eat pizza in front of the TV on Friday nights. I am not super strict, but I also want them to have good habits. I don't want them to eat dinner in front of the TV *every* night or anything like that." The nonnegotiable rules that parents named for their children often centered on treating others with courtesy or respect and getting along with others, especially siblings and peers. Bettina, a black middle-class mother, said that the rules for her kids are "just really minimal compared to what I grew up with" and include "common courtesy kinds of things. I hope my children are courteous to people. That is one example. You know? Say thank you, say please . . . Basics." Madeleine, a white middle-class mother, also expressed learning to get along as a cornerstone leading to nonnegotiable rules in her parenting: "I want to give him the tools to navigate the world. All of us are sort of, there is something about all of us that is annoying or really obnoxious. Each of us has difficulty dealing with other people, with things in the world. Whatever those difficulties are for him, I want to be able to see them and then give him things that will help him navigate with other people, with events, with life as it comes." These relational behavioral boundaries are often seen as becoming more relevant when kids are away from home than the older behavioral boundaries, which placed more emphasis on the orderly management of daily activities at home and respectful, unquestioning obedience to parental directives.

SUMMARY

In the first half of the twentieth century, popular parenting advice moved away from emphasizing strict control based on behaviorist methods and moved toward a more permissive view that emphasized the child's lead in activities of daily living. As children came to be regarded as the experts on their own developmental needs, many routine activities that had previously been regarded as important matters of discipline came to be seen as less in need of strict parental regulation. The prevailing theme of today's advice about everyday discipline for children is to set a few clear, nonnegotiable boundaries around matters of safety; at that same time, parents recognize children's natural insights into their own growing needs for independence and allow children a great deal of autonomy in negotiating daily routines and expressing disagreement with their parents.

This model not only allows a great deal of personalization of appropriate rules and boundaries but also requires a constant active negotiation between parents and children in setting and maintaining those rules. Discipline methods abound in popular parenting advice—family rule posters or contracts, counting to three (or ten), time outs, sticker charts, reward jars; and parents are told to select those concepts that seem most appropriate for their situation or that work for them. Moreover, the ultimate decisions about what constitutes acceptable behavior are left to each family. Many parents with whom I talked in various ways described the importance they place on helping their children develop autonomy by giving them an active role in making decisions about their day-to-day lives. At the same time, middle-class parents—probably the most likely to allow or encourage their children to express their autonomy through negotiation and bargaining—also expressed sheer exhaustion with the routine defiance they encountered over simple daily activities like meals, bathing, brushing teeth, dressing, and getting from place to place. Nonetheless, to a large degree these parents regard children's autonomy over daily life at home as beneficial for the independence it teaches, and they constructively tolerate conflicts over these issues because they believe this will help children become emotionally competent problem-solvers. Working-class respondents were somewhat less likely to tolerate as much open defiance from their children, but they, too, saw value in openly discussing rules with children and encouraging children's self-expression, within limits.

CHAPTER 3

Keeping Tabs on Kids

CHILDREN'S SHRINKING PUBLIC AUTONOMY

> Growing up we ran around outside everywhere. Now you are always worried about who could be out there to snatch your kids or something like that. —Stan

A NUMBER OF SOCIAL CHANGES—anxieties about children's safety, increased reliance upon private automobile transportation, the construction of public space as adult space, changing work patterns and time pressures in families, and the introduction of new media technologies—have contributed to contemporary expectations that parents must know the exact whereabouts of their children at all times. Keeping tabs according to today's standards often means keeping children at or very close to home and making sure that they are supervised at all times by a responsible and trusted adult. As a result, children at the beginning of the twenty-first century enjoy a great deal less autonomy over their own movements in public than did previous generations throughout much of the twentieth century. Most parents I interviewed identified this as one of the most noticeable differences between their own childhoods and those of their children.

Since the early 1970s, parents have been increasingly charged with individualized responsibility for keeping children safe from both strangers and traffic.[1] Parents also form the primary group charged with ensuring that children and youth are not allowed to be nuisances in public spaces that have increasingly been constructed, both physically and socially, to exclude children.[2] These cultural shifts in the construction of parenting are apparent in descriptions about how children get to and from school and other activities and how they spend their free time. The increasing level of supervision required by "good" parenting practices means that children have come to experience greater constraints on their use of public spaces and have less autonomy over their own mobility than did past generations. In addition to keeping tabs on children's movements through space, parents must also keep tabs on children's use of various media that sometimes complicates and blurs the boundaries between private and public: while some uses of media extend the private space of home outward, others raise additional safety concerns about public intrusions into the private space of home. Here, too, responsibility for monitoring children's use of media technologies at home is privatized as the obligation of individual parents.

TIGHTENING THE REINS ON CHILDREN'S MOBILITY

Early twentieth-century parenting advice showed evidence of a strong emphasis on children's need to develop independence and competence apart from their parents. In recent decades, however, children's freedom of movement and their opportunities for independence outside their homes have been considerably reduced. The loss of children's autonomy is apparent in comparisons between historical and contemporary advice to parents, especially in advice about children's mobility—to and from school or other activities—and in changing depictions of children's play and use of free time. Loss of public autonomy for children is also readily apparent in parents' recollections of their own childhoods in the 1960s and 1970s, compared with the practices they follow today as parents. In short, children now have fewer opportunities to conduct themselves in public spaces free from adult supervision than they did in the early and mid-twentieth century.

In the early twentieth century, even young children were more independent from their parents in ways that have become proscribed by contemporary standards of safety and parenting practices. In depictions of children in advice texts from the first half of the twentieth century and continuing through the 1960s and 1970s, children are described as moving relatively unhindered through various public spaces. For example, children walked unaccompanied to school, roamed around and played in neighborhoods alone and in groups, rode their bikes all over town, hitch-hiked around town, and ran errands for their parents, such as going to the corner store or post office. These descriptions of freedom to roam have disappeared from contemporary advice. Instead, parents today are admonished to never take their eyes off of their children in public places and to make sure that children are adequately supervised by an adult at all times, whether at home or away from home.

School Journeys

Children's opportunities for independent mobility are indicated in historical changes in descriptions of their routine journeys to and from school. Walking or riding a bicycle, formerly children's primary means of getting to and from school, served as viable alternatives to school buses. In 1969, nearly half of American children walked or biked to school.[3] Many parents with whom I talked remembered walking unaccompanied to school, either alone or with other kids, in the 1960s, 1970s, and 1980s. Several mentioned that they began walking unaccompanied when they were in kindergarten, and a few even recalled walking home for lunch and back to school in the afternoon. In the last several decades, though, because of the decline of neighborhood schools, the construction of many newer schools on busy roads, and increased anxiety about stranger dangers, few children today experience the freedom (or drudgery) of walking independently to school. Instead, most American children are driven to school by parents, a practice that congests traffic around schools and raises additional safety concerns for those who might otherwise prefer for their children to walk.[4]

In magazines, "back-to-school" advice for parents often suggests ways to prepare kindergartners for beginning school and to ease the transition for other children from summer schedules to school-year routines. In the past, such advice commonly recommended that parents make sure their new students (both kindergartners and children changing schools) became familiar and comfortable with the route to school and knew how long it would take them to walk. An excellent example of this advice comes from a 1956 article about school preparation:

"LET me go to school by myself, please," pleaded five-year-old Mike. "You said I could, and I'm old enough. Five is old enough to go alone, 'specially since I know the way." It was the first day of the fall session. The previous Thursday had been registration day and Mike and I had gone together for that. Now, on this long-awaited Monday morning, Mike was asserting his independence. As I looked at his determined little upturned face, I knew he was right. His babyhood was irrevocably over now. He was asking for the right to be a real boy and for a responsibility for which he had been prepared. I started to help Mike get ready for school a good year before he entered kindergarten. We usually took an afternoon stroll, weather permitting. We began walking in the direction of Glenwood elementary school, the school that Mike would attend. It is four blocks from our house. We followed the route that Mike would take going to and coming from school, so gradually the streets, the houses, the trees, all became very familiar to him. He began to know the proper crosswalks to use, and he became friendly with the genial crossing guard near the school. . . . His eyes sparkled as he waited for my answer. Might he go alone? "Of course, darling," I smiled as I bent to kiss him. With a "Yippee!" he was out of the door and down the front steps. At the corner he waved just before he disappeared from sight.[5]

Fifty years later, an American parent who would allow a kindergarten student to walk, unaccompanied, four blocks and across streets to school, would be considered reckless and neglectful by the standards of both popular advice and many local cultures. Since the early 1980s, anxieties about child victimization by strangers have coupled with increased dependence on automobiles to drastically reshape our cultural conception of appropriate public autonomy for a five-year-old child's journey to school.[6] What some observers have called the "infantilization" of children is perhaps most obvious in our diminished cultural expectations of independent mobility for children between the ages of five and ten.[7]

Back-to-school preparedness advice now mostly focuses on knowing bus schedules and drop-off routines, instead of walking routes. Either way, most children arrive at school accompanied by an adult, whether a parent or a bus driver, where they are transferred into the supervisory care of a teacher or other staff member. In contrast to little Mike's assertion of independence, contemporary back-to-school advice frequently focuses on soothing small children's anxieties about riding school buses. A typical example comes from a 2006 *Parents* article titled, "Stop School Anxiety":

> SCARY SITUATION: RIDING THE SCHOOL BUS
>
> A 10,000-pound school bus can strike fear into the most confident child, especially when it's noisy and filled with big kids. "Children also worry about getting on the wrong bus after school;" says Lisa Locke-Downer, Ph.D., a clinical psychologist and assistant professor at the University of Virginia. Soothing solutions: If your district offers kindergartners an orientation bus ride in the summer, sign up. You should also talk up the bus trip before the first day, says Mary Pat McCartney, elementary-level vice president of the American School Counselors Association. Say, "This is really neat—you don't get to ride in a bus very often." When the first day of school arrives, introduce him to the bus driver, and ask the driver if she'll seat your child in front—your kid may feel more comfortable being near an adult. If he's concerned about finding the right bus after school, ask whether a teacher or an aide can guide him.[8]

Although more may be expected of them academically in kindergarten, the dominant message in our culture is that at five years of age children are too young for independent and autonomous mobility. Even when their children ride school buses, parents are increasingly likely to accompany (or drive) their children on the short journey to a neighborhood bus stop. In fact, in some localities, risk reduction policies require that children be met at the school bus stop by a parent or designated caregiver in order to get off of a school bus when returning home from school.

Kindergartners, however, are not the only children who have anxieties about riding the school bus. Although buses are considered the safe way to get kids to and from school, shielding them from the dangers that might be posed by traffic and strangers, some kids experience significant anxieties about school buses as a frequent site of bullying. For example, one parent's letter about school bus bullying became a Q&A "Problem of the Month": "My seven-year-old daughter has a problem with two other girls on the school bus. They tease her mercilessly and won't stop even though my daughter has asked them to. Ignoring them doesn't work either. She wants me to call their mothers. What is the best way for us to handle this?"[9] At the school-based parents' group I observed, school bus bullying, a topic of great concern to parents, provoked an animated and agitated discussion at one meeting. Several parents were at their wits end with children who were fearful about bus rides and with what they saw as inadequate adult supervision on school buses. Bullying is not new, of course, but kids today often find themselves "trapped" with their tormentors in the small space of a school bus; many children today do not have temporal or spatial forms of autonomy that might allow them to avoid bullies on their journeys to and from school (such as walking an alternate route home and delaying or speeding up departures from school). In efforts to control bullying, schools, parents, and popular advice-givers rely heavily upon increasing children's emotional competence—teaching them emotional awareness and social skills to handle peer conflicts. The elementary school where the parents' group was based, for example, had incorporated a popular social skills curriculum into all of its classes. Contemporary advice about bullying also recommends increased adult surveillance and monitoring of children; however, it does not include recommendations that might stem from giving children greater autonomy over their activities, schedules, and use of public space.

Free Time and Neighborhood Play

A second way that children's decreased public autonomy is evident is in changing descriptions of children's free time and neighborhood play. In popular advice texts throughout most of the twentieth century, it is apparent that school-age children roamed and played in neighborhoods without adults accompanying them. Teens and preteens were described riding bicycles, buses, and subways all over towns and cities. Kids were commonly sent on errands, such as going to a grocery store or post office, by themselves. Hitching rides around and between towns was apparently a common practice. Sometimes mobility was a source of conflict between parents and children when kids asked for rides from parents who believed that kids should be more independent in their mobility. More than one parent's letter described some degree of conflict over whether parents were obligated to chauffeur kids around town.

A mother's helpful hint in 1971 illustrates this tension and one family's solution:

> Travel Money. Rather than walk or ride his bike, my 12-year-old son preferred to have me drive him places. As a result, I often felt uncertain about where to draw the line between reasonable chauffeuring and over-indulgence. Finally, after several talks on the cost in time and money of using the car, we agreed on a plan that's proving workable. Our son now gets a dollar a week that's designated travel money, over and above the regular allowance he gets. I then charge him 10 cents a mile for each trip I take him on. At first I was getting back most of the dollar, but soon he was going places on his own steam—and he found he could use the extra money as he pleased.—Mrs. P. J. Hassler, Phoenix, Arizona.[10]

In past generations, parents even expected toddlers to be capable of going into the yard and playing without direct supervision. A letter printed in a 1946 lay advice column in *Parents* describes the freedom even very young children were allowed over their coming and going:

> Our daughter, not yet two years old, enjoyed playing out in the yard as long as I was with her. As soon as I went into the house to do my many household tasks, she lost interest in her play. She would come and pound on the door, screaming continually, but still refusing to come in when given the opportunity. Finally, her father and I decided that her cries were not caused by anger at being left alone; rather, she was afraid of being shut out where she could not come in to see me. So we put a second handle on the door within her reach. When she discovered this new addition she was so thrilled with it that she was in and out all day long. The novelty soon wore off, and her trips were less frequent. Now after only a week, she plays happily in the yard for hours, on good days.—Mrs. L. S. F., Mass.[11]

In contrast, contemporary advice to parents of toddlers advises that young children at home should never be out of sight, even for a moment, because the consequences of leaving children unsupervised may be tragic. As a result, there are any number of products and suggestions for ensuring that toddlers cannot open doors on their own, but none to give young children *more* independence over their coming and going.

A particularly striking example depicting children's freedom of movement in the mid-twentieth century is a 1951 *Good Housekeeping* article offering advice to parents about what to do "When a Child is Missing."[12] The major premise of the article is that it is normal for children to be out on their own and that they occasionally may not come home at the expected time: "Almost all of us have waited anxiously for a child who did not come home when he was supposed to, and we all know the feeling of fear until the door opens and all is well. Fortunately, far fewer of us have not heard the door open and have had to call the police; to report: 'My child is missing.'" The advice reassures parents that most of the time there is no need for panic because children usually turn up quickly enough and explains that most of the time they have simply become distracted or lost track of the time. However, the article also describes when parents should call authorities, what information will be required, and what to expect if the police search for a child. The article indicates the greatest level of concern for "very young" children: "under seven or eight years old, as a rule." Some of the advice for preventing young children from "straying" includes an admonishment for parents to check on children at least once an hour when they're playing around the house; the advice explains that "police say that some parents who watch their children closely in public places will ignore them for hours at a time around the house." In clear contrast to contemporary advice and sensibilities, there is no indication whatsoever that a parent whose young child is (temporarily) missing will be considered negligent or inadequate as a parent. Parents who lose track of their children from time to time are not a few bad or unfortunate souls singled out as cautionary examples; instead, they are "almost all of us."

Also in contrast to the tone of contemporary advice, "When a Child is Missing" expresses a level of trust in strangers that is quite startling by contemporary standards: "Sometimes the police find—and they are justifiably annoyed when they do—that a total stranger has seen the child sitting wearily on a doorstep and has quietly taken him in, fed him, and let him lie down for a nap. Usually such strangers intend to help the child get home as soon as he has had a chance to rest. It simply does not occur to them to notify the police." In stark contrast to contemporary warnings about strangers, the total stranger of this midcentury advice is a helpful (even if misguided) person, but is not considered dangerous!

Despite mentioning that the FBI will need to be called if the parents have received a ransom note or phone call indicating kidnapping, the advice of "When a Child is Missing" ultimately reassures parents that kidnappings are rare, and "often the child is found snug asleep on a porch or wandering along a street." The article asserts that most older children who are missing have intentionally left home but will usually come home on their own. Parents are instructed to "call the police department at once *when* the missing child turns up" so that the police assigned to the case can be freed up for other duties.[13]

The freedom of movement depicted for children in popular parenting advice continued into the 1960s and 1970s. A 1966 advice article laid out guidelines for children's autonomy to navigate public space and handle emergencies: "In general a child about five years old can be expected to know his name and address, be able to dial 'O' for the telephone operator, and to report small accidents such as cuts, splinters and bruises to an adult. A six- to eight-year-old can be expected to follow simple routes to school, be able to find a telephone or report to a policeman if he is lost, and to know he must call home if he is going to be late. A nine- to eleven-year-old should be able to travel on public buses and streetcars, apply some simple first aid and exercise reasonable judgment in many unfamiliar situations."[14] A 1961 *Parents* article titled "Danger from Strangers" focused on teaching children to be aware of the potential dangers that strangers could pose in public places, but the writing did not advise against allowing children to leave home alone or to move through public spaces unaccompanied. One scenario recounted in the article describes: "Typical, perhaps, is the twelve-year-old boy who came into a large city for a youth conference. His mother was to pick him up for the return home. But he had an hour to kill and wandered into a drug store. While he was drinking a soda, a man sidled up, engaged him in lengthy conversation, lured him with enticements, and suggested they meet after the conference." As the advice regarding the scenario ensues, the focus is on ensuring that children are not attention starved and building their instincts for recognizing people who would take advantage of them; in stark contrast to current sensibilities, there is no indication that a twelve-year-old is thought to be too young to be in a strange city unaccompanied by a parent.[15] In a more colloquial mode, a 1971 feature in *Good Housekeeping* asked various celebrities to describe the mistakes they had made with their first children and how they had learned from them. Actress and singer Debbie Reynolds described her "mistake of being over possessive" and "smothering" her older child by refusing to let her out of her sight: "Without realizing it, I was making our home seem like a prison to my child. It took a while, but I learned that my child would never develop her own personality, her own interests and friends, if I didn't stand back, out of the way." Reynolds explained that with her second child she had allowed much more freedom from the start and had happy results.[16]

The autonomy to move relatively freely around neighborhoods and towns shapes adults' memories of their own childhood play in the 1960s and 1970s. Most recall free time during which they had a great deal of latitude to direct their own activities and movements. The impact is that they remember taking most of the initiative for coming up with things to do in their free time. Much of this consisted of finding other kids in the neighborhood and together inventing or negotiating some kind of peer-planned play. Even when they were involved in more structured pursuits, such as sports leagues, they were independently responsible, at least some of the time, for getting to and from their activities.

> So we had a lot of freedom. I think neighborhoods were safer back then. There was not as much traffic and not everybody had two cars. We ran around the neighborhood a lot and we had freedom to go to [other] kids' house. Their parents were not involved. They did not make a play date. You had to go find your own friends. They did not take you to the park. You had to bicycle over there. My partner was saying, "Nobody took us to little league. I put my glove on the back of my bike and I biked over, I played the game and then came home." . . . I remember walking a mile to go skating on the pond or whatever, going to the park to play for two hours by myself when I was six, seven or eight years old. I am not sure they even really knew where I was. (Madeleine)

Like Madeleine, most other parents similarly recalled a great deal of freedom to play outdoors in neighborhoods and woods, to form their own clubhouses and games with other kids, and—as they got older—to roam more widely around their towns. In particular, they remembered the freedom of largely unsupervised and wide-ranging play "all day long" during the summer, ended by various signals that it was time to go home, such as "when you heard church bells," "when dad whistled," "when it was dinner time," and "when it got dark." Of course, as adults now looking back, these respondents are in some ways collapsing together memories from a variety of ages in such a way that makes their entire childhood seem unstructured and carefree; in fact, the independence they gained, they accrued as they got older and showed greater maturity. It is clear, however, from both their remembrances and the historical record of popular advice that children are gaining independence away from home at later ages than their parents and grandparents did.

When some parents describe the freedoms they enjoyed as children, they describe those days wistfully, with nostalgia for the past, and explain that they feel like their own children are missing out on something valuable. However, a few parents pointed out that although they enjoyed a lot of freedom as children, they now consider their own parents to have been neglectful and say that they are glad that today's standards are higher for parental supervision. Still others acknowledge with realism that both the times and the public standards for parents have changed. For example, Pauline described both her memories of what she did as a child and her knowledge that today's parents face tighter constraints:

> It is so different. It is just very, very different. How times have changed. . . . We used to walk up to the shopping—we were right near a strip mall. You had a grocery store and a card store. It had a Friendly's and a drug store, something like that, and a thrifty sort of store . . . we would go up there and shop around. We would hang out behind that building. Now, you think "Oh, my God." Then we would hang around by a pond and catch frogs. No concern that somebody might drown in the pond. Meanwhile, nobody ever knew where we were. We would either walk or we would hop on our bikes. We would be down at the Dairy Queen all the time. It was amazing. I talked to my mother about that. The funniest story my mother told me was—I obviously would not have known—she said, "Oh yeah, when you kids were little

and it was nice and warm out ..." She would put the old playpens—you know I was 18 months old, in a playpen in the front yard. She would not be out there. She would be in the house doing house work and we would just be outside getting some fresh air. I think, could you imagine if you drove by somebody's house and you saw a kid? I mean DSS would be knocking at your door. So it is very, very different.

As Pauline points out, parents today feel constrained by cultural and legal standards that require much closer parental supervision than some of them recall from their own childhoods. Parents worry about safeguarding their children from a world they perceive as more dangerous than it was in the past. However, both middle- and working-class parents also worry about being judged by neighbors and other parents as falling short on their duty to protect their children and facing state intervention or legal repercussions for any lack of adequate supervision. These worries about state intervention are most pressing for less-affluent parents, who describe the feeling that they are being watched and judged by others who may disapprove of their parenting methods.

Constant Supervision Required

In contrast to past freedom of mobility, children and adolescents since the 1980s have been much more constrained in terms of what they are allowed to do and where they are allowed to go by themselves. In the 1980s, a number of widely publicized and sensationalized incidents of child abduction and victimization changed public perceptions of safety for children and heightened parents' awareness of the dangers posed by sexual predators and other would-be child abductors.[17] Media reports of actual incidents of child victimization mingled with urban legends, such as stories of Halloween candy containing razor blades, to make parents increasingly wary of their children's safety in public.[18] In popular mainstream advice, parents are admonished to know exactly where their children are at all times and that it is ultimately their responsibility to protect their children from situations that might leave them vulnerable to abduction or molestation by strangers.

Since the 1980s the need for careful adult supervision is stated often and unequivocally in parenting advice. From the time their children are born, parents are charged with being constantly vigilant about knowing their every move and protecting their safety. Playpens, safety gates, infant swings, bouncy seats, wading pools, sandboxes, and swing sets all come with prominent warnings: "Never leave child unattended." To that end, increasingly sophisticated monitors are marketed that allow constant surveillance of babies and young children at home.[19] But as children grow, the fear that grips parents most is not of household accidents, but of child abduction. Magazines and other media disproportionately report stranger abduction cases and remind parents that unaccompanied children are vulnerable to abduction and murder. One striking example of a cautionary tale is a 1991 article titled "A Secret Too Terrible to Remember": "Neighbors made remarks about my not letting my children out of my sight. But I knew better than most people that even in nice neighborhoods children are not always safe. When I was eight, my best friend, Susan Nason, was murdered. . . . Susan's mother, Margaret, a tall, slender woman in her late twenties, first began to think something was wrong when her daughter failed to return home from running an errand in the neighborhood."[20] A recent Mother's Day feature made close supervision an explicit criterion in answering its title question, "Are You a Good Mother?": "The world now seems a much more dangerous place. 'My mother would let my sister and me go for 20-mile bike rides alone. I would never let my kids do that,' says a Midwestern mother who home schools her kids (and has recently taken in two foster children). 'I'm always careful; I always make sure I know who my kids are with, and where.'"[21]

It is clear that the parents I interviewed take to heart advice and prevailing standards that charge them with monitoring their children's movements and being vigilant about their safety. Chris, a white middle-class dad, described his anxieties about his children's safety and how he constrained their movements: "Are there predators around? You can go to any of the federal buildings and any of the local offices and sex offender's posters are hanging up and you are like, 'Where do they live? Are they anywhere near me?' [My eight-year-old] is not allowed to go past the neighbor's mailbox right now. She can go there, the cul-de-sac and our backyard. That is it. She cannot go anywhere else." Although professing different comfort levels with outdoor play, Michelle and Nadine, both middle-class stay-at-home-mothers, described fearfulness and tight boundaries for their primary-school-aged children:

MICHELLE: I don't know when I would feel comfortable just saying, "Yeah, you can go down the street by yourself." I don't know. I don't right now. I am uncomfortable even letting my kids go in the backyard by themselves. I let them go together when there are two of them. I will not let my daughter go by herself. Only if the window is open and they are within ear shot of everybody. It makes me uncomfortable. I don't know. I am worried somebody is going to get their attention. They are going to want to go out front and I don't know what is there. I don't know. I am very fearful.

NADINE: And I am a little more lenient. Our backyard is fenced. [My daughter] goes back there and they will play whatever . . . I will let her out in the front when she goes to get the mail and the newspaper. She will play hippity-hop or something like that in the front yard. I am more cautious about watching her. Literally, I am keeping my eyes on her when she is in the front yard. Even though it is a cul-de-sac, there are woods there. Conservation land is right there.

MICHELLE: Right. And I would let my kids go to friends' houses. It's not that I have to be with my kids every minute. I sort of think they need to be with an adult. I am not very comfortable with them being unsupervised. . . . It is just not the comfortable thing. I don't know. I feel like there are just so many more things that we know. We know more about what is going on. I just feel like it is not safe.

NADINE: In forty years I guess, a lot happens. It sounds like a very 'old person' thing to say but the world is a different place. There was some of that but I think of people just stopping and talking to my children and . . .

MICHELLE: And a lot of people who have bad intentions with my children.

NADINE: Fifty percent of them have good intentions. They might say, "Oh, what a beautiful little girl," and the other fifty percent say, "Oh, what a beautiful little girl, why don't you come into the basement with me?"

Despite the fact that children are statistically much more vulnerable to injury and victimization at home, like Melanie and Nancy, most parents

today frequently voice their fears that the world "out there" is a dangerous place for children. In contrast to the image of the helpful, if misguided, stranger of the past, Nadine's statements illustrate contemporary
parents' sense that *half* of the other adults in their communities pose
threats to their children.

Even when parents consider their children safe, they must sometimes contend with local standards that dictate tighter boundaries and
closer supervision than they feel is truly necessary.[22] Kimberly, a white
middle-class mother of three, who lives on a cul-de-sac in a very quiet,
manicured, suburban neighborhood, feels that even though she thinks
her kids are safe playing near her home, she will be judged inattentive
and inadequate by others if she is not visibly monitoring them: "I feel
like I'm supposed to be involved in their every move. If I'm not aware
of where they are at all times, like, I wonder sometimes when I let my
kids play out in the front or ride their bike, what do people think of
me—that I just allow the kids to roam freely?" Cassandra, a Hispanic
middle-class mother, similarly disclosed to me what she called her guilty
secret—she has left her children in the car when she had to make a quick
stop at a store. "I feel I can go into a store for ten seconds and someone
is not going to take them. That is not rational. I think a lot of parents are
afraid of that." Although she described a careful risk assessment that con-
vinced her that her children were safe, she did worry about the potential
consequences of being found out and charged with neglect. The fact that
as a society we have increasingly individualized parents' responsibility
for children's safety is apparent in parents' fears, whether justified or not,
that they could be charged with child endangerment for allowing their
children to do things that the parents judge as safe and that parents and
children in past generations considered routine. Instead of building safer
communities where children can enjoy rights to move and play, we have
increasingly individualized the burden of ensuring children's safety.[23]
Parents no longer feel that they can trust neighbors and other community members to assist in supervising children; therefore, they must keep
them close at hand.

Of course, parents make informed judgments about their children's
safety based on not only the cultural consensus of other parents but also
the actual conditions of their neighborhoods and towns.[24] Children's
safety outdoors, in their neighborhoods, and on routes to school varies

significantly by geographic and social locations. Thus, differences in urban and rural areas, neighborhood characteristics, social class, race, and gender create marked disparities in the amount of public autonomy afforded children.[25] A number of studies by geographers indicate that despite changing expectations about gender-typed behaviors, boys tend to gain earlier freedom of mobility and enjoy wider home ranges than girls.[26] Kim Blakely found, for example, that in a sample of nine- to eleven-year-olds in New York City, boys who had bicycles were permitted to ride an average of eight hundred feet from home, often including going around a corner; girls who had bicycles were permitted, on average, to ride only half that distance—about four hundred feet from home—and were not permitted to ride outside of clear sight lines.[27] Some research indicates that children of working-class parents enjoy greater autonomy over their free time and outdoor play than do children of middle-class parents.[28] In some impoverished neighborhoods, however, high rates of violent crime and a lack of public resources for children affect both parents' and children's risk assessments about the safety and desirability of *any* outdoor play.[29] In addition, many public spaces are increasingly constructed, both physically and socially, as adult spaces where children are subject to suspicion and interference if they attempt to use them independently.[30] Children's and adolescents' age, social class, gender, and race characteristics affect the extent to which they are regarded as public menaces or threats and thus discouraged or barred from using public areas. These meaningful differences in children's experiences are poorly represented by the often-idealized cultural images presented in popular magazines; that is, some children's actual experiences of autonomous mobility may be even more tightly constrained than would be indicated even by mainstream parenting advice.

The result of individualizing the charge to protect children is that children, kept more constrained and dependent upon their parents, are gaining autonomy over their own activities and movements at later ages than was true in the past. Although it is certainly not true that children have lost all freedom to play in neighborhoods, it is generally the case that younger children have lost much of this freedom. In general, even when parents assess their neighborhoods as reasonably safe, children now gain public autonomy over their local movements two to three years later than their parents did.[31] In 1966, the prevailing wisdom was that

six- to eight-year-olds were competent to travel independently to school
and other activities.[32] Today this license is more typically granted when
children are eight- to eleven-years old. When I asked her at what age she
would allow her children to play in her neighborhood outside their own
yard, Tatiana, the mother of two- and four-year-old girls, described a
two-year lag for children's autonomy for play: "We live right next to the
neighborhood I grew up in. To me, I used to go out at five and six and
be able to run around in the neighborhood and that was fine. But that
was also a different time. That is a very good question. Like, if I were to
pick a number, I would feel like seven or eight is where I would feel
comfortable. I would not like her to cross a main street at seven or eight
but being able to go back into the neighborhood, I would say around
seven or eight." Liz, who lives in another suburban neighborhood,
described a comparable standard for her children, saying that her older
children, who are ten and twelve, have freedom to play near home but
that she is not yet ready for her youngest to be out of sight. "They do
have a really good neighborhood so they can go anywhere in the neighborhood as long as I know where they are going. I am having a little
harder time with my five-year-old son because I feel he is really young
to be hanging out in the neighborhood alone if I don't know exactly
where he is. He is sort of at this awkward age. If he were eight years old
it would be different. With him I feel like I really have to know, I have
to watch him a little more closely."

KEEPING TABS ON PEER RELATIONSHIPS

As we have seen, children's independent mobility has become more
tightly constrained, particularly for young children. Instead of sending
children off to school and activities on their own or out to play, parents
now spend a considerable amount of time chauffeuring children.[33] At
times, this creates the potential for conflict between parents who feel
obligated to escort their children and children who feel they are old
enough to be free from their parents' watchful eyes. A 1991 article titled,
"Keeping Tabs Without Being a Nag" advised: "Respect your preteen's
wishes. . . . Make plans that address her need for independence without
compromising her safety. Drop her off a block from the soccer field so
that her teammates won't see her with you. If you're driving a group of
her friends to a middle-school dance, make sure another parent picks

them up so that your child isn't the only one under parental supervision."[34] While they are driving the carpool, hanging around during scout meetings and soccer practices, and supervising play dates at the park, parents are not simply present; they are also monitoring the behavior of their children. In fact, the latest generation of parents is frequently advised to seize upon teachable moments in the time that they spend present with children, such as when children are watching television, playing with friends, and riding in carpools.

Even though expert advice sometimes recommends allowing children to exercise autonomy in their peer relationships, especially when it comes to kids working out disagreements between themselves, much advice focuses on how parents ought to intervene in situations in which they are supervising children who, a generation or two ago, might have been unsupervised. Consider this example: "You take your 5-year-old to the park. When another little girl won't get off the swing to give your daughter a turn, your child calls her stupid. Keep your comments short and simple. 'Point out with a tone of voice that's not overly angry that those words hurt people's feelings,' Dr. Scarlett recommends."[35] In fact, advice to let children work out their own peer relationships seems to be so necessary and prevalent because children are rarely, if ever, away from adult surveillance. This leaves parents uncertain about how and when to intervene and results in a lot of conflicting advice on the matter. Nonetheless, the need for constant supervision is never questioned: an article about middle-school-aged children advises, "Read the signals— when your children want you and when they don't. Don't take over a group situation that is primarily theirs. But just as important, don't withdraw completely and neglect to supervise them adequately. They need and want your guidance—just not front and center."[36]

Not only must children's movements be monitored and constrained to protect them from strangers and traffic, but their peer relationships also require a great deal of monitoring. Thus, even as children get older and begin to have additional opportunities for activities and leisure time spent away from home, parents are advised to keep tabs on their children's peer relationships. "Supervision is a simple but pivotal parenting technique. It should be so much a part of life that parents and children take it for granted. Supervision of peer activity should begin with toddlers and last through the teens. The cardinal rule of supervision is: Keep your eyes and ears open and your words to a minimum."[37] In fact, some advice warns parents not to let down their guard as their children get older, reminding them that "preteens still need to be monitored—even if from a distance."[38] For example, a cautionary tale in 1996 told of a teenager who went missing while unsupervised in her own back yard. After a search of several hours, she was found dead near the air conditioning unit, where she had been "huffing" (inhaling fumes to get high).[39] With such high stakes, some advice even suggests that adolescent children require more parental time and supervision than they did as infants and toddlers because at later ages peer pressures become a source of concern: "It is when youngsters are between the ages of ten and fifteen that they are most actively asking questions and experimenting with behaviors that will shape their attitudes, habits, and values for a lifetime. This is when they are most vulnerable to negative peer pressure. They need their parents' help to make wise choices. Studies show that parental involvement is a key factor in students' academic achievement at this age. There is also evidence that teenage pregnancy, delinquency, and other problem behaviors are less likely when parents continue to be actively involved in the lives of their children and monitor their activities."[40] Several parents I interviewed echoed this line of reasoning that children need more, not less, supervision from parents as they get older.

Adequate supervision of older children and teens often involves carefully limiting and monitoring their mobility as well as ensuring that they spend most of their free time in adult-organized activities: "It's important for kids to have activities and be in supervised situations after school so that they don't experiment simply because they're bored."[41] In fact, as I describe in chapter 4, children are currently spending so much of their out-of-school time in structured and supervised activities that we must question whether they actually have much "free" time at all. Middle-class children, in particular, participate in a round of near-constant enrichment activities that leave them supervised at all times by adults and give them little control over their own leisure time.[42]

All of this constant supervision has consequences for how children experience peer relationships. One consequence is that kids have fewer opportunities for age-integrated and gender-integrated play, both of which are sources for learning important social skills. Barrie Thorne's ethnographic study of children's play reports that kids are more likely to cross both age and gender lines when playing in smaller neighborhood groups than in larger groups at school.[43] Age and gender sorting likely extends from school settings to many organized after-school activities as well, a development that leaves kids without the opportunity to form alliances across these boundaries. Another consequence is that kids who rely on adult intervention to settle peer and sibling disputes do not gain experience managing and solving these conflicts on their own. Instead, the concerted cultivation style of middle-class parenting, with its high level of adult involvement and attention, results in not only more adult engagement in settling kids' disputes but also more frequent instances of peer and sibling conflicts.[44]

Spurred by desires to teach problem solving and conflict resolution, as well as by concerns about bullying, many schools are beginning to incorporate social development curricula to teach children skills for negotiating peer relationships. These curricula reflect the growing emphasis on children's private, emotional autonomy that I describe in chapter 5. However, seen in the light of children's lack of independent mobility and near-constant surveillance by adults, these curricula also reflect, ironically, children's decreased public autonomy. Kids are often excluded from autonomous use of public space and instead corralled together in school and in various "private" activities, often with little choice of companions. With fewer opportunities to learn early in childhood how to "work it out" on their own with peers in age- and gender-integrated neighborhood play, children are regarded as lacking interpersonal skills for solving conflicts and getting along with one another.

Some sociological evidence suggests that limitations on more public forms of youngsters' autonomy are actually contributing factors in the development of the very peer relationships that are problematized by such curricula. Murray Milner, for example, has argued that some adolescent behaviors that adults find disturbing—clique formation, put-downs and meanness, and a preoccupation with who is "in" and "out"—are a consequence of teens exercising power in the arena of status relations, the only form of social power readily available to them.[45] Although avoidance is the preferred method of social control and conflict management among suburban adults, both children's reduced autonomy and the greater density of their peer relationships make avoidance a less feasible strategy for them; that is, open conflict and violence are more likely in response to youngsters' peer conflicts.[46] While neighborhood bullies can sometimes be avoided, when peer conflicts occur either at school or at home, kids often have no escape and so must turn to other forms of conflict resolution. Increased demand for social development curricula therefore reflects children's decreased autonomy as well as the desire to steer children toward therapeutic, or "talking," forms of conflict management rather than violence. Most recently, concerns have arisen about bullying in the new space of online social networks, highlighting the ways that media technologies introduce new avenues for and new concerns about keeping tabs on kids.

KEEPING TABS ON MEDIA

Although I didn't specifically ask parents about media technologies, most of them raised the topic on their own during their interviews. It became apparent that there was a relationship between how parents thought about their children's opportunities to experience independence and how they conceived of media technologies as blurring the boundary between home and public space. Parents talked about media technologies affecting their children's freedom of movement in three key ways: various forms of media serve as alternatives to outdoor play and play away from home; media technologies extend the reach of home outward; and such technologies publicly intrude into the private space of home.

For some parents who talked about media technologies, media provided a convenient explanation for the contrast parents saw between their remembered childhood experiences and what they now observe. Marcos, a Hispanic working-class father, said that he would like for his daughter to spend "less time on the Internet. I would like for her to go outside more. . . . When we were kids, we always played games outside. Well, there would be a whole yard full of kids. We always got involved playing outside. You don't see that too much [anymore]." Naomi similarly recalled that when she was a kid, "there was only so much on TV. We went outside and played a lot with our friends. And other parents were working just like my parents. But still we were able to stay in the neighborhood. We just did things. We did not have to be transferred from slot to slot."

Like Marcos and Naomi, many parents explain that kids' greater involvement with media—watching television, playing video games, surfing the Internet—is keeping kids indoors. They observe that they do not see many kids playing in their neighborhoods, and they attribute this not to decreased autonomy for children, but rather to kids' choice of activities. From this perspective parents often assume that the opportunities either to play outdoors or to consume media entertainment indoors are equally available and viable to kids as options. For some kids this may be true, but not for others. In fact, we know that when parents are concerned about children's public safety, parents often encourage media entertainments to allow them to keep a closer eye on kids at home.[47] Saying that children are not playing outside because they prefer to watch television or surf the Internet, however, frames children's decreased mobility as an independent and individualized choice that children are making. Therefore, the convenient use of media as a scapegoat sometimes obscures the increased obligation that many parents feel today to provide constant supervision for children and the tighter constraints on children's freedom of movement.

Parents also describe media technologies as a way to extend the reach of home into public space. Kids' use of media technologies at home may allow parents to physically keep an eye on kids, but parents also value the fact that kids can learn about the world "out there" from the safety and security of their own homes. Parents describe the ways their kids use media technologies to access information, expand their knowledge, practice their communication skills, and express themselves. Furthermore, parents allow their children to experience monitored mobility by extending home outward through the reach of the cell phone. These parents describe beginning to give children limited licenses to leave home when children are around nine to twelve years old. Julia, whose daughter is twelve, said that her daughter "walks the dog around a lot. She will leave our house and walk the dog and wander around the neighborhood. I make her have a cell phone. . . . I worry about safety issues." Belinda's explanation is similar:

BELINDA: For a long time she wanted a cell phone. It was like the biggest thing. I think she was asking since she was eight years old. We did buy her one on her eleventh birthday. The only reason I think was to let her have a little bit of freedom and to allow her to have a little bit of independence that way. . . . I started dropping her off at activities instead of being able to stay. . . . If she is at the YMCA for forty-five minutes and I am not there I want her to be able to call me if she needs me.

MARKELLA: If she is at the Y for forty-five minutes does she call you?

BELINDA: Oh absolutely. She does. She will call me twice. "I am in, I made it, I am safe, I am happy, I am putting my phone in the locker." Whatever. Then she will call me to make sure I am outside before she comes outside to meet me.

Thus, licenses to leave home are enabled by the reach of technology, but they are accompanied by the requirement that children stay in touch so that their growing mobility can be carefully monitored.[48] In fact, new communication technologies mean that even as children move away from home and into adulthood, parents are still expected to keep tabs through an "electronic tether."[49]

Media technologies allow parents to keep tabs on kids by keeping them at home or monitoring their mobility away from home, yet media technologies also publicly intrude into the private space of the home and introduce the need for new forms of parental supervision. Keeping kids at home is one way parents try to keep them safe, but new media technologies bring additional threats directly into homes. Kimberly, a white middle-class mother explained that she worries a lot about "safety, keeping your kids safe. Keeping kids safe while, at the same time, being open to the opportunities that are out there with Internet and travel, and cell phones and the technological advances that have opened up new avenues for exploring life. . . . Trying to help them navigate that and learn those roads and keeping themselves safe." Marcos, a Hispanic working-class father, worried about leaving his teenage daughter at home because of the reach of technology. This was something about which he had specifically sought advice from his friends and family: "If we want to go somewhere would it be safe to leave her at home at age fifteen? Do you think that is a good age? It would be sort of, 'Would you feel too comfortable leaving a teenage girl home?' There always could be guys there. If she does not know any better they could try and call, this and that. People now-a-days, they will speak in different forms. Someone will be calling and keeping in touch by Internet, texting, and things like that." Parents like Kimberly and Marcos worry that Internet and phone technologies allow children to be victimized in their own home. These concerns are not just about Internet predators, though; parents are increasingly worried about the ways that new forms of mediated communication (email, texting, social networking media) are impeding children's development of social skills and ability to deal appropriately with peer conflict. Recent public concerns about cyber-bullying also illustrate the ways that parents conceive of media technologies as blurring the boundaries between public and private.

Beyond their fears that media technologies create new avenues for their children's victimization, parents also worry about negative cultural influences introduced by television, movies, video games, and the Internet. Concerns about negative influences from media are not new, but the forms of media have changed. In 1941, Clara Savage Littledale, editor of *Parents' Magazine*, wondered:

> Have the children of this country gone "comics" mad? . . . Parents and teachers are worried and asking what to do. Surveys have been made and they bear out what parents say—that virtually no child escapes the influence of the comics. Most of the comic magazines are cheap and lurid—some are even worse—yet these publications are holding children spellbound. What do comic magazines offer? Except for an occasional feature, the comics do not pretend to be funny. They dish up fantastic excitement and portray impossible, often grotesque characters who achieve their hearts' desires no matter what the odds. It is not a reading diet that any responsible adult would wish for a child, and yet it is a diet which is unbelievably popular with children.[50]

Alarm about comics in the early twentieth century was no trifling matter: Littledale quotes an observer who refers to comics as "sex-horror serials" and "lurid publications [that] depend for their appeal upon mayhem, murder, torture, and abduction."

Parents in the early twentieth century clearly worried about media exposure, but letters from that period reveal why contemporary parents may feel nostalgia for the ease with which parents could screen media influences in the past. For example, a mother wrote to *Parents' Magazine* in 1936 to describe her solution:

> We live in a small town where there is only one moving picture show. Our thirteen-year-old does not go out on school nights, so that leaves only the week-end for pictures. But sometimes they had a gruesome murder mystery and other times unwholesome grown-up stories on weekends. So I would say, "Arthur, the picture this week is one that I don't think would be at all interesting to you. Wouldn't you rather have the thirty cents admission to do with as you please?" He never fails to have a dozen uses for the money and never has preferred the show. Then when there are good pictures for him, I make it a point to say, "There is a good picture this weekend and I know you will enjoy it—plan on going."[51]

Since the era when parents worried about the comics and whether this week's moving picture show was appropriate, the range and amount of media that children consume has increased exponentially, as has the difficulty of effectively monitoring it. Douglas, a white working-class father, explained: "Everything on the Internet, you have to be, I'm afraid of those things in a sense. . . . Don't get me wrong—I go on the Internet. I am a thirty-two-year-old man. I can navigate it, but I don't want my ten-year-old son looking at whatever could pop up. You click on the wrong thing and then—boom! I know there are parental locks on cable vision and things like that. That part kind of worries me a little bit. Other influences, outside just in general." Other parents voiced numerous concerns about their children's exposure to violence, sexuality, negative body image messages, materialism, and the glorification of unrealistic celebrity lifestyles.

PRIVATIZING RESPONSIBILITY

In popular advice, parents are told that it is their responsibility to keep tabs on their kids' media usage. Although they are advised about technological aids—"use filtering software" and "make sure your television has a V-chip"[52]—parents are told that ultimately only parental vigilance stands between their children and inappropriate content: "Everyone agrees that the most effective way to monitor kids' online activity is . . . to monitor it. Literally. To stand beside the computer from time to time when your son is at the keyboard, watching his every mouse click. . . . Accompanying your child to a website he frequents is no different from 'checking out a playground where your kids go, to see that it's safe, to see who hangs around there.' . . . Parents are the ultimate filter."[53] *Good Housekeeping* reported in 2006 that mothers "have the sense of spitting into the wind in terms of how hard it is to counteract messages of greed, commercialism, and sexuality"; nonetheless, they promote the idea that shielding kids "from inappropriate music, TV, movies, and Internet sites" is a requirement for being "a good mother."[54]

The privatization of responsibility is internalized and accepted by parents, who see media monitoring as one duty of parenting: "'I'm C.J.'s mother, so I'm responsible for what he does,' says Kelley Jones, a Detroit single mom who generally allows her thirteen-year-old son to browse just about any website he wishes on the computer in the living room, as long as he discusses what he finds. Says Jones: 'It's a waste of time to blame technology for parents' mistakes.'"[55] Given the concern that both parents and experts express for how controversial media content affects children's development and increases the burden of parenting, it is surprising how little either group has promoted any kind of collective response that might demand more public oversight of media content or advertising to children. Instead, most popular advice frames the issue as private, rather than public. Advice-givers simply tell parents that they should not expect to successfully shield kids from all inappropriate media content; rather, they should seize upon "teachable moments"— for example when watching television with their children—to discuss how their family's values compare with media portrayals. Such advice reflects the widely taken-for-granted character of the belief that parents should individually determine what is appropriate for their own kids and then somehow try to enforce their own boundaries. This view evidences both parental freedom to make their own value choices for their own families and the degree to which parenting has become a private role without public support.

Despite their willingness to accept the responsibility for vigilantly keeping tabs on kids' media use, parents also see media influences as changing the very nature of childhood. Although children may receive licenses to travel through physical public space at later ages than in the past, in other ways living in a media-saturated culture makes them grow up sooner. Articles like "Too Sexy Too Soon," "Teenagers and Credit Cards," and "Raising Kids Online" all present worries that kids are being pushed into certain kinds of adult situations and behaviors before they are ready.[56] Liz explained: "I think they are just older. I feel like they act older than I did at this age. I think it's the media, I think they do have access to the computer, although, we try to limit it. We limit hours and what they are on. I just think they see things. I am not quite sure how." Parents also worry about the ways that media messages and precociousness affect children's peer relationships. For example, one mother and school social worker talked about the "mean girls issues":

> A big issue throughout kindergarten and fifth grade was mean girls issues. Little cliques of mean little girls bullying each other with name calling and sort of power playing with each other which I would say I don't remember. Maybe we wipe it out when we are older. I don't remember it being this bad when I was in school. I think it's because of the access to the media that these kids have. And mean girls in general. There are movies about it now. Kids in fifth grade are watching Hannah Montana which is about a high school student. They are seeing peer issues that high school students are dealing with. It's not them. They are adapting some of that idea.

Parents' assessment of the ways that media alters the nature of childhood do not end, though, with fictional representations. Parents also expressed a great deal of concern about the effects of growing up in a media-saturated, post-9/11 world. Several of these parents worried about the ways that contemporary news media portray the world as a scary place. Therefore, they supervise their children's exposure to not only sit-coms, movies, and music but also news and current events. They wanted to make sure their children were not being unnecessarily frightened by reports of real violence like crime, wars, and racism. Naomi, a black middle-class mother, described the "media blitz" as the biggest challenge facing parents today: "What is out there in the media. What is portrayed in the media. I mean, I could not turn the news on the last few days because of what happened in New Hampshire [a brutal killing of a woman and her daughter at home]. So, we like to watch current events but we cannot watch current events so they don't know about the sports that just happened last night because I could not risk them having to hear about the story." Cassandra, a Hispanic middle-class mother, also described the news as a particular challenge: "I tried to tell [my son] when he was little, I told him the reason we don't watch the news is that it focuses only on the bad. There is all this good and then this little bad and that is what the news is about. It confuses you. You only show them the dangers and scary stuff. They dream about it. They absorb it all and are so fearful." Quite a few of the parents with whom I talked describe their children as anxious, and they conceive of this as a qualitatively new feature of childhood in a media-saturated age.

SUMMARY

In the current social construction of childhood, kids are both getting older and younger.[57] Although children may be maturing faster because of some things to which they are exposed in the media, they are also more dependent upon parents until later ages. Both the record presented by popular advice and the observations of contemporary parents indicate that children have lost substantial public autonomy over their own mobility. Whether because they are viewed as angels or devils,[58] children are less welcome in many public spaces, their mobility is tightly constrained, and they are under nearly constant surveillance and supervision. Closer adult supervision alters children's experience of peer relationships, leaving kids fewer opportunities for spontaneous and unsupervised recreation. And even as they do gain mobility beyond home and neighborhood—usually at a two- to three-year delay from their parents' generation—their movements are monitored carefully through the use of cell phones or other new technologies.

While they are kept "safely" at home, kids' use of media technologies also requires individualized parental monitoring and supervision, to keep them both safe and innocent. Children's exposure to new media technologies and popular culture has been a longstanding source of ambivalence and anxiety in popular parenting advice. Although the specific concerns have changed with time—for example, from comic books to the Internet—much advice on these topics reveals anxiety about the ways that popular culture and mass media undermine parental authority and encourage children toward earlier independence from their parents by bringing public cultural messages directly to children in the private spaces of their homes. Concerns about mass media often focus on children's exposure to controversial subjects, such as violence and sexuality. Today's parents are advised to maintain strict controls on their children's movements away from home in order to keep them safe, but they express perplexity about how to control the dangerous elements that seem to reach into their homes through television, video games, Internet, and cell phones. Like the other sites of negotiation between parental authority and children's autonomy, dilemmas about entertainment media result from reordering the line between public and private realms of experience.

CHAPTER 4

Mixed Messages about Responsibility

CHILDREN'S DUTIES AND THE WORK OF PARENTING

I have looked online for different [chore] charts, chart systems for the kids. One of my daughters actually made up a chart, not that anybody has looked at it one time yet. But it is there. It is exhausting trying to implement it for me.　　　　　—Deborah

[My biggest challenge is] just trying to get children to be self-motivated. That is real difficult for us in our household. To get our children to be self-motivated is constantly, "Did you do this? Did you do that? Your lunch is on the table. If I had not said anything you would have been going off to school and I would have had to bring it to you." That kind of thing is really just having to be alert and focused. I know they are young but I did not come home from school and have my parents sit down with me and say, "Okay, let's do homework." I just did it. So to me that is really, really stressful.　　　　　—Naomi

IN THIS CHAPTER, I explore the decreased recognition of children as public participants and contributors through the twentieth-century cultural construction of childhood as a period of sharply limited responsibility. At the beginning of the twentieth century, American culture was accepting the notion that the proper social role of children was not work, but education. Even taking into account this starting point, popular advice reveals substantial historical changes in children's opportunities to experience meaningful independence and responsibility in their homes and communities. To be sure, children do still have many duties: they are required to go to school and do homework; many are expected to help out at home by doing chores; increasingly, children and youth are required to perform community service; and for a growing number of children, even extracurricular "leisure" activities can become one more "have to" in busy schedules. Although children's lives are full of duties, I argue, however, that contemporary parenting advice offers very mixed messages about these duties; while advice claims that children need to be responsible, suggestions undermine those opportunities to demonstrate responsibility with a persistent focus on necessary adult supervision. This advice, then, contributes to the very limited public recognition of children as capable members of their communities who might make autonomous and meaningful contributions to the common welfare.

Sociologist Viviana Zelizer describes a major transformation that took place in the social valuation of children at the turn of the last century, as the "economically useful" child of the nineteenth century was replaced in the twentieth century by the "economically useless but emotionally priceless" child.[1] Zelizer argues that this transformation, which included an intense battle over child labor, was about not only changing economic interests but also new cultural understandings of childhood as children were sentimentalized and sacralized. By the beginning of the twentieth century, middle-class childhood was already well-established as economically unproductive, and by 1930 legislation prohibited most forms of child labor, thereby establishing working-class and poor children, too, as "useless." Prohibitions on child labor and the advent of mass schooling greatly altered most children's experience of childhood by establishing it as a period of education and training for future productivity.

In the popular parenting advice I examine, it is clear that from the beginning of the twentieth century the transformation from child worker to child scholar was complete in the middle-class family ideal. These magazines include very few references to children's paid work. Some discussions of paid work, like a 1966 article titled "Girl Dropouts," problematize paid work as a barrier to sufficient education, explaining that "a few years ago a girl could drop out of school and drop into a job. Today automation is steadily decreasing the number of unskilled jobs—the kinds that don't require a high-school education or special training."[2] Most other articles that mention paid work acknowledge that kids need ways to earn spending money, but that their opportunities for earning money are severely limited. For example, a 2006 *Good Housekeeping* article featured "Jobs for Kids," explaining: "Lots of jobs aren't open to kids until they turn 16. So what if your child is bored by babysitting . . . or not cut out for a paper route? Encourage him to start his own business: With any luck, he'll learn about taking responsibility and managing money." The "businesses" featured in the article, though, have a distinctly childish nature: a lemonade stand and making crafts to sell to friends and neighbors. Acknowledging the difficulty kids have when they want to earn money, parenting advice frequently recommends volunteer work as an alternative to paid work, both for kids too young to have jobs and for teens who may want to work but encounter a limited labor market.

Twenty-first-century work in the sociology of childhood has begun to direct attention toward the work performed by children, revealing that children in some social categories take on vital responsibilities that have been overlooked because they did not fit the mainstream, middle-class ideal of a carefree childhood. Ethnographer Miri Song has described the importance of children's labor "helping out" in the small ethnic businesses run by immigrants in Britain.[3] Marjorie Orellana has illuminated the household work performed by immigrant children in California, including their responsibilities as "cultural and linguistic brokers" who ease the immigrant transition for their families.[4] Lisa Dodson and Jillian Dickert report that low-income mothers rely on their daughters to help with household work and caretaking for younger siblings.[5] Studies like these are important because they reveal the myth of a universal childhood by highlighting instead the many different childhoods of children in varied social locations. Recognition of these variations and of the labor of the "industrious minority,"[6] however, have yet to influence the more widespread cultural construction of a "real" childhood as a time of freedom from responsibility.

Jens Qvortrup, a leader in the new sociology of childhood, has offered an insightful theoretical critique of the cultural construction of childhood as a stage of irresponsibility; he advances a macroeconomic argument that all children have a place in the contemporary societal division of labor.[7] In contrast to Zelizer's argument that children have become "economically useless,"[8] Qvortrup argues that childhood education is a form of socially necessary labor in modern economies. Children's usefulness, he argues, has been transformed from work to education, but children are still constructive and useful social participants, whose work is economically vital even if unremunerated. In thinking about children's level of responsibility, then, we need to take into account not only economically recognized paid work and the particular family responsibilities of children who fall outside the mainstream but also the variety of unpaid duties that make up most children's social participation today—household work, schoolwork, enrichment activities, and community involvements. In describing these duties, does parenting advice portray children as responsible and capable social participants?

Although I agree with Qvortrup's theoretical analysis of children's macrosociological usefulness, I do not find this theoretical view reflected in popular representations of children and their duties at home, at school, or in their communities. Although popular advice explicitly reminds parents that it is essential to teach their children to be responsible, it implicitly sends the message that parents should maintain relatively low expectations about children's capabilities and that ultimately parents shoulder responsibility for children's work. It is ironic that as popular advice has increased the emphasis on teaching children to be responsible it has simultaneously required greater hands-on parental involvement and adult supervision for such teaching. Thus, children's autonomy and responsibilities as social participants are obscured as attention is directed instead toward parents' responsibilities. That is, discussions of childhood duties in this popular medium reinforce the boundary between adults and children. To be an adult is to be a responsible social participant in the public sphere; to be a child is to be irresponsible, dependent, and relegated to the private sphere.

HOUSEHOLD HELPERS

Despite the fact that parenting advice has always included tips for getting children to pick up after themselves, do the dishes, and be responsible about their chores, this advice indicates that the amount and kind of household work and responsibilities expected of most children decreased substantially in the course of the twentieth century. In the first half of the twentieth century, popular parenting advice depicted household chores as a largely taken-for-granted feature of children's and adolescents' lives. Entire articles designed to persuade parents about the advisability of assigning chores did not appear in my literature samples until the 1960s. Prior to that, although experts did advise parents about topics such as how to instill tidy habits in their children, most expert advice that mentioned chores did so in passing, typically in the context of discussing other topics, such as children's developmental stages or fitting chores into the back-to-school routine. For example, a September 1929 *Parents* article, "Make it the Best Year Ever," primarily focuses on school preparations, but the article does include a reminder to build chores into the school routine before children's schedules become crowded.[9] Another article from 1946 addresses chores in passing as part of a discussion about helping children adjust to their parents' divorce: "The fundamental objective is to provide the child with a home, a family circle, of which he feels himself to be a cooperative member. . . . The more he plays on that home team—the more he runs errands for it, makes beds for it, cooks for it, mows the lawn for it, really cooperates in its chores—the more it will mean to him. Therefore he should not be 'spared' chores."[10]

Whether mentioning chores in relation to back-to-school routines, health concerns, developmental stages, or divorce adjustment, early twentieth-century experts largely took for granted that household chores and responsibilities were a normal feature of children's lives, and their concern was to ensure that this normalcy was maintained despite any unusual circumstances that might arise. In contrast to more recent expert advice, which is more likely to describe which chores are appropriate for children of various ages, expert articles through the 1950s mentioned children's chores as a given but did not offer many detailed descriptions of the work they performed. More detailed descriptions of children's chores, however, abounded in the letters by parents and lay advice printed in magazines.

Letters and features written by parents in the first half of the twentieth century described adolescent and pre-adolescent children as shouldering responsibility for a wide range of household work. In addition to cleaning their rooms, taking out the trash, and helping wash dishes, the children's duties described in early twentieth-century parenting advice included many chores: routine household cleaning; menu planning, food shopping, and regular meal preparation for the family; running errands for parents; budgeting, balancing checkbooks, and keeping household accounts; household decorating and furniture rearranging; maintaining furnaces; carpentry and household maintenance; automobile maintenance; and nursing sick family members and neighbors. These duties were obviously more routine and substantial for teenagers than for younger children, but even very young children were assumed to be capable of contributing to necessary tasks. One mother's letter in 1931 describes how she taught her four-year-old to lay kindling and wood and strike a match to start a fire. "After that, if she was at hand when it was time to light the fire, I permitted her to do so. She soon came so accustomed to doing it that she could be trusted to start the fire while I prepared vegetables and other things about the kitchen."[11] A father similarly described his two-year-old daughter's delight in dumping out his ashtray on the rug and how he transformed her fascination with this problematic activity into teaching her to empty the coal scuttle and be "a helpful little girl."[12] And, of course, parents have perennially discovered that by including preschool-aged children in housework they can keep the youngsters occupied and profitably engaged rather than bored and constantly underfoot.

Competent Children

Despite a long history of parents writing to complain that children will not keep their rooms clean, a consistent theme in early twentieth-century parental descriptions of household chores was that parents found their children to be more capable and responsible than they initially thought. In their letters, parents described increasing their children's responsibility over household work as the solution to a wide range of parenting problems, including childish rowdiness or carelessness, teenage listlessness and boredom, sibling rivalry and neighborhood bullying, and children's lack of understanding of household budgets. In quite a few of these letters, greater responsibility for household duties was ironically the answer to children's shirking of chores. Consider this example from 1931:

> My three children made every possible excuse to get out of doing the dishes. I was discouraged because I thought children nine and

fourteen should do the dishes while I did the other housework. Finally, I decided to do all the dishes myself and let the children help with the other work, even though it might not be done as well. The children began to take the greatest interest in the home. The nine-year-old twin boy took all of the care of the furnace when his father was away. With a little direction and help from me, he washed the kitchen floor and wanted everyone to help keep it clean. He also cleaned the kitchen stove every week and enjoyed taking it all apart to clean. His twin sister ironed napkins and towels, helped mix dough for cookies and biscuits and ran the vacuum cleaner. The fourteen-year-old girl is very artistic and developed a real pride in the way she kept the living room and sun parlor. She made a new shade for the lamp. She rearranged the furniture and enjoyed seeing the rooms in order. My housekeeping has been much easier and I have been surprised to see how capable the children really are. And as for the dishes—we get them done! The children even come in and say, "Mother, let us wipe the dishes." —Mrs. W. H., Toledo, Ohio.[13]

In a 1936 column on "Teenage Problems" another letter writer similarly explained: "Helen took no interest in helping do the housework or cooking. As she was very brilliant in school, I did not think she was lazy. One day I suggested to her that I would like to have her manage the business side of the household for me. She was enthusiastic about the idea. She carefully planned the budget, kept the accounts. She now plans menus, does the buying, and helps with the housework in many other ways, seeming really interested.—Mrs. S. J. F., Iowa."[14]

In these discoveries of children's competencies, parents describe their children as having both real skills and the capability to gain skills that can be useful around the home. Many parents discovered that, although their children complained about rote chores that had little meaning, they enthusiastically embraced tasks that allowed them to develop or display their autonomy, competence, and creativity. A 1933 *Ladies Home Journal* article, for example, commented that a child who was only assigned "repetitive tasks that required little imagination or planning" often had a "sulky or resentful air as she went about her duties," but this same child took pride and made spontaneous contributions when her mother learned to recognize and respect the difference "between doing monotonous tasks that were so commonplace as to go entirely unnoticed, and those in which there was room for creative originality, in even a small degree."[15]

Expert advice backed up parents' discoveries of childhood competence, writing about the skills and abilities that children could gain and contribute around the home and the benefit to children of experiencing their own usefulness. A 1929 article, for example, reports that "Mr. L. E. Wolfe who has devoted more than a quarter of a century to superintending the school systems of several cities . . . says: 'The industrial plant in the homes—where cooking, sewing, care of rooms, gardening, chicken raising, and repairs are done—should teach boys and girls one hundred times more valuable lessons than all the industrial plants in schools.'"[16] A 1946 article about the developmental readiness of eight-year-olds similarly refers to the "work skills" they can contribute at home, including "mowing the lawn, hoeing weeds, making baskets, embroidering, crocheting, knitting, doing plain sewing, using a saw, a plane or a brace and bit, and using a pocket knife."[17] This persistent focus on skills and competence in both parents' letters and expert advice reveals that, although children were typically understood to have diminished responsibility compared with adults, they were portrayed as capable of demonstrating autonomous responsibility for many household tasks.

The portrayal of children's chores as part of a household's routine functioning was further reinforced by occasional references to the idea that children should not be paid for their regular household contributions: "Allowances or extra money should not be payment for ordinary household tasks which a child would normally be expected to do as a family member. If a youngster wants to make extra money, he can be paid for something which ordinarily would be done for pay by someone outside the family."[18] As Zelizer points out, ambivalence about whether to pay children for routine chores has long revealed a cultural discomfort with the ambiguous boundary between household work and economic labor.[19] However, early twentieth-century advice also reveals that many parents did not consider it necessary to pay children to do household chores because the chores were already the children's responsibilities. The general tenor of advice offered by both experts and lay people through midcentury was that children could and would, when they were asked, contribute to household work in appropriate and meaningful ways.

Good, Old-Fashioned Chores

Beginning in the 1960s, expert articles began to appear in popular parenting advice that more specifically focused on the necessity and profitability of chores for children. One interpretation of such focused articles might well be that children's chores could at that point no longer be taken for granted as a regular feature in the middle-class ideal of family life. Instead, experts began to advise that parents revive or reclaim the old-fashioned practice of assigning chores to children. A 1966 *Good Housekeeping* feature asserted: "Let's face it: In this day of dishwashers and vacuum cleaners, it's often a lot easier to do things yourself than to insist on a helping hand from the kids. It's not just the constant reminding they need to complete the simplest chore. It's the fact that they frequently bungle the job. As a friend of mine said the other day, averting her eyes from a lumpily made bed, 'It really does hurt me more than it does them!' All the same, most of us have a feeling that chores are good for children. The very word has a gritty, honest-Abe sound to it."[20]

The call to return to "good old-fashioned chores" heralded a shift that became increasingly apparent in advice at century's end; recent advice makes specific recommendations about the appropriateness of chores for children at different ages and developmental levels, but it has been less likely to depict chores as either simply children's share of the necessary household work or an opportunity for children to display and gain useful skills. Instead, contemporary beliefs are that, as the *Good Housekeeping* feature quoted above asserted, "doing meaningful work . . . gives the child a good opinion of himself" and "to be of real value, chores mustn't be too difficult—the child should be able to take pride in what he's accomplished."[21] This focus on building children's self-esteem has become the prevailing undercurrent in most contemporary advice about chores.

In the 1970s and 1980s, descriptions of children's household chores in these popular magazines all but disappeared. Parents' letters no longer described children's household tasks. Only three items from these two decades of the sample mention children's chores at all, and only one includes a substantial statement about children's household work. In response to a mother's query regarding her husband's failure to share in housework following her return to paid employment, a 1981 advice column recommends that not only the husband but also the children take part in chores, with the mother responsible for organizing lists of chores for every member of the household.[22] Although the expert advised the mother to involve children in household work, the mother's letter showed no indication that she considered her children potential household helpers. Instead of household chores, the dominant responsibility mentioned for children and adolescents during this time period was education and the building of outside interests through extracurricular activities.

Children's chores made a noticeable reappearance in parenting advice in the 1990s and 2000s in feature articles such as "Raising Responsible Kids," "Can Do Kids," "The Power of No," and "Whose Chore is it, Anyway?"[23] When compared with the chores recommended and described in earlier eras, contemporary chores are notably gender neutral; gender-specific recommendations for boys and girls have disappeared from popular magazines.[24] Articles from the last twenty years, however, tend to discuss chores mostly in regard to very young children and typically refer to relatively trivial tasks when compared with the chores described in earlier eras. Even though contemporary authors show concern that children and teens learn responsibility, most chores they recommend involve either having kids pick up after themselves or such simple tasks as taking care of a pet, clearing the table after dinner, or assisting with laundry by sorting clothes. There are numerous reminders that young children benefit from feeling useful at home; the admonishment that "children as young as 2 or 3 can be asked to pitch in" is typical of contemporary discussions of teaching children to be responsible.[25] Beyond recommending that very young children be allowed to help with simple tasks, older children's and adolescent's chores are rarely discussed as constituting part of the ongoing work necessary to family life. Instead, these articles tell us that parents have "a sense of uncertainty about what chores make sense" and that "few parents ask kids to do anything around the house because they think their kids are already overwhelmed by social and academic pressures; adding lawn mowing or laundry almost seems cruel."[26]

Furthermore, the acknowledgments of children's skills and competence seen in earlier decades have largely disappeared in recent years. Instead, while parents are encouraged to require responsible behavior from their children, they are also cautioned to keep their expectations about children's competencies fairly low. For example, a 2001 *Parents* article tells us that "Donna and Dan Gephart, of Palm Beach Gardens, Florida, assign their 6- and 8-year-olds the tasks of cleaning their rooms and putting away their laundry. 'I realized that as long as they were doing the job, I couldn't be too particular about how it gets done,' Donna says. 'So I let them do it their way.'"[27] The bulk of the evidence from popular advice, then, is that children are no longer expected to make autonomous contributions to their households in the ways that children in their grandparents' generation were.

Household Help or More Work for Parents?

Despite abundant explicit messages to parents that children need to learn independence and responsibility, children's chores are implicitly constructed in popular advice as a form of work for parents. Instead of describing children's skills and competence, this contemporary advice ironically focuses on parents' duty to teach children responsibility. This parental duty is necessary because contemporary advice insists that a sense of responsibility is tied to children's developing self-esteem and that enhancing children's self-esteem is a key task of parenting. One article tells readers, "In Third-World countries . . . a child of 4 is given a spoon and told to stir the pot because the parents are too busy doing other chores. As a result, these children often have a high sense of self-esteem—they know they are helping the family. In this high-tech age of microwaves and Crock-Pots, we no longer need to have our children 'stir the pot,' but we still need to let them know they are an important part of the family." Parents are therefore responsible to invent, assign, and oversee children's chores, not because it is expedient to have children help in household work that needs to be done, but because they believe the children need to perform some task in order to enhance their sense of self. In Zelizer's words, "the usefulness of children's chores is secondary; child work is supposed to train the child, not help the parent."[28] We might say, then, that chores have become child centered rather than work centered. Or in economic terms, we could express this shift by saying that children's chores are now valued more for their potential contribution to human capital, oriented to future goods and services, than for their present production of useful goods and services.[29]

Contemporary portrayals of children's chores as a form of parenting work include detailed descriptions of the verbal resistance and complaints parents must endure when requiring children to do chores, the constant negotiation between parents and children over what chores will be done by whom, the managerial task of setting up various reward systems to motivate kids' compliance, and the parental drudgery of reminding and nagging children until chores are accomplished. Instead of relieving parents of work, children's chores actually create more work for parents: "Who wants to nag a 12-year-old (for the fifth time) about taking out the garbage?"[30] Parents frequently acknowledge that it would be easier to complete the assigned tasks themselves, but they believe the completion of chores is in some way "good for" children. Despite the belief that chores contribute to children's self-esteem, the recent focus on external rewards and payments—such as points that can be redeemed for toys, games, or outings—is in contrast to earlier advice that saw the immediate benefit of chores as children's opportunity to take "pride in a job well done."[31]

In portraying children's chores as a form of parental drudgery, popular magazines have mirrored the writings of feminist scholars, who in their efforts to document gender imbalances in household work and care-work have given voice to women's experiences but obscured children as agents. In her review of feminist literature on housework, Pavla Miller comments: "In most of this writing, children and young people appear as objects of care, consumers of emotion, goods and services, sources of mess, worry and expense—as well as of love and satisfaction when all goes well. Only rarely are they seen as fellow workers, as people whose individual and collective agency helps shape and redefine the social relations in which they take part."[32] Anne Solberg makes a similar observation about feminist writings: by taking women's experiences as their point of departure, children are "described as the receivers of women's work and attention," with the effect that "while uncovering women's work, women's research has effectively covered up the work of children."[33]

Constructing Childhood Irresponsibility

In contemporary advice, children appear to have freedom to challenge and direct how they will participate in household chores. These portrayals reflect the greater recognition of private forms of autonomy such as children's emotional agency and the right to challenge parental authority (see chapters 2 and 5). These popular depictions, however, obscure recognition of a more practical and publically significant kind of agency: children are not portrayed as capable of demonstrating meaningful and autonomous responsibility over necessary work. It is important to note that mainstream depictions do not always accurately reflect reality; both my own small interview sample and several other studies show that children do, in fact, participate in household work.[34] Furthermore, children's considerable contributions to their families' well-being in the global South and developing countries confirm that neither chronological age nor developmental stage determines usefulness; cultural meanings of childhood shape expectations and recognitions of work.[35]

Children's chores are one area over which American parents have considerable autonomy in personalizing their individual family rules: in some families, children have no obligation to help at all with household work; in other families, there are expectations that children will help in substantial ways. The variance derives from not only individual preference, but studies have also shown that family size and structure affect the amount and nature of household work children perform: children contribute more, for example, to household work in larger families and in single-parent families.[36] Within my interview sample, working-class and minority parents were more likely to tell me that their children have routine chores at home. Consistent with my finding that parenting advice constructs chore assignments as a form of parenting work, middle-class parents were much more likely to tell me that their children contributed relatively little to household work but that they felt that they ought to be assigning their children more chores because, in failing to require more housework of their children, they were in some way neglecting their children's development and falling short as parents. Several expressed a sentiment similar to that of Karla, a stay-at-home-mom: "I think we need to give him some more responsibilities. We don't give him enough chores and things like that . . . [but] we would need to be stricter about enforcing them, you know." Middle-class parents were also more likely to describe themselves and their children as overscheduled, leaving little time either for kids to complete chores or for parents to oversee them. In short, those whose families most closely match the ideal portrayed in most mainstream magazines were least likely to have substantial chores.

Thus, even though kids in some families demonstrate considerable responsibility in households that are interdependent upon everyone's contributions, the trivial portrayal of children's household work in mainstream popular magazines contributes to the social construction of childhood as a time of dependency and incompetence, rather than autonomy and competence, helping to render children's actual work and duties invisible. For example, sociologist Virginia Morrow demonstrates in her studies of children's after-school activities in Britain that a key task performed by children in many families is care for siblings, yet "assuming responsibility for other (younger) children is rarely mentioned in the sociological literature about children's everyday lives."[37] Similarly, I found that children's caretaking responsibilities are almost completely absent from the present sample of popular parenting advice; they appear in only three brief passages in the entire century-long sample—and two of these appearances are cautionary statements that children should not be responsible for the care of siblings. Morrow notes, "the social construction of childhood dependency, based as it is on conceptions of children as developing objects, and therefore as incompetent and irresponsible, precludes us from acknowledging the extent to which children are capable, competent, and have agency and responsibility in their own lives."[38]

A number of explanations can be offered for the historical decline in children's chores, including decreasing family sizes, the increased outsourcing of household labor, and, as I describe in chapter 5, the privileging of children's emotional autonomy and self-esteem over a more hierarchical structure of family authority. However, an important factor to consider further is the degree to which children's primary realm of responsibility has shifted—especially in middle-class families—from household helpers to targeted objects of education and enrichment. Middle-class parents told me that their children do not help out much around the house because they as parents want to make sure kids have some leisure time. Liz, a white middle-class mother, explained: "I feel like they need down time, time when they can come home and not be hounded to do anything, so I want them to have that time too. I hate to, just the minute they get home, say do this, this, this." Other parents similarly described their children as needing a break when they are home from school and activities, which raises the question of how we conceptualize school and extracurricular activities as work and responsibilities for children. The apparent shift away from expecting children to undertake substantial housework toward prioritizing children's education and schoolwork coincided with the general increase in attention in advice literature to children's cognitive development, education, and need for "enrichment" activities.[39]

SCHOOLWORK AND HOMEWORK

A great deal of parenting advice contributes to an understanding of children's education as a necessary period of training for future work rather than a substantial form of children's work in the present. Even though sociologists have begun to credit the importance of recognizing the production of human and social capital that will be used in later careers as a form of productive work in itself,[40] popular representations have resisted the portrayal of education as productive work. Although school is commonly regarded as children's "job," the social construction of education as work for children is ambiguous.

Children's education has clearly become more demanding of both children's and parents' efforts. Though educational concerns were well-represented in popular magazines in the first half of the twentieth century, after the 1960s the number of feature articles, some quite lengthy, that offered extensive analysis of schools and educational trends dramatically increased. For example, the September issues of *Parents* in the 1970s had not one or two education-focused back-to-school features each, as had been typical in previous decades, but four and five feature-length articles per issue examining various aspects of children's school readiness, school quality, teacher training, and educational trends. Given the slow declines in manufacturing jobs and the increasing importance of higher education in the postindustrial information age, the increased emphasis in parenting literature upon children's educational needs is not surprising. With the widespread sense that ever higher levels of education are necessary to ensure employability and a middle-class standard of living, school has increasingly become children's most important and publicly visible responsibility. It therefore makes sense for parenting advice to give attention to how parents can ensure children's educational success, from kindergarten through college. The increased emphasis on education in advice literature is mirrored by parents' and teachers' assessments that educational standards have crept steadily upward over the last generation, particularly for young children. Kindergarten, for example, has become a full-day, academic experience for most children, rather than a half-day, social experience. A long-time second-grade teacher described the increasing work load for children she has observed in her grade level over the past twenty years, saying that they had gone from no homework to expectations of forty minutes per night. She concluded, "I think there is a lot more responsibility on these kids, a lot more work than was expected twenty years ago." Nonetheless, to the extent that children are accorded responsibility over schoolwork, this responsibility is highly individualized; parents and children are told that a child's education ensures his own future success and self-support but not that his work at school contributes to any greater public welfare.

In parenting advice, the emphasis is not on education as a form of work for children but on the responsibility of parents to ensure that kids are getting an adequate education. Parents are therefore encouraged to be actively involved in their child's curriculum, classroom, school, and school district. One typical back-to-school article advised in 2001:

> Boost your child's chance of academic success by forging a good relationship with his teacher. "Writing a brief note to the teacher at the beginning of the year sets a positive tone," says Robert Brooks, Ph.D., coauthor of *Raising Resilient Children* (NTC/Contemporary Publishing, 2001). "Tell a bit about your child's strengths, weaknesses, and interests." Include contact numbers at home and at work, including an e-mail address if you have one, and invite the teacher to share any concerns with you. During the first few weeks, the most important thing you can do is carefully read all the handouts from the teacher. These will be the key to understanding classroom rules and routines. Open-school night will probably be your first formal introduction to the teacher. When you visit the

classroom and hear about the curriculum, pay attention to the teacher's expectations for parents.[41]

These kinds of encouragements for parents to be actively involved in their children's education may be welcome and laudable, and certainly there is ample evidence that parental involvement contributes to children's educational success. In thinking about how this advice contributes to the social construction of childhood, however, we should note that, by emphasizing parents as the responsible party, parenting advice obscures children's agency in their own education and diminishes public recognition of schoolwork as real work for children.

Furthermore, parents receive mixed messages about how the responsibility for homework completion—typically regarded as a critical component of educational success—is to be shared by parents and children.[42] The teachers I spoke with as informants for this research all insisted that they attempt to communicate clearly that children, not parents, are responsible for schoolwork and homework. At various grade levels they emphasized that children should be responsible for managing their own school supplies, books, and papers and for organizing and completing assigned work without nagging or reminders from parents. A typical statement about homework from a teacher was "we are trying to get these kids to understand responsibility and time, why they are doing it, and that it's not mom's job." Some parents told me that they received this very message from their children's teachers. One mom described the message to me:

> [My daughter] had a remarkable year last year with a teacher who helped me become more hands off and just say, "Let her go. She needs to take ownership of her life at some point in time." She gave me that freedom just within the school setting as far as me kind of saying, "You have to do your homework," "You have to do your homework." The teacher was like, "You know what? So what if she does not do it? It is your job to remind her but it is her job to take ownership of it." So that teacher really allowed me and freed me up to "just be Mom," as she said. The teacher let me not have the consequences of her actions. We need to give her the consequences for her inactions. . . . Now I don't think about her homework.

I know she is doing it. . . . It really was me being more hands off. Giving that permission to not feel like it was my fault.

Parents also receive plenty of normative messages that discourage a hands-off approach. Parents are advised frequently that their active involvement is required for homework to be successful; in fact encouraging parental involvement is sometimes the legitimating rationale for assigning homework. Although the advice in popular magazines certainly never tells parents to do children's homework for them, it likewise does not portray homework as children's solo responsibility. Over the last thirty years, popular advice has told parents to stay on top of kids' homework, coaching them to: "take homework seriously" and "make sure that you are present and available";[43] "let your child know how involved you are";[44] "check daily assignments and provide encouragement and assistance" and "tell your child you want to go over all returned papers regularly, always keeping a sharp eye out for chances to encourage and reward progress while avoiding excessive attention to poor performance";[45] and to teach "basic study skills and habits basic study skills and habits," "check your child's notes to make sure he is writing down key words and also keeping track of the things that the teacher would be likely to point out as most important," and "make sure your child pays special attention to the summary sections of each chapter and masters the comprehension questions."[46] Thus, although it is unquestionably children who are completing homework, parents have the ultimate responsibility to manage and direct the task. Liz, a white middle-class mom, described in detail the mixed messages about responsibility that she felt were prevalent from her children's school:

> I think as much as our schools are saying we want your children to be independent and be remembering things on their own, doing things, there is another message, especially with the Internet now . . . there is this parent board where parents have access to grades and they have access to exactly what their child's grade is at every point in time, when projects are due, when tests are. I find that to be a very contradictory message. Like, yeah, you want us to be letting our children make mistakes and fall . . . yet you are telling us we have to be looking at this parent portal and knowing what is

coming. I struggle with that because I feel like, you know what, . . . I don't want to know every test she has. Again, I think certain children, everybody says if you had children who were not doing well you would want to know that because you would want to be able to help that. I think it totally depends upon your child, but I feel like there is more and more asked of parents. Email is just—your band width is only so much for three children getting 80 emails a week. To me it's over the top. . . . Yeah, and now the textbook is online. Another sheet of paper came home from science in fifth grade. Here is how you access this particular website so you can help your child with their science homework. Well, like I don't have anything else to do. And then when I talk to the teacher about it she says it's only if they need help or guidance or if you want to explore it more. I just feel like there are lots of those things and I just feel like it's giving us mixed messages: I can even be more of a helicopter parent, which is what you are telling us not to be.

Both parents and children are thus left uncertain as to whether schoolwork and homework constitute a realm of real autonomy for children. Even though kids are told that education is their main "job" at this point in their lives, prevalent cultural messages also work to diminish the sense of responsibility that children may feel over that job.

Mixed messages do not end with school, however. Over the past few decades, children's enrichment through structured activities has increasingly become regarded as a necessary component of their development. The various extracurricular, cocurricular, and other structured activities that have become standard features of American childhood carry their own set of mixed messages about responsibility and work. Do these activities constitute leisure or work for children?

EXTRACURRICULAR ACTIVITIES: LEISURE OR WORK?

Children's structured activities form a key component of the "concerted cultivation" model of middle-class parenting described by sociologist Annette Lareau.[47] The broad array of activities in which children participate outside compulsory school time are often referred to as extracurricular and cocurricular activities when they are sponsored by schools, but "enrichment" activities also encompass many nonschool sponsored pursuits, including after-school programs, participation in sports leagues or other competitive activities, membership in various clubs and civic or religious organizations, and an array of private lessons. Despite vast differences in the experience of a child joining her school's chess club, taking a private flute lesson, participating in Girl Scouts, attending extended-day programs for after-school care, receiving religious training, and playing on a soccer or Little League team, both parents and parenting advice usually lump all these pursuits together under the catch-all label of "activities." Since the early twentieth century, these activities have been a notable feature of how children spend the "leisure" time that was created when child labor laws ended most of children's paid employment and compulsory schooling structured their days into school time and free time.[48]

Structured activities for kids serve the dual purposes of both opportunity enhancement and social control.[49] In the last century, popular parenting advice has encouraged children's participation in structured after-school activities and touted the many positive benefits of these activities for kids, including providing opportunities for having fun and spending time with peers, encouraging physical activity, developing skills and interests, building teamwork or leadership abilities, and promoting positive self-esteem. Extracurricular activities have become regarded as one means by which children establish a sense of self, an identity, with experts urging that "children must go through a process of determining what they can do and what they enjoy by trying out a variety of activities" and that parents should "help by providing ample opportunities for them to explore any avenues that interest them."[50] In addition, as more and more parents have become dual-earners, parenting advice has also encouraged children's participation in after-school activities as a way of ensuring that kids have adequate adult supervision and are involved in safe and pro-social (not delinquent) activities, reminding parents that "it's important for kids to have activities and be in supervised situations after school so that they don't experiment simply because they're bored."[51]

As children's participation in structured activities has become increasingly prevalent since the 1980s, a number of sociologists have offered insightful analyses of the role that these so-called leisure activities play in cultivating cultural capital and reproducing social class differences.[52] Patricia and Peter Adler, for example, have argued that kids' "extra-curricular careers" begin recreationally but continue through increasing levels of competitiveness, thus socializing children—especially the privileged middle-class children who can afford participation at elite levels of competition—to the corporate work values of American culture.[53] In addition to thinking about activities as a way of passing on cultural capital, which casts children as passive recipients, recent sociological work has also pushed us to consider the meaning of children's activities in terms of their own roles as active social agents. For example, Hilary Levey, who has studied children's involvements in a number of structured and competitive activities, argues that a variety of children's activities might usefully be conceptualized as a form of work, "either because the children are producing goods and services in the present, acquiring various forms of capital, or learning how to orient themselves toward future careers and production of goods and services."[54]

In the race to succeed, parents and kids are told that involvement and achievement in activities is necessary for building the kind of resume that will secure college admission, which certainly prompts us to conceive of activities in terms of producing career-oriented human capital. A recent *Newsweek* article quipped about the pressures of parenting today: "It's not enough to raise a nice kid; she's got to be ahead of the developmental curve and involved in arts and athletic activities (while fueled only by nutritious, organic snacks, of course)."[55] Another *Newsweek* feature opined that "this generation of parents has always been driven to give their kids every advantage, from Mommy & Me swim classes all the way to that thick envelope from an elite college."[56] The parents I spoke with took these messages to heart and talked about the pressures their children face. One social worker and mother described the situation: "There is more expectation for achievement than I think there was when we were growing up, when I was growing up. You have to be the best in everything. You have to be involved in everything. Kids don't have a minute to sit down and breathe before they are off to another hockey, soccer, baseball lesson or gymnastics or whatever." The middle-class parents with whom I spoke, particularly those whose children were teens and preteens, were certainly aware of the role that extracurricular activities play in college applications, describing the many activities kids do as a way that they "sell themselves" as well-rounded achievers. Even while describing the pressures that their children's sports and extracurricular activities put on their family life, parents are resigned that "you have to do all these things to get into the right college" (Liz).

Both the middle-class and working-class parents I interviewed described their children's involvement in a wide array of structured activities, and parents' reasons for encouraging their kids' involvement in activities are not purely instrumental or focused on college. They also described wanting to provide their children with opportunities to build skills and abilities, as well as to develop a strong sense of self and find their passions in life. These reasons for wanting kids to undertake activities often left parents in a dilemma about whether they should direct their children's involvements or allow kids to exercise more autonomy over their own extracurricular pursuits. Parents who might turn to popular magazines seeking answers to the question of how much direction to provide for their children's activities are likely to find contradictory advice and be left on their own to decipher a suitable arrangement for their own children. On the one hand, they might find advice to develop a "disciplinary guideline" that specifies "suitable activities."[57] On the other hand, they might be advised to "try to abide by his preferences" or to "say, 'The hours between school and dinnertime are your time. Which activities interest you most?'"[58]

Parents, therefore, devised their own individual strategies for kids' activity schedules: some parents were more heavy-handed, some left all the choices up to their kids, and many fell somewhere in between on a continuum. Madeleine, a full-time professional and single mother explained that her efforts to "mold" her twelve-year-old son through extracurricular pursuits like music, language, and sports had been the source of some arguments between them: "I don't think, at age five through nine, however old your child is, children are not capable of understanding the big picture. My job is to provide that context of the picture, what is the long-range goal . . . I actually think I feel very strongly about forcing him to do things he does not want to do for his better good." Other parents, like Pauline, took a more hands-off approach: "We sort of always gave our kids the option." Many parents, though, expressed some uncertainty about whether they should be allowing their children to make more decisions for themselves about their extracurricular involvements. Kimberly, a mother of three, said that she was "overwhelmed," by both the array of activities on offer and her own feelings of uncertainty about whether she or her children should be making the choices among these many activities. Although Kimberly clearly found it stressful to find the right balance between directing her children's activities and allowing them to express their own preferences, she was committed to having them participate on teams and take lessons because she saw these as crucial to their discovery of their passions and burgeoning sense of selfhood. Referring to her four-year-old daughter, she said: "If I don't have her in extra-curricular activities she is going to totally not get to find herself. I am not going to be providing her with the opportunities that she needs."

The cultural pressure to help children find themselves starts when the children are very young. Parents of preschool children describe the invisible but palpable push they feel to make sure that their children have ample activities that allow them to explore their interests. Stan, the middle-class father of twin four-year-olds, said: "they are supposed to be really well rounded. They are supposed to take music classes and swim classes and piano and some of those things come from inside of us. Some of them, it seems, it's just like what you are supposed to do and I don't know where that comes from." Furthermore, because of the competitive nature of many of children's structured activities—especially sports—several parents described a common anxiety: if they did not sign their kids up at three or four years old, then they might never have the later opportunity to join the travel team.[59] Most parents described directing young children's involvements in numerous activities, often to "sample" the offerings, but gradually they gave the children more choices over their activities as they grew older.

Not only do parents struggle with questions of how much autonomy children should have in choosing activities, but they also must somehow strike an appropriate (but unspecified) balance between "structured" and "unstructured" time for their children. This, too, raises the question of whether activities constitute leisure or work for children. Parents are increasingly being cautioned by experts to "leave some time unbooked"[60] because there is growing concern in popular advice that children are "overscheduled" and "overprogrammed." Even as they encourage parents to provide enrichment opportunities for their kids, experts also tell parents to put on the brakes: "Sure, the soccer team will help make a kid well-rounded. So will chess club, gymnastics classes, and the countless other activities you dash him off to each day. But having plenty of downtime with you is even more critical to developing his character."[61] Parents are therefore supposed to ask themselves, "'Am I demanding too much of my child? Does my child have too many activities?' If you think the answer is yes, then you might lighten your child's schedule by cutting back on play-dates and activities to give him more unstructured time."[62] Many parents I interviewed expressed concerns about the need for balance between activities and "down-time," but found little concrete guidance other than somehow striking a balance that changes from year to year and season to season. As Stan put it: "It seems like so many kids are overprogrammed with activities and so we want to get them involved but we don't want to overdo it. That is one thing we are going to have to try and figure out."

Beyond the instrumental concern of building a resume and the more expressive desire to develop interests, parents describe their children's involvement in structured activities as an important building block for character traits like teamwork and responsibility. Therefore, although most parents said they did not force their children to sign up for activities unless they wanted to, many parents described rules for continued participation once a session or season had begun. A white working-class father explained: "we have always taught our kids . . . you cannot quit the team. You signed up, you are part of a team, you have to do it." Many parents with whom I spoke fully subscribed to this belief of teaching kids to honor their commitments. In fact, a discussion in a parenting group I observed centered on the struggle to find effective disciplinary consequences for kids' behavior, revealing the ambiguous nature of extracurricular activities. Parents lamented the fact that it was difficult to "find consequences that really matter to the kids" but are also "realistic" because, although activities are supposed to be fun and a privilege for kids, they are also a commitment and responsibility. A mother exclaimed: "You cannot say, 'Well you can't play soccer,' because of teamwork or whatever." Therefore, although many activities are supposed to be designed for children's fun or leisure, parents' unwillingness or inability to revoke them as privileges may make them appear more like work to kids.

As with housework and schoolwork, fostering kids' sense of responsibility through extracurricular pursuits also creates a lot of work for parents, who not only finance kids' activities but must also rearrange their own lives to meet the demands of their children's involvements in highly structured and tightly scheduled activities. Lareau and Weininger point out that much of this responsibility is gendered, falling to mothers rather than fathers.[63] Indeed, employed mothers were most likely to describe to me the strain of juggling children's activity schedules on top of other responsibilities. Julia, who had down-shifted her work hours in order to spend more time at home, still exclaimed: "How much of my life is spent in a bloody spreadsheet trying to figure out, how am I going to work, get the kids to flute?!" For Kimberly, another down-shifting mom trying to balance full-time parenting with part-time work, the pressure to be heavily involved in her children's activities was a source of what she called the "not good enough" messages directed at parents: "If you make mistakes the kids are going to be totally messed up. . . . You know, if I'm not involved in the PTO at school, I don't care about my kids. I feel like there are lots of judgments that are out there. Society is constantly sending messages that you are not a good enough parent. Not coming to help with the fair, not taking them to Sunday School regularly, like going twice a month is not good enough. . . . Yeah, I mean, I think there are all different 'not good enough' messages." Liz, who works full-time and has three children, also described the stress created by sports schedules and parental contributions: "One of my examples is I am really tired of cutting up oranges and taking them to soccer games. The parents have to rotate who is going to take oranges to soccer. All of a sudden, it occurred to me, as I am running late, frenzied to go buy my stupid oranges, cannot these girls for one-and-a-half hours not eat anything? You know? I mean, can they just take a water bottle?! If you want your daughter to have oranges then send them, but why are we making the parents do all this work?"

Although children's activities are usually considered a form of leisure, a number of indications in popular culture point toward the ways that children's activities occupy a much more ambiguous category of play-work. In this ambiguous category, it is also unclear whether structured activities represent a realm of autonomy or constraint for children. To the extent that activities represent opportunities for children to demonstrate their ambitions, skills, or responsibility, activities may represent an arena in which children experience a vital sense of their own self-development and autonomy; structured activities, however, are typically adult-directed, strictly scheduled, and place children under constant adult supervision, representing greater constraint over the more freestyle and child-directed play of the past.

CITIZENSHIP AND COMMUNITY INVOLVEMENT

In earlier generations, children and adolescents had meaningful opportunities to be responsible by doing well in school and extracurricular activities and contributing not only to their households but also to their larger communities. A 1931 *Parents* article illustrates the importance of this, especially for adolescents:

> [An] imperative aim for the adolescent is the development of social interests, right social attitudes and interests in great social movements, such as the interest in organized philanthropy, positive effort for public welfare, and the like. . . . The individual adolescent desires to do something really significant in the social groups of which he is a member. If he acquires the ability to render some service, this brings a reward to which no other is comparable. Every youth desires such opportunity, and nothing is more tragic, nothing perhaps more menacing to the mental health, than lack of opportunity and lack of ability to achieve social success. Every boy and girl may well be trained to such superiority in something that each will be able to render a distinct service in some social group and thus to receive the stimulus that comes from success.[64]

Greater autonomy and responsibility were emphasized as antidotes to both teenage listlessness and teenage rebellion. The adolescent autonomy advised was not typically participation in youth culture unsupervised by parents; instead, it was greater autonomy in the adult spheres of productive work and community involvement, and it frequently placed adolescent children in mentoring relationships with adults other than their parents. One father's letter about the destruction of a neighborhood playground and his subsequent mentoring of the offending gang of boys illustrates the attitude that adolescent misbehavior could be effectively countered through meaningful work, community involvement, and mentoring:

> I inquired among the children and learned the identity of the boys who committed the destruction. In the spring of 1944 I took these boys into my basement shop, explained the use of various tools and asked if they would like to use them. The response was overwhelmingly affirmative. We labored in the shop and on the playground evenings, Saturday afternoons, and Sundays. The other parents were dismayed at the sight of a gang of boys, some of them pretty big, over-running the playground in perfect freedom. . . . The boys kept at work until we had rebuilt and re-painted all the equipment in the playground. . . . The playground is more attractive than before and not one bit of malicious damage has been done during the past year.[65]

During the eras of World War II and the Cold War, children's active community participation was recommended to parents as a means to foster their development as good citizens. In the early twentieth century, national citizenship and local community involvement were linked, and, because children were engaged in their communities, they could be engaged as citizens as well. A 1951 *Parents* article, "How to Raise Good Citizens," told parents: "Though you may not dream of his one day becoming President, your child should become increasingly interested in the business of government. It's his business because it's his government. That's why it's your business to see that his interest is encouraged as soon as he becomes concerned with his neighborhood, the school, the community center."[66] Another article advised: "Children of school age have not much concept of the whole of America. They may, however, have first-hand experiences with their own part of America—their community. These are the years for building habit patterns of personal investigation to find out, of consulting varied sources before forming judgments, of finding in their environments all sorts of problems the solution of which will lead to intellectual and social activity."[67] Although civic education entailed a view toward future civic participation, parents were also encouraged to view their children as citizens— active and engaged members of local communities—not just as bystanders or citizens-in-training. "In your home the responsibilities of the 'office of citizen' should be taught to your children. . . . Provide opportunities for attendance at meetings of city councils, county commissions, sessions of the legislature, and special hearings and civic gatherings."[68] "Don't offer your children the tourist-view of government buildings from the outside but enable them to find out what goes on inside."[69] In 1946 one mother wrote: "I want my daughter and every young person in our community to know about local government. It is there, I feel sure, that democracy must be nourished or die. I want them to understand town meetings, taxes, the alderman and commission systems."[70]

Evidence of youth autonomy in civic involvement and community government and was present in parenting advice into the 1970s. A 1961 article, "You Can Trust Your Town's Teens," describes the importance of handing over some types of community planning and decision-making to organized and responsible teens:

> For several years now, teen-age problems in Battle Creek, Michigan, have been effectively handled, in large part, by the teenagers them-selves. It started when a mayor's committee was set up in response to a general fear that juvenile delinquency was increasing. Two teen-agers with obvious leadership talents were invited to join the group. The two guests voiced such sharp insights into what was wrong with their town's facilities for teen-agers, offered such intel-ligent suggestions for revitalizing the city's recreation program, and thereafter rounded up reinforcements with such contagious enthusi-asm, that the mayor's committee soon disbanded and turned over its problems to a Youth Board elected by the teenagers.[71]

The author, describing several other similar initiatives to involve teens, advanced the argument that "the more scope young people are given for making their own plans, exercising their own initiative and solving their own problems the better the result."[72] A 1971 article described the inde-pendent contributions that youth could make to their communities in "Good Projects for Teenagers without Summer Jobs": "Many teenagers try to find paying jobs for the summer vacation. But for those who cannot find jobs, they can still make a rewarding contribution to their communities in unpaid work."[73] The article describes opportunities for kids to volunteer on their own in hospitals and veterans' homes, tutor-ing children or helping out in children's summer programs, and at the

YWCA and Red Cross. Though the article appeared in *Good Housekeeping* and was therefore presumably aimed at mothers to make them aware of the opportunities available for teens, it does not direct mothers to accompany their children or set up schedules for them; rather, the article indicates that teenagers can seek out volunteer opportunities, arrange for those that interest them, and treat these volunteer positions just as they would a paid summer job.

Since the 1970s, the rhetoric of citizenship that was prevalent during the cold war has disappeared from popular advice. Following the social upheavals of the Vietnam War and the women's movement, there has been limited recognition that the private roles of parents at home are conducted in service of national welfare. However, there is no shortage of nostalgic yearnings for children to establish a sense of connection with their local communities (necessary, of course, for their self-esteem). There are also plenty of suggestions that volunteering in their communities is a good way for children to develop a sense of responsibility. Although responsibility is touted, in a rather vague sense, as being critical to kids' development, several recent articles lament the loss of opportunities for children to demonstrate responsibility. For example, a 1996 article reports: "According to clinical psychologist Elizabeth M. Ellis, Ph.D., author of *Raising a Responsible Child* (Birch Lane Press), a great number of children brought to her for counseling have never been given the opportunity to learn a sense of responsibility, which she defines as being able to meet the goals you've set and use problem-solving skills. Such children tend to be dependent on parents to make decisions for them and have low self-esteem and poor coping skills when faced with everyday stress. 'That can mean problems as children get older.'"[74]

In contrast to the successful community involvement possible for (at least some) children in the past, both contemporary limitations on children's and adolescents' freedom of movement and contemporary emphasis on increased adult supervision constrain kids' ability to organize activities that allow them to feel they are making independent contributions to their communities. Some schools have begun to encourage or require community service projects, but in recent decades most expert recommendations for encouraging children's sense of responsibility have centered not on children's role as volunteers but on family volunteering. Parents who are concerned that their children become more socially conscious are instructed to "find a volunteer activity you and your child can do together. The Kids Care Clubs, for example, with chapters around the country, sponsor programs in which kids and parents together help improve their neighborhoods."[75] Busy parents are reassured that single-day commitments are worthwhile and that "helping others doesn't necessarily commit you to a single cause. Many families volunteer for one-time special events or projects. That might mean a bike tour, a walk, or a fishing contest to raise money for a worthy cause."[76] Of course, the growing preference for one-time special events may itself be a contributing cause of the decreased community solidarity and trust that can make it hard for parents to imagine allowing their children to participate on their own.[77] While the continued advocacy of community involvement and volunteer work reflects a clear sense that children benefit from developing empathy and contributing to the well-being of others, the idea has largely disappeared that children can develop a meaningful sphere of competence and autonomy from their parents through their own independent community involvement. Instead, children's participation in their local communities is one more area in which parental supervision is required.

SUMMARY

Parenting advice is very clear that children need to learn responsibility, but the evidence of the past century's advice is that their opportunities to exhibit and be recognized for meaningful responsibility have become tightly constrained. Whereas evidence from past advice shows that children in the early and mid-twentieth century still were regarded as competent and capable of demonstrating meaningful responsibility in their homes and communities, parents today receive mixed messages from advice. On the one hand, they are told to look for ways to build their children's independence and sense of accomplishment by having kids participate in household work, take responsibility for their own schoolwork, and engage in structured activities and volunteer opportunities that can give them a sense of achievement and connection to their wider communities. On the other hand, parents are implicitly reminded in the same advice that kids need so much parental supervision in these endeavors that it is unrealistic for parents to expect kids to show real responsibility.

Contemporary advice frames children's duties as learning exercises designed to foster self-esteem rather than real contributions to household functioning, community well-being, or social productivity. By emphasizing parents' supervisory responsibility, popular advice contributes to a social construction of childhood as a period of dependence and incompetence. Children and adolescents receive similarly mixed messages: they must demonstrate autonomy and responsibility in order to grow into adults, but at the same time they are denied opportunities to take on independent responsibilities because they are not adults. In recognizing parenting—especially mothering—as a form of work (even if private and unpaid), contemporary culture emphasizes only the work that children create and not the work that they perform. Even when children's actual contributions in homes and communities are substantial, they are obscured by a cultural definition of childhood that renders them invisible. This reinforces the boundary between childhood and adulthood, whereby only adults are recognized as autonomous public actors. The requirement of adult supervision thus constrains children's public autonomy and places parents as intermediaries between children and social institutions.

CHAPTER 5

Psychology's Child

EMOTIONAL AUTONOMY AND THE PRIVATIZATION OF THE SELF

My biggest push [is] to make sure they are able to control their emotions and understand what their emotions are and to be able to feel they understand what they are feeling and how to control or express what they are feeling . . . I hear myself a lot saying, you know, it's fine to cry. You can cry as much as you want. But you need to get control of yourself and figure out where to put those kinds of words in.   —Nadine

I do feel kids are encouraged more to express themselves. I do think, once again, generational thing, children were to be seen and not heard and now we are always asking them, "How do you feel about this?" "Tell me about your day. Tell me what you liked and what you did not like." I think kids are definitely way more apt to express themselves because their parents or people around them are giving them that chance to express themselves. It did not necessarily appear years back. I definitely think they have a chance to express themselves more.   —Tatiana

IN THE TWENTIETH CENTURY, the growing emphasis in parenting advice on children's emotional development revealed that emotional agency has become increasingly central to childhood socialization. In the last few decades, parenting advice has stressed the importance that children become emotionally self-differentiated and that they be encouraged to express their own unique ideas, thoughts, and feelings. This emphasis on children's emotional competence has had a significant impact on the disciplinary strategies of contemporary parenting. I argue that such advice indicates that emotional self-concept and self-expression have become core aspects of how we culturally conceive of individual agency, a development that has caused the public-private trade-off I describe in the forms of autonomy expected from parents and children. Psychological understandings of childhood development have made children much more culturally visible as emotional agents in the private sphere, but they have simultaneously contributed to the diminishing possibilities for envisioning children as active and autonomous public agents in their communities.

POPULARIZING PSYCHOLOGY

Childrearing advice at the start of the twentieth century focused overwhelmingly on issues of physical health, but in the interwar era advice began to shift toward a concern with children's emotional and intellectual development.[1] As infant mortality rates fell and many childhood diseases were successfully reduced or eliminated, expert advice to parents shifted ever more toward shaping children's behavior through an understanding of mental and emotional development. Since the 1930s and 1940s, popular parenting advice has represented the dominance of psychological explanations of children's behavior and has relied heavily upon the expert opinions of psychologists, psychiatrists, and family therapists.[2] Indeed, psychology's colonization of childhood as its special area of expertise and the close alliance between psychology and education were enabling factors in psychology's rapid growth as a profession during the twentieth century. Historian of American education Barbara Beatty reports that there was "a tenfold increase in the number of professional psychologists between 1919 and 1939, from a few hundred to some three thousand, and exponential jumps to more than thirty thousand by 1970 and nearly a quarter of a million by 1995," an increase largely owing to the positions created within the psychology of education.[3]

Academic psychology, popularized through various popular media including magazines and television, has resulted in a widespread "pop psychology" that relies heavily upon a therapeutic understanding of the self as a developmental project of discovering and repairing emotional traumas, many of which are believed to be rooted in childhood and family of origin.[4] Since the 1940s, parenting magazines have been among the greatest promoters of pop psychology—both contributing to the cultural authority of psychology and "watering down" some of its scholarly insights.[5] In particular, parenting magazines have advocated that parents use expert psychological knowledge to understand the stages of children's intellectual, social, and emotional development. A 1951 *Parents* article describing a community mental health initiative is illustrative of the new therapeutic attitude that parents need to understand children's mental and emotional development. Describing a psychiatric health initiative, the article quotes a medical director who argues that preventative mental health is "as important for the welfare of the normal child as vaccination against whooping cough or smallpox." The article reports that "more and more often now Group Health's obstetricians suggest that expectant mothers, too, have at least one pre-delivery consultation [with a psychiatrist]. Parents awaiting a first child often feel the need of guidance in the emotional as much as in the physical development of the infant."[6]

Whereas eighteenth- and early-nineteenth-century childrearing advice had been dominated by moralists, and physicians had stepped in to offer medical advice to early twentieth-century parents, by midcentury child psychologists and family therapists were regarded as the crucial experts on children's healthy development. This sea change in parenting advice from physical to psychological concerns was represented by the 1952 release of "A Healthy Personality for Your Child," a U.S. Children's Bureau pamphlet distilling the advice of psychiatrists and psychologists regarding children's personality development. The *New York Times* reported: this booklet "may well be as important to the emotional welfare of many generations of youngsters to come as 'Infant Care' and its successors have been to children's physical health. . . . As medical science and public health measures have cut down the tolls of disease and disability, emotional difficulties have become the primary child health problem today."[7] Although neither moral nor medical concerns have disappeared completely from popular advice, in the second half of the twentieth century these became overshadowed by the assumption that parents foremost require an understanding of children's psychological and emotional needs.

In the second half of the twentieth century, psychological advice about children's development not only explained the stages of intellectual and emotional growth but also began to stress the importance of children's self-esteem and emotional self-differentiation, and parents were urged to create opportunities for children to express their own unique ideas, thoughts, and feelings. By the 1960s the growing attention given to children's emotional development and self-image reflected the ascendancy of a psychological understanding of the human person, which has dramatically shaped the contemporary American view of the self and family relationships. Freudian psychoanalysis, initially inspiring this therapeutic ethos in the early twentieth century, quickly permeated professional and academic knowledge as well as popular culture.[8] As a result, twentieth-century American culture became preoccupied with emotional life, and public enactments of therapeutic narratives of suffering and self-help significantly altered the boundaries between private emotionality and public reserve.[9] In popular parenting advice, the therapeutic ethos has not only shaped how we understand children's developmental needs and the work of parenting, but it has also helped to shape the ways that children are culturally visible and invisible. The overwhelming emphasis of parenting advice in recent decades on children's competency recognizing and expressing emotion has made children more visible than ever *as emotional agents* and indicates that emotional self-concept and self-expression have become core aspects of our cultural conceptions of individual agency.

Emotional Development and Age-Grading

In educating parents about psychological development, advice in popular parenting magazines often describes specific age-graded stages and the level of social and emotional maturity that can be expected from children at each stage. The assumption that the self develops through psychosocial stages is a key aspect of all psychological models of the self and represents a particular, historically contingent concept of the self that arose during the twentieth century.[10] Theories of self-development through well-defined stages were first popularized in America by G. Stanley Hall, whose theory of childhood development was grounded in an evolutionary philosophy of history.[11] Following Sigmund Freud's lectures at Clark University in 1909 (where he had been invited by Hall), Freud's theory of psychosexual stages and Freudian psychoanalysis found fertile soil in America and sank their roots deep into the American psyche.[12] Neo-Freudian Erik Erikson later elaborated Freud's stages into eight stages of psychosocial development that span the human life course from infancy to late adulthood. In each stage, Erikson posits that individuals confront new challenges that are tied directly to their sense of self and identity.

In the 1940s and 1950s, Dr. Arnold Gesell, a leading authority on child development, founded the Clinic of Child Development at Yale University. Based on his intensive observations of infants and young children, he developed the Gesell Developmental Schedules, which measured mental growth as exhibited through motor characteristics, adaptive behavior, language, and personal-social behavior. Gesell and his colleagues Frances Ilg and Louise Bates Ames wrote a number of books that described children's mental development in the first five years of life, from five to ten, and from ten to sixteen. These were later broken down into year-by-year parenting books by Ames, with titles suggesting the emotional side of each age, such as "fun-loving, fussy" ones, "terrible or tender" twos, "wild and wonderful" fours, "sunny and serene" fives, and "loving and defiant" sixes. By the 1960s, Gesell's ideas, which stressed the physiological basis of development, were superseded in American psychology by Jean Piaget's four stages of cognitive development, which placed greater stress on the importance of environmental rather than internal influences on development. Piagetian theory has informed much of the psychological work on child development since the 1960s.

Age-grading in popular magazines has drawn on a loose understanding of the developmental stages posited by developmental psychology and has been further encouraged by the overlap between psychological and consumer market research.[13] In the early twentieth century, it was common to see only broad distinctions between infants, young children, and teenagers (with lines only sometimes being drawn between preschool and school-age children). Age compression, however, has led to increasingly fine distinctions between children based on age. Typical developmental stages described in contemporary magazines are represented by the categories of infants, toddlers, preschoolers, school-age or middle childhood, tweens, and teenagers. In *Parents*, for example, a significant portion of each issue for the last several decades has been comprised of the "As They Grow" section, which is broken into stage-by-stage descriptions, explanations, and advice, sometimes broken into the categories just mentioned and sometimes proceeding year-by-year. Children's developmental stages are often described in terms that especially highlight children's emotional development. A typical developmental stage explanation in a 1991 article, "What it Feels Like to be Two," explains that children this age experience "intense feelings. It's not that two-year-olds' feelings are unique. They experience many of the same emotions as adults but haven't yet developed the ability to control them. . . . As a result, they feel love, sadness, fear, and other emotions with an intensity that is probably difficult for adults to imagine. Two-year-olds are at the mercy of their untempered feelings almost all of the time."[14]

Continuing well beyond the toddler stage, a great deal of advice about school-age children and adolescents similarly recommends that parents, teachers, and school administrators consider emotional development as an important aspect of formal education. An article from the 1960s about private schools, for example, describes schools with "philosophies [that] place more emphasis on the emotional and social development of children. They will pay a great deal of attention to a youngster's relationships with his classmates, his ability to participate in group activities, his capacity to handle his emotions, and his sense of personal freedom and self-expression."[15] Another article points out this concern with children's emotional development in a public school system in the 1970s: "The tone of concern for each individual, and for the complete individual, is set by Dr. Theodore Wiesenthal, Community Superintendent, who feels that concentrating on the three R's is not enough. His commitment is to educating for the present and the future, and he is interested in the students' thought processes and emotional development in addition to their academic skills."[16] Even in the era following No Child Left Behind, when the overwhelming attention given to standardized testing has squeezed out many curricular "extras," like physical education, some schools are adopting social development curricula that emphasize the age-graded learning of emotional and social skills.

EMOTIONAL INDIVIDUATION
AND SELF-ESTEEM

In popular advice, children's emotional agency is emphasized by a prevailing understanding of developmental stages as steps to emotional individuation. A 1986 *Parents* article explains that "for a two-year-old, being able to feel good about oneself stems from a sense of achievement in the many aspects of development. . . . *In her emotional and social development she is experiencing herself as a separate person from you.* She develops a sense of strength as she is able to make decisions and choices for herself."[17] Advice about older children and adolescents similarly reflects the understanding that emotional development toward greater individuation is taking place. For example, a 1981 article about early adolescence explains that children's behavior at this age "is part of an effort to become less emotionally tied to parents and more secure as independent persons. In most cases it is not caused by real dislike but by the very fact that the emotional ties to parents are so strong. Putting down Mom and Dad is a way to gain emotional space and distance from them."[18] This emotional agency for children and adolescents is seen as a prerequisite for achieving positive self-esteem, which in the last generation has come to be regarded as a principal marker of healthy childhood development. In fact, attention to children's emotional individuation necessitates a concern with their self-esteem precisely because it reflects a conception of selfhood that rests heavily upon emotional agency.

In the second half of the twentieth century, the parenting space occupied by self-esteem expanded both quantitatively and qualitatively. Although implicit discussions of children's positive self-concept were present in earlier advice, the term "self-esteem" did not appear in my sample of magazines until 1951. Before the 1950s, references to positive self-feelings were couched in terms of building confidence through social connectedness. Early twentieth-century references to building a child's sense of self discuss parental tasks of fostering self-confidence and a sense of accomplishment in their children. For example, a 1931 *Parents* article titled "Cultivating a Wholesome Personality" counseled: "Every boy and girl may well be trained to such superiority in something that each will be able to render a distinct service in some social group and thus to receive the stimulus that comes from success. . . . The boy and girl should thus develop self-confidence and hence should have opportunity for taking responsibility and for initiative."[19] Another 1931 article notes that "giving him confidence in himself is not obtained by protecting him too zealously from failure or defeat."[20] This early twentieth-century advice claimed that parents who provide opportunities for children to develop independence and feel a sense of accomplishment help them gain the confidence they will need as adults. Problem solving and self-reliance were the recommended goals: "There are bound to be in store for our children bitter disappointments. But the child who is allowed to face his own problems, instead of having his way always smoothed ahead of him, is on his way to the attainment of a self-reliant, wholesome, well-rounded personality."[21] A 1951 article, "So Much to Learn Before Six," advised: "It is our responsibility to help our boys and girls to develop judgment and confidence in order to become adults who can meet problems realistically, enjoy their lives and get along happily with others."[22] In the first half of the twentieth century, then, children's self-confidence had less to do with their emotional individuation and more to do with their successful integration within a social group.

Through the 1940s, advice reveals that self-concept was understood to be more grounded in outward accomplishments than in inner feelings. One article advised, for example, "there should be praise, light but appreciative, for the orderly act . . . with the emphasis put on the accomplishment, rather than on the child."[23] Although there were encouragements for parents to build children's self-confidence by showing unconditional love, there were also warnings that excessive attention and affection from parents would make kids unpopular and self-conscious. A 1929 article, for example, warned that a mother who praises her child and makes her the center of attention "will do well to realize that such treatment leads to unpopularity and avoid it."[24]

By the 1950s, popular magazines had begun to refer explicitly to "self-image" and "self-esteem" as topics of concern. The earliest use of the term "self-esteem" in my samples comes from a 1951 *Parents* article, "Father's Changing Roles," in which fathers are encouraged to see that outward behaviors like bragging, teasing, and bullying may mask a child's own inner difficulties. The article calls for greater emotional involvement of fathers, especially with their school-age children: "Instead of punishing the child who pushes others around, a man needs to face the fact that such a child has a problem involving a lack of enough self-esteem. He needs a build-up rather than belittlement or scolding."[25] In contradiction to earlier advice that warned against too much praise, another 1951 lay advice column claimed: "We are much too free with advice and criticism, too chary with praise."[26] The insistence that parents be generous with praise of their children has continued unabated into the twenty-first century, and it is typically seen as a key component of building children's positive self-esteem.[27]

From the Inside Out

Since the introduction of the term in the 1950s, parents and commentators have increasingly seen self-esteem as centered in the child's emotional core, rather than based primarily upon outward accomplishments. Praising and drawing attention to children's strengths and accomplishments have remained regular features of the advice for building self-esteem, but the message since the 1950s has been that praising children for their accomplishments helps them to feel good about themselves—that is, to develop a positive sense of *who* they are, rather than just taking pride in *what* they do. "Father's Changing Roles," illustrating the early signs of this shift from the outward accomplishment to the child himself, asserts that a good father will "avoid setting up over-ambitious expectations for a child to meet. He will make it plain that he loves his children for themselves alone and not for their A's on report cards. He will assure them that trying is what matters most whether they always succeed or not. He will approve of each one as a person who is trying hard and is entitled to a few mistakes in the process. Approval is a source of strength for the individual."[28] Other early examples of this shift toward children's sense of self as more grounded in their emotions than in their actions come from articles that deal with issues of sibling rivalry. For example, a 1961 *Good Housekeeping* article describes the help offered to a child at a psychiatric child-guidance clinic:

> Take the case of Betsy, a shy, withdrawn child who daydreamed in class and never played with other children. Her teacher noted Betsy's unhappiness and tried to draw her out. Betsy, however, was afraid to emerge from her shell. At the child-guidance center, it became clear that much of Betsy's trouble lay in the admiration received by her beautiful, talented older sister. Betsy felt she simply couldn't compare, so she gave up trying. Her grades in school fell off, and her daydreams provided her with the sense of satisfaction she lacked in real life. The guidance center helped Betsy's parents to understand her feelings. In addition, the psychiatrist was able to

make understandable to Betsy her feelings of rivalry for her sister. Becoming more secure in her relationships with her parents, she began to feel that she, too, had fine qualities and could make a valuable contribution to life.[29]

Articles such as this one point out that a child's self-concept may not be rooted so much in actions and accomplishments as in general feelings of self-worth that are formed primarily through the emotional attachments parents forge with each child as a unique individual. By the 1960s, references to self-esteem in popular magazines were commonplace and had begun to serve as the occasional thematic subject of articles such as "Help Your Child Like Himself" and "What Injures a Child's Self-esteem?"[30] Still, through the 1970s, a great deal of the advice about self-esteem was primarily concerned with improving self-worth for troubled children or those experiencing specific problems, such as learning difficulties in school, extreme shyness, or family disruptions.

In *Good Housekeeping* the late twentieth-century therapeutic emphasis on children's self-esteem can be seen in the "My Problem and How I Solved It" articles that were a regular feature from the late 1960s until the early 1990s. These first-person stories, written and submitted by readers, describe families facing and overcoming dramatic crises, many involving a child with an issue such as a learning disability, addiction, or mental illness.[31] These stories follow a common therapeutic narrative form, in which outward behavioral or relational problems are discovered to have an inner, emotional cause. In this narrative form, problems are resolved by seeking out therapeutic professionals who help individuals to recognize, express, and alter their feelings. In *Good Housekeeping*'s particular narratives involving parents and children, the parents' initial view of the problem is having ineffective discipline strategies for dealing with a child's behavior problems. The "My Problem" stories always include seeking expert help from professional psychologists or psychiatrists, through which the parents learn a diagnosis that medicalizes the child's behavior and shifts the parents' view of the problem from having an out-of-control child to having a child with a treatable illness or disability. The turning point in the narratives, however, always comes when the parents *themselves* change by accepting the child's emotional individuation and stop trying to control the child. One such narrative relates: "We learned that in order to change Janie's behavior we first had to change our own. Most important, we had to stop trying to solve Janie's problems for her and allow her to start taking responsibility for her own life."[32] Another story turns when the parents realize: "Most important of all, we had to remember that Andy was thinking of himself as a failure. That self-image had to be changed. . . . His rages and fights resulted from his frustration at not being able to do what he felt we expected of him . . . To help Andy, we had to change ourselves, and it wasn't easy."[33] The positive outcomes of these therapeutic narratives always include improved family communication skills and better self-esteem for the children. For example, one narrative concludes, from the daughter's point of view, "I look back on those years before my illness was diagnosed, and I think if only I could have been treated then. But I guess I really wouldn't want to go back and change anything. After all, it's part of me. And I like who I am."[34]

Overdoing It?

Since the 1980s, concern with children's self-esteem has moved to a more central and visible place in popular parenting advice. Such concerns began to appear much more often as the thematic focus of articles about "normal" kids. For example, in recent decades *Parents* has included numerous feature-length cover articles that revolve around the theme of helping all kids—not just those with extreme or atypical difficulties—to develop positive feelings about themselves, including "Help Your Child Feel Great," "Boosting Self-Esteem," "Can-Do Kids," and "How to Raise a Really Good Kid."[35] At the same time, self-esteem has been featured more prominently in parenting articles that are thematically about other topics.[36] Even "The Me! Me! Me! Generation," a 2001 article about how parents can curb their children's narcissism, tellingly contains ample advice about helping children to feel good about themselves.[37]

Not only has building self-esteem moved away from outward accomplishments toward inner emotional security for all children, but increasingly in recent decades parents have been advised to "stack the deck" in their children's favor by managing their children's activities and involvements to make sure that kids experience more successes than failures. In the 1970s Joyce Brothers was dispensing advice about helping children to accept failure: "help her by looking for areas where she can excel and at the same time, teach her that everyone must fail from time to time. Help her to regard failure as a stepping stone to learning, rather than as a major catastrophe or a reason to retreat into her own world."[38] At the same time, parents were also being told to "make sure that your child's efforts are successful most of the time so that his pride and sense of self aren't damaged."[39] Parents in the 1970s began to be cautioned, for example, about rushing their preteens into organized sports because win-and-lose activities could damage kids' self-esteem.[40] As a long-time physical education teacher explained to me about this transformation, "When I started teaching [in the 1960s] everything was black and white. You won, you lost. There wasn't any 'Oh, but you did a good job.' No, it was, 'You lost. You've got to accept it.' And I do think there is some value to that. You do need to learn how to accept it—you need to learn to be a good loser. . . . And then we had the era where we did partner-cooperative kinds of activities and problem solving. And nobody lost, nobody won. Now, there are hardly any games where you win or lose. . . . Now, you never keep score. There is never a score. Supposedly, it is for self-esteem." Although schools implemented changes, parents have not always been receptive to psychologist's concerns about competition. Sociologists Peter and Patricia Adler point out that when schools acted on the prevailing psychological advice in the 1970s to eliminate competitive team sports for young children, many parents reacted by signing kids up for private-sponsored leagues, some of which were much more competitive than school play.

Several parents expressed skepticism about the effectiveness of some contemporary practices aimed at building self-esteem; they wonder if they send messages that seem phony to kids and fail to prepare them for life's ups and downs. Several parents and teachers, for example, mentioned doubts about the practice of giving all kids trophies for participation in sports. Chris, a white middle-class dad, voiced a reservation that was typical of the concerns discussed by several parents:

In the little grades you don't keep kids back anymore. . . . If they do keep a kid back there is a really serious reason. They push them on because they don't want to hurt their self-esteem. Well, I don't want to bring a kid down. Don't get me wrong. But, you are not going to go out in life and have everything perfect. You know, not every kid is going to write an A paper. . . . [My daughter] has so many trophies up there in her room. Softball and T-ball and soccer and swimming. Everything you participate in you get a trophy for. There are winners and losers in life. I certainly don't want [her] feelings crushed. No parent wants that, but there is a fine line you walk between crushing a kid and making them, you know . . . I mean, [she] played soccer this year and this spring they kept score but they do not keep stats. This is the first year they kept score. They never used to keep score. Nobody wins and nobody loses. T-ball, everybody gets up and bats. Everybody gets a trophy and everybody wins. Everyone does not win in life.

In arenas other than sports, parents have been similarly cautioned to avoid setting overly high expectations for kids. An article about children's chores, for example, argued that "building a child's self-esteem is more important than mastering perfect bedmaking."[41] And a 1996 article about social skills warned, "Don't expect too much . . . try to avoid pressuring children to adopt skills that go beyond their emotional and developmental maturity; this will only deflate their self-confidence and impede them socially."[42] Some parents with whom I talked echoed this message: a child's pride in his or her effort is the ultimate accomplishment. For example, Pauline said, "I think trying to be the best person that you can be is the most important thing. Not everyone is going to be Albert Einstein or a famous sports personality. Do you know what I mean? But striving to do the best you can do and be the best you can be. I think that is the most important thing. If you put forth 100 percent effort on whatever you do then you can feel good about yourself. You can be proud of what you have accomplished." At the same time, some parents and teachers worry that the overwhelming push for parents to protect kids from failure might be taking away from children's opportunities to experience independence and build emotional resilience. Mark, a dad and teacher, expressed his opinion: "I don't think we allow them to fall down, pick themselves up, brush themselves off, and figure out what the next step is. We are always right there as parents, teachers and so forth to pick them up. We make sure they are okay. I think we need to do a little less of that. I tell parents that when I talk to them all the time. Let them fail sometimes. Let them fail." Although opinions differ about how best to foster self-esteem, advice-givers and parents all agree that self-esteem is critical for children's development.

EMOTIONAL COMPETENCE

In the advice directed to the latest generation of parents, the development of an inner core of self-esteem has entailed children's growing autonomy and individuation as competent emotional agents. In fact, in the intense focus on self-esteem since the 1980s, we can see a qualitative expansion in its meaning. In the last three decades self-esteem has encompassed not only children's sense of accomplishment and emotional security but also what Illouz terms "emotional competence"; that is, children's self-concept has become increasingly tied to their self-awareness, their ability to recognize and express their own emotions, and their ability to empathize with the feelings of others.[43]

Emotional Vocabularies

Concern over how kids feel about themselves is tied to a deeper current of attention paid to building up children's awareness of feelings in general. Whereas descriptions of children's emotions have been present since the early twentieth century, advice about helping children to recognize and talk about their feelings was rare before the 1960s. In early twentieth-century parenting advice, emotional expression was most often considered in connection with physical symptoms: either emotional excitement was pinpointed as the cause of temporary physical discomforts—such as abdominal pain—or emotional outbursts were taken as evidence of an underlying chronic physical disorder. For example, to identify hearing disorders, "Parents . . . should watch to see if the child is overactive or even violent in play or throws temper tantrums when trying to communicate. These can be signs that he is frustrated because he cannot hear words properly and is unable to express himself well enough to be understood."[44] This early advice assumed that, unless there was a physical problem of development, children would naturally show appropriate emotional development and communicate adequately. Although children were portrayed as emotional beings, their expressions of emotions were typically regarded as evidence of immaturity. Emotional maturity was assumed to consist of an individual's ability to control their emotions, rather than to express them verbally. Prior to the 1960s, then, children were taught to "*substitute* speech or reasoning for the more emotional forms of response," but the focus was upon controlling or suppressing emotional display, rather than delving into, understanding, and talking about emotions.[45]

During the first half of the twentieth century the association of emotional display with childish immaturity was also evident in the marriage advice included in parenting magazines. This advice was specifically aimed at women and regarded women as immature if they did not control their negative emotions. One psychologist advised: "Remember that control of the emotions is possible for most people. Persistence of childish emotions means that the job of helping you develop thoughtfulness of others was not finished by your parents. You must finish the job of being controlled and kind by disciplining that child within yourself."[46] Even though this article was about marriage, it contained an assumption that it was a parent's job to teach disciplined control of emotions. Francesca Cancian and Steven Gordon report that marriage advice in magazines in the mid-1960s began to advise women to express, rather than suppress, their anger.[47] Similarly, since the 1960s, talking about feelings has been viewed as an increasingly important way of helping children to recognize and experience both their emotional life and themselves. Furthermore, it is significant that emotional socialization since the 1960s has largely assumed that children's emotional needs and expressions are androgynous and has recommended similar strategies for teaching both girls and boys to understand and talk about their feelings.

Contemporary norms about freedom of emotional expression mean that today's parents may be more likely than their own parents to tolerate tantrums and other extreme emotional displays. Tatiana, a white middle-class mother, explained: "when you are out in a grocery store and a kid starts throwing a fit I think it depends on your generation. . . . In our generation we all understand now kids are going to have fits. If you need to ride it out by letting them scream around the grocery store I don't think people are going to judge you." According to contemporary advice, however, parents should not just tolerate emotional tantrums; rather, they should use them as opportunities to teach kids to channel emotion into language. In contrast to earlier understandings, emotional maturity is now assumed to consist of the ability to talk about feelings. An expert advised in a 2001 Q&A column: "One of the most valuable skills we can help our kids develop is an ability to understand and describe emotion."[48] Contemporary parenting magazines are full of advice about teaching children to "expand their emotional vocabulary."[49] The therapeutically inspired insistence that kids should be emotionally autonomous and verbally express their feelings is the primary cause of the shifting behavioral boundaries that I documented in chapter 2, the apparent growing tolerance of children's defiance toward parent authority.

Empathy

The most common ways parents are advised to help children understand and describe emotion is through modeling empathetic responses and encouraging children to label and talk about their feelings. A 2006 article about preschoolers instructs parents to "show empathy. Your howling child isn't merely mad. 'Anger hides feelings such as disappointment or anxiety' explains Dr. Pickhardt. Support her emotions by labeling them. Say, 'You're frustrated because your blocks fell down.'"[50] Parents are encouraged not only to be empathetic with their children's emotions but to model talking about their own emotions as well: "sharing your own feelings will help her expand her emotional vocabulary. When you say, 'I'm a little sad because my friend is sick and I'm worried about her,' you send the message that we all have moments of anger or sadness, which we can identify and discuss."[51] Another means of helping children develop an emotional vocabulary is by teaching children to decipher body language: "Help them read faces. Being people-smart means tuning in to nonverbal cues like body language and facial expressions. Look at magazine ads with your child and ask what the people in the photos seem to be saying or feeling, suggests Domash. Or, point out a group of people you see on the street and together try to decode their attitudes. Do they look secretive? Relaxed and open? The goal is to get your child to pick up on unspoken messages."[52] Advice to help children recognize and label their own feelings attributes emotional autonomy to children and directs parents to further support children's individuated self-concepts.[53]

The recent focused attention to helping children build their awareness of and ability to talk about emotions is not, however, purely self-centered. In the last two decades, this attention to emotional competence has also abounded in advice about helping children to develop social consciences and civic awareness through learning empathy for others' feelings. Thus, although positive self-esteem is predicated upon a high degree of emotional individuation, it is also regarded as contributing to the wider social and civic good. Teaching children empathy is often recommended as both a means of establishing behavioral boundaries and building a sense of social connectedness with others: "When children mistreat friends, use specific 'feeling' words to discuss the incident. ('So you pushed Jessica because you were jealous that she was playing with Amy instead of you?') 'A child needs to be able to recognize and communicate his own emotions before he can respond to another's,' explains Dennis Meade, Ph.D., a psychologist for the Port Washington, N.Y., school system. 'By naming a feeling, you help your child understand his own reactions as well as those of others.'"[54] Advice scenarios in which parents ask, "How would you feel if . . ." are common, and teaching children to consider the feelings of others is recommended as the basis of good manners, discipline, and the development of a conscience.[55] For school-age children and teenagers, especially, concerns about teasing and bullying prompt many occasions for teaching empathy. An article on resisting peer pressure advised: "When your teenager is quick to label someone a 'weirdo' or 'nerd,' say, 'You've got a couple of habits that make you different, but they don't make you weird or bad.'"[56] Both verbalizing feelings and considering another person's point of view are frequently recommended as ways to "help him to view himself as a good person in your eyes and his own."[57]

Quite a few of the parents with whom I spoke agreed with the tone of popular advice in describing the necessity of empathy to teaching right and wrong. David, a white, working-class father, described this as a matter of teaching his son respect:

> He is two and a half. I mean, he is going through a little hitting thing. He hits. I tell him, "You cannot hit." This is a problem. This is an aspect of being a parent. I tell him, well I ask him, "Do you like to get hit when your cousin hits you?" He will say, "No." Well then I will say, "How do you think this person feels? How do you think I feel? Or when you yell . . . how do you think I feel?" I try to tell him to communicate and to use his words and to take a step back. I even said, count to five, count to 10 or whatever. He can do that.

It is simple enough I guess. It is some good advice, as opposed to hitting or whatever. Then I say you have to really think about what you are doing and respect other people's feelings. "How do you think, how would you feel if [your cousin] hit you? You would be upset, you would be mad, maybe you would cry. You would be hurt. You don't want to do that to somebody else so you have to respect their feelings and respect them as it hurts them." I tell him that now. I figure the earlier the better.

Beyond immediate peer relationships, empathy is also seen as a way to engage children's sense of connectedness with others. Even though popular parenting advice sees emotional competence as requiring a high level of individuation, the resulting emotional agency accorded to children is sometimes understood to serve as a contemporary basis for social and civic engagement, as in this 2006 article on "How to Raise a Really Good Kid":

> Emphasize empathy. . . . It's up to you to develop that quality by tuning your kids in to what others feel. If your preschooler bops her friend on the head with a Barbie, make sure she realizes that her friend is crying. Ask how she would feel if her friend hit her. With older children, you can use current events to help make them more sensitive to others. "Let your grade-schooler watch coverage of a hurricane or earthquake on television, for instance, and ask her if she can imagine what it would be like to lose her home," Dr. Borba suggests. Helping her understand what other people are going through will show her why it's nice to call a sick friend or bring cookies to an elderly neighbor.[58]

Nadine, a middle-class stay-at-home-mother, called this "emotional and civic mindedness" and said that it is her biggest goal in her parenting. She explained that she wanted her children to be able not only to understand, control, and express their emotions but also be in tune with feelings because that is a way to "learn the respect of every other person. We don't do this not because generally it is wrong, we do this because it would bother other people, it would be rude to other people. We pick up after ourselves because we want to respect other people who are coming in to use the restaurant. We want to respect other people who will be playing here. . . . So I think a lot of what I do in even raising my children, and the lessons that I teach, are expressing emotions, accepting emotions and understanding how other people would feel if we do these things." Therefore, empathy is regarded not as a mere individual skill to be learned but rather a common basis for morality. Thus, children's individual emotional autonomy is understood to form the potential basis for their sense of connection with others—from their parents, siblings, and peers to other members of their community, society, and world. Nonetheless, the contemporary emphasis on emotional competence gives priority to a decidedly privatized understanding of children's autonomy, with social engagement predicated upon a successfully individuated self.

MANAGERIAL PARENTING: EMOTIONAL CONTROL AS DISCIPLINE STRATEGY

The highly emotional, individualized, and privatized conception of childhood autonomy can be clearly seen in the disciplinary tactics recommended in popular parenting advice, with significant effects upon the prevailing cultural conception of what constitutes good parenting. Talking about feelings has become the primary means of experiencing emotional intimacy between parents and children, and it has also become a widely recommended disciplinary strategy. Given contemporary public disapproval of corporal punishment, the primary form of discipline left to parents is talking, and much of this talk revolves not around explaining rules but around understanding, managing, and expressing feelings as a means of ensuring compliance. Following Eva Illouz's excellent description and analysis of the therapeutic emotional style of contemporary corporate capitalism,[59] I call this feeling-focused disciplinary strategy a "managerial parenting" style.

Certainly the idea of parents—especially mothers—as household managers is not new. I described in chapters 3 and 4 how parenting since 1980 has come to involve increasing parental management of children's mobility, schedules, duties, and community involvements. Here, however, I am considering an additional dimension of management that has become central to parenting: emotional management. In two key ways, parents are encouraged to enact the therapeutic ethos in conformity with the expectations of good corporate managers supervising employees. Parents are encouraged to exert "soft power" over children, to impose parental will through keeping their own emotions in check. Parents are also encouraged to practice a therapeutic communication strategy of active listening that helps to channel the child's expression of emotion and direct the child's behavior. The therapeutic emotional style that dominates popular parenting advice thus disciplines both parents and children.

Soft Power

In her study of the emotional style of corporate managers, Illouz notes the typical therapeutic managerial advice: "if a person is to control the situation he must not allow himself to be stimulated by the emotionality of the other person."[60] There is a great deal of discursive continuity in this emotional style between the private and the corporate realms, and recommendations of emotional control are long-standing features of advice literature aimed at parents. A very early example comes from a 1926 *Good Housekeeping* article on discipline that denounced spanking long before outcries against corporal punishment had become the norm; in "Discipline," Josephine Kenyon, author of *Healthy Babies are Happy Babies* advised: "divest the times when you have to say 'No' of your own passionate emotion and the incident will make little impression. If you let yourself get worked up about it that little tension edge will show in your voice and the whole point is emphasized in a negative way."[61] While many early twentieth-century magazine advice columns assumed that mothers were often sabotaged by their uncontrollable emotionality, Kenyon advocated emotional reserve and control for women of a type that has since become commonplace in both family therapy and contemporary corporate settings.

Kenyon's advice for mothers foreshadowed the common parenting advice that appeared seventy and eighty years later. For example, one of the 2006 "20 Commandments of Toddler Discipline" is: "Be a good role model. If you're calm under pressure, your child will take the cue. And if you have a temper tantrum when you're upset, expect that he'll do the same."[62] Another article warns, "If you're tense yourself, your child is a lot more likely to follow suit."[63] Even lighter and humorous stories point out the necessity of parental control of emotions, such as a 1991 article relating a father's tongue-in-cheek story of his own misadventures in parenting while his wife was away for the weekend: "I flew into a rage. . . . I stormed about the kitchen, cursing and slamming things out of the way. My tantrum, however, simply made things worse. Besides rousing Annie, it scared Alex. Terrified, he began screaming louder than ever, his toothless mouth agape, his limbs flailing in every direction. . . . I was coming unglued as Annie's shrieks echoed through the house. My mind was suddenly flooded with horrific visions of me staggering outside in a stupor, disheveled and glassy-eyed, laughing while paramedics dragged me into an ambulance."[64] In 2006, one mother wrote that instead of giving vent to negative emotions in the heat of the moment, she "realized recently that I talk the same as my mother; that when my feelings are hurt, I get very quiet, hold my breath, and count to ten like she used to do." Her letter was tellingly written in response to the Mother's-Day-themed prompt, "Are you a good mother?"[65] The message of popular advice is clear: a *good* parent is in charge of her or his own emotional expression. In an alignment similar to the one Illouz describes in the corporate hierarchy,[66] parents' exhibition of emotional self-control subtly signals and confirms their social superiority, while children's lack of emotional control indicates not only their weaker position in the social structure of the family but also the child's weaker *self*, that is, their self-in-formation. Thus, even as older notions of status hierarchy in families have faded, a psychological definition of power based on emotional control reinscribes traditional child–adult power relations on the basis of emotionality and self-development, rather than simply age status.

The insistence that parents maintain managerial emotional control highlights a certain tension and contradiction in the therapeutic demands of parenting. Because parenting takes place in the private, family sphere, emotional expression is believed to be central to the project of parenting. However, the demands of maintaining order and control under the "teamwork" model of family life, as well as the imperative to foster children's self-formation in such a way that they gain the emotional self-control necessary for corporate success, means that advice urges parents to maintain their own emotional self-control, especially in (not) reacting to interpersonal conflicts with their children. At the same time, though, parents must be both emotionally involved with and available to their children. Popular parenting advice resolves this contradiction primarily through the cultural model of communication. Parents are not supposed to *show* emotion (at least not negative emotions), but they are supposed to *talk about* emotions.

Communication and Control

In contemporary parenting advice, parents are clearly admonished to model a particular emotional style that is both emotionally communicative and highly controlled. Furthermore, they are also expected to help shape their children's style similarly: "Acknowledge that she's upset. Say, for example, 'I can see how mad you are that you can't play with your toy car right now. Would you like to punch a pillow to get rid of some of that anger?' This helps her identify her emotions, and gives her a more socially acceptable nonverbal way of dealing with her feelings. Finally, pay lots of attention to her when she uses a more appropriate way of venting her anger."[67] Because such "feeling" talk encourages children to verbalize emotion and simultaneously redirects behavior into acceptable forms, this parenting advice is not just about teaching communication skills but also represents a distinct disciplinary strategy. This highly communicative approach to discipline has been a key cause of the increased autonomy that children have over their verbal behavior at home, which results in the "seen and heard" image of children that I described in chapter 2.

In recommendations of a managerial style of parenting, the emphases on communication and empathy with children serve both strategic and moral ends. Effective communication based upon empathy with children's feelings is rational and strategic because it helps parents to efficiently manage conflicts and direct children's behavior. At the same time, it is a moral imperative that good parents try to understand children as separate persons and consider their points of view. Consider the conclusion to a *Good Housekeeping* therapeutic narrative: "Though Janie hadn't changed at all, Bill and I had. We had stopped focusing on Janie and her problems. I was no longer angry at my daughter, so I was now able to respond to her outbursts with love. Rather than shouting at her, I'd simply say, 'I'm sorry you're so upset, Janie.' I soon realized that by avoiding arguments, I was opening the way for Janie to talk to me about her problems. And I listened more closely than I had before."[68] By recognizing her daughter's emotional agency and responding with an empathetic emotional vocabulary, this mother reported that she was better able to strategically handle disciplinary conflicts and to be a good, loving parent. Furthermore, her recognition of her daughter's emotional agency supported the daughter's positive self-development and self-image.

Whether as cause or effect, popular advice seems to accurately reflect contemporary parents' views. Most parents to whom I talked described in various ways that keeping their own cool is a key goal in disciplining their children. For many of them, controlling emotional expression means raising their voices less. Especially for parents who disapprove of corporal punishments, yelling is the next frontier. Although a few explicitly disavow both spanking and yelling as abusive, most described yelling as a site of personal struggle. Liz, a white middle-class mother, for example, talked about her own need to "turn the volume down" in order to avoid "escalations." Like Liz, several other parents talked about yelling with an unmistakable element of guilt. Although yelling contradicts their image of the ideal parent they aspire to be, they admit to yelling when they feel out of control, especially in response to discipline situations. They are, however, proud of their parenting efforts when they are able to maintain personal emotional control in discipline standoffs with their children. Some parents described their own self-monitoring to recognize when they are "about to lose it" so that they can step away from a conflict before they resort to emotional responses or raised voices. In fact, parents described one of the most common strategies for dealing with children's refusals and defiance: parents simply take a short break, when possible, with several moms even describing it as putting *themselves* in "time-out."

There are some good reasons to believe that such managerial parenting strategies and messages of communicative control may resonate particularly well with twenty-first-century middle-class parents. Because of the congruence between the corporate managerial style and managerial parenting style, middle-class professionals are readily able to borrow strategies from work to use at home and vice-versa. The connection between emotional control at home and at work was made explicit by Naomi, a black middle-class mother who is a full-time professional: "I find if I get loud it is not going to serve any purpose. . . . I say when everyone is yelling and screaming at you that is not appropriate. I would not go to work and have someone yelling and screaming at me. Nor do I want you to go to work in the future with people yelling and screaming. Therefore, I am not going to yell and scream." One group of parents who are particularly likely to successfully enact the strategy of managerial parenting are "down shifting" mothers—women who have temporarily left or scaled back on corporate and professional careers to devote time to mothering young children. Many of these mothers approach parenting as a professional enterprise, where they can apply the skills they learned in their careers to socialize their children to be successful achievers.

To be the kind of effective and good parents who can foster their children's reflexive self-development, managerial parents must master "reflexive selfhood."[69] As Illouz describes the cultural model of communication, it is a means of "providing linguistic and emotional techniques to reconcile diverging imperatives: namely to assert and express the self, yet cooperate with others; to understand others' motives, yet manipulate oneself and others to reach desired goals; and to be self-controlled, yet personable and accessible."[70] Like corporate managers supervising employees, parents are advised to deal with children using therapeutically inspired communication strategies to reconcile the diverging imperatives inherent in family life.

Active Listening

One specific strategy recommended by both popular managerial guidelines and parenting advice is that of "active listening." Illouz notes the following description from a corporate training seminar: "the technique of active listening . . . has several functions. First, the listener permits the venting of emotion. The speaker feels heard and tension is released. The listener's body posture and gestures, such as head-nodding, confirm for the speaker the sense of being heard. His feelings are reflected back by the listener (e.g., 'It really was important for you that . . .'). She re-states or paraphrases what the speaker has said, again checking with him for accuracy. She then asks clarifying questions for further information. The telling-listening function is extremely important in conflict resolution."[71] This same active listening communication technique is abundant in advice about how parents should deal with children: "Listen effectively. If your child comes to tell you something, stop what you're doing, focus on her, and concentrate to hear the full story and any underlying message. Then, make sure you have understood: 'It sounds as though you didn't like what he said.' Encourage your child to suggest solutions. If you are busy, ask if she can hold the thought until you can devote yourself fully, and agree on a time to pick up the conversation."[72]

Although they did not use the specific terminology of "active listening," most respondents described this form of communicating with their children. Liz offered a good example in describing one particular "escalation" that centered around her thirteen-year-old daughter getting to the school bus on time. Later that evening, she talked with her daughter about the morning's emotional situation: "[My daughter] said, 'You screaming at us does not help. I know exactly what time it is.' She is telling me, 'I know exactly what time it is and how close I have to make it, Mom. You don't have to make it worse by rubbing it in.' I heard that. I said, 'I know. I'm going to start working on trying not to be anxious for you. But, you need to understand when you miss the bus it has consequences for me. It makes me late for work and that is why I get grumpy.'"

Active listening involves a great deal of empathy on the parent's part, especially for the younger child's unverbalized feelings. For example, a 2001 "Behavior Q&A" advice column instructs:

> "At age 5, children haven't developed an inventory of language to adequately describe how they feel," says Andrew Cohen, Ph.D., a school psychologist at the Dalton School, in New York City. "When your daughter says, 'I hate you!' she is actually saying, 'I'm angry, disappointed, sad, hurt, tired, agitated, worried, or stressed.'" Dr. Cohen says. Take a step back and assess the situation before you react. Is your daughter exhausted after a day at school? Is she hungry or ticked off about something? Your response can help her pinpoint her feelings: "I just said no to something you really wanted—that's frustrating and probably makes you angry." Try to avoid a protracted conversation about how hurtful her remarks are, Dr. Cohen advises, focusing instead on her emotions.[73]

Occasionally, advice even includes recommendations to have children who are too young to talk point to pictures or use sign language to help them identify and communicate what they are feeling. Parents are thus given the clear message that even very young children's emotional agency should be recognized and encouraged.

This advice is not limited to teaching young children the appropriate words to name their emotions; it also extends to showing empathy for older children and adolescents and encouraging them to talk to their parents about how they are feeling. For example, in a 2006 advice column parents are advised not to take their school age children's bad behavior or insults personally; instead parents should "try to figure out the source of her negative feelings—they may actually have nothing to do with you. When kids this age are bothered by fights with friends or things that happen at school, they'll often take it out on Mom simply because it's a safe way to get angry. 'Do encourage her to open up, try simply saying, "I get the feeling that you're upset about something,"' advises Dr. Cohen-Sandler. 'Your daughter may not be able to articulate the problem right away, but this will leave her an opening to talk when she's ready without putting any pressure on her.'"[74] Another 2006 article about test anxiety for school-age children encourages: "You do need to talk to her, though, to help her understand what she's feeling. So ask questions instead of making statements that may sound critical. For example, rather than 'You'd better study for the math test next week, I've heard that it's really hard,' try 'Do you know what's covered on the math test? Do you feel prepared?' You can also comfort her by acknowledging that you were scared about big tests too; it will reassure her that she's having a normal reaction."[75] Empathy for adolescents is depicted as more trying for parents but crucial to helping them to weather the storms of puberty:

> Youngsters at this age often appear to be on an emotional roller coaster—going from high to low and up again in a short period of time. During the lows, they are often petulant and silent. If they comment at all, it is brief and often sarcastic and tinged with anger. Being helpful to them at these times is a real challenge for parents. . . . When an effort to talk about the child's moodiness fails, a parent might say something like, "Okay, I can see that you are too unhappy to talk now. I hope you can talk to me about what's bothering you when you feel better." Once your child appears to be less upset, and before she forgets about a passing problem, you might ask her again if she would like to talk about why she was upset. Often she won't know, or the reasons she gives will be vague or will appear to be unimportant. Don't worry about that. Try to treat with respect all problems presented—and don't belittle or reject the explanations your child gives.[76]

The Emotional Self

Throughout such advice for parents to be empathetic and emotion-ally communicative with their children is a common idea: validating children's emotions is necessary for building children's self-concept. Illouz argues that "'communication' is a technique of recognition that can be transposed from the private to the public sphere . . . because it contains the elementary forms of modern selfhood."[77] First, this emo-tional recognition helps children to develop a self-concept—that is, to recognize themselves as separate from their parents, constituting a unique *self*. Second, there is insistence that parents should never belittle or dismiss children's feelings because this would be damaging to chil-dren's self-esteem. Parents' empathy and emotional involvement are portrayed as key ingredients in building up an inner core of resilience that will see kids through life's ups and downs: "Be empathetic. The ability to see the world through your kids' eyes is essential for fostering resilience. You don't have to agree with everything they do, but try to appreciate and validate their point of view. . . . In order to be empa-thetic, you need to continually stop and think about how you'd feel if someone said to you the same things you're saying to your children."[78]

In the therapeutic understanding of personhood, the self is anchored in childhood and primary family relationships.[79] Therefore, parents have come to be regarded as solely and privately responsible for children's emo-tional well-being, self-concept, and their future possibilities for success and happiness. Attention to emotional expression and empathetic involve-ment from parents are thus portrayed as not only part of helping children to develop their emotional awareness but also part of building up their self-esteem. This is how parents can "Help Your Child Feel Great":

A good self-image develops and thrives in an atmosphere of warmth, understanding, and respect for a child's unique traits and abili-ties. . . . [S]he needs you to be aware of her successes and to pull her through her inevitable failures. She needs an encouraging comment, a pat on the back, a proud recognition of her achievements. She needs you to have reasonable expectations regarding her abilities, to be aware of her age-related struggles, and to recognize that her sudden maturity is not yet consistent maturity. *She needs you to be tuned in to her feelings, to be involved with her, and to appreciate her unique qualities.* And she needs you to provide routines and structure in her life. As you create an environment in which your child can feel good about herself, you put in place the most vital cornerstone for her healthy development.[80]

Parents are told that unless they establish the right kind of relationship with them, their children cannot develop individual identities as fully formed and healthy selves. In this therapeutic view, a healthy self depends not upon the health of one's society, a sense of duty to others, or adherence to moral guidelines; instead, the self is precariously dependent upon an emotional calculus that includes an elusive balance in the parent–child relationship between intimacy and individuation.

Therefore, the therapeutic emphases on emotional development and positive self-feeling as the foundation for a "good" childhood undergird a contemporary notion of selfhood in which privatized and expressive forms of autonomy are privileged over more public experiences of autonomy. The psychological emphasis on children's emotional development has made children highly visible as emotional agents in the private sphere of the family, but the same therapeutic worldview that undergirds this advice also limits children's experience of public autonomy. Advice about building children's self-esteem, for example, assumes that children's emotions and self-concept are especially delicate and easily damaged. Therapeutic victimization narratives not only root emotional traumas in childhood and family relationships, but they have also encouraged a widespread sense of risk and a protectionist stance toward children that tends to "infantilize" and "deresponsibilize" childhood.[81] Therefore, at the same time that children have been attributed emotional agency, they have also become publicly regarded as fragile, potential victims who need considerable protection. By encouraging a strongly protectionist stance toward children, a therapeutic understanding of childhood has made children less visible than ever before as responsible public agents. The growing emphasis on private forms of self-expression that I examined in chapter 2 has therefore accompanied the constraints on children's public autonomy that I examined in chapters 3 and 4; both result in large part from the increasingly privatized view of the self supported by the contemporary psychology and the therapeutic ethos it has engendered.

SUMMARY

In the twentieth century, psychology became the dominant discipline promoting understandings of childhood development and offering parenting advice. Much of this advice revolved around psychological models of development that emphasized emotionality and the need for building and protecting children's self-esteem. By the 1980s, self-esteem had begun to occupy a central and prominent place in popular parenting advice, and the qualitative meaning of self-esteem had moved decidedly toward emphasizing children's individuation and emotional competence as critical to successful self-development. In service to these goals, contemporary parenting advice recommends a model of parenting built upon emotional management and soft power. Psychological views of personhood have shaped not only how we understand children's developmental needs and the work of parenting but also the ways in which parents and children are culturally visible and invisible. Although the recent therapeutic emphasis on emotional competence may provide a basis for certain forms of civic mindedness, it first privileges an understanding of the self as an individuated entity, making children and parents highly visible as private and emotional agents but largely invisible as public agents.

CHAPTER 6

Conclusion

DURING THE TWENTIETH CENTURY, demographic, cultural, and economic changes intensified the privatization of the family, with significant implications for both parenting and childhood. Parents have been granted (and are forced to acknowledge) greater autonomy in deciding what is best for their children and families, and children are readily recognized as individuated and emotional actors with greater freedom in the private sphere. Such privatization, however, also means that little public attention is given to either parenting as an activity fraught with political implications or children as participants in public life. This trade-off for parents and children indicates a deeper cultural shift in the ways that we conceive of private and public arenas of social life and of an increasingly individualized and psychologically driven concept of agency.

The cultural frameworks of privatized family life in contemporary America inadequately acknowledge the real ways in which parenting is both a private and a public activity. Current cultural constructions of childhood also fail to recognize children as public actors. Full recognition of parents and children as public actors might mean, for example, that we could regard both parenting work and children's education as forms of socially necessary labor and compensate these labors monetarily. It might mean providing for a social safety net so that the majority of children living in families headed by a single parent would not be impoverished. On a more realistic scale (but still a reach in the United States), we could recognize the public provision of benefits like health care, family care leaves, and universal preschool as necessary supports to parents and children. Taking children seriously as public actors might also mean directing considerably more funds toward improving the quality of public education, planning for built environments that take into account children's independent mobility, and providing more opportunities for children and youth to experience meaningful work and gain independence from their parents through mentoring relationships with other adults. Ultimately, the changes in the discourse of parenting that I have analyzed in *Adult Supervision Required* reveal that contemporary American culture provides readily accessible categories for understanding individuals as private and emotional entities but does not provide robust categories for imagining the individuals who make up families as public and civic actors.

THE TRADE-OFF FOR PARENTS

Parenting in the twenty-first century is an expert-guided endeavor, but most parents today exhibit attitudes toward experts that have changed from those of the early twentieth century. At the start of the twentieth century, medical science was rapidly gaining cultural authority as advances in bacteriology and vaccination began to eradicate many deadly diseases. Physicians were soon joined by psychologists and other child scientists as childrearing advice shifted away from moral prescriptions toward the new scientific understandings of health and behavior. Although mothers in the early twentieth century were active in interpreting the new scientific advice, they largely regarded the advice of these men of science as holding authority, and many mothers strove to conform to the prescriptions they read in manuals, pamphlets, and magazines. This attitude toward childrearing authorities held until the postwar era, but by the 1970s larger social and cultural upheavals meant that people began to view the authority of both science and experts more skeptically.[1] Although parents still seek out expert knowledge and rely upon it to help them make decisions, they are both more aware of contradictions among experts and more confident of their own right to determine what suits their own desires and what works best for their family structure. In collecting information and advice about children, therefore, parents today are likely to "take it with a grain of salt" and to feel a sense of autonomy over many parenting options.

Many Americans now see a one-size-fits-all model of family as outdated. This does not mean that there are no cultural models against which families are judged; the two-parent, heterosexual, nuclear family is still the favored cultural ideal, and middle-class preferences still determine what is regarded as "mainstream." However, the favored ideal no longer insists upon the strictly gendered roles that characterized the breadwinner-homemaker model that was culturally dominant for much of the twentieth century; instead, individual families feel considerable freedom to determine for themselves their roles of economic work and caregiving. Furthermore, single-parent and blended families have been significantly normalized as alternatives to the two-parent nuclear family structure, and families headed by same-sex couples are becoming less stigmatized. In addition, America's increasing diversity has meant that immigrant and ethnic groups have added still more patterns to the already varied landscape of family forms.

Cultural changes in the mainstream definition of a proper family did not simply happen; many alterations have been the result of hard-fought political campaigns to recognize the rights of individuals and couples to make private choices about family structure and gender roles. Most parents are glad to have greater freedom to tailor their practices to suit their family's particular needs and social location. The resulting diversification among families, however, has increased burdens for parents in other ways. Private choices and culturally legitimated variation have meant that at the same time that parents have gained autonomy as individuals they have lost some of their solidarity as a social group. Because many parenting decisions are highly individualized, parents may feel that other homes are different enough from their own that they find it difficult to trust other parents. Increasingly, parents are wary of outsiders, and Americans "don't want to get involved" in other families' private affairs.

The lack of trust and solidarity between families means that parents are wary of one another and that children experience fewer involvements with other adults in their communities; children, therefore, depend more solely upon their own parents who are more individually responsible for children's upbringing. Without local community involvement to both support and monitor parents, extrafamilial supervision of parenting has increasingly been transferred from the informal relationships and organizations of civil society to the formal professions and impersonal bureaucracies of the state. I have described this as a bifurcation of authority whereby individuals gain considerable autonomy over private matters at the same time that public authority is concentrated at the state level. This bifurcation means the loss of social authority by the community-level relationships, networks, and organizations of civil society. Parents have thus gained private autonomy as individuals at the same time that they have become less recognized as a public group and more subject to the impersonal supervision of the state.

THE TRADE-OFF FOR CHILDREN

This trade-off for parents between the privatization of certain family choices and increasingly bureaucratic regulation of others has precipitated a corresponding trade-off between the private and public forms of autonomy that are understood to constitute childhood. The psychological view of the child that gained dominance during the mid-twentieth century focused on children's individualized progress through stages of mental, emotional, and social development. Parents were therefore advised that childish behavior is a natural and healthy result of children's development and that children should be allowed a greater measure of autonomy over a range of their everyday behaviors at home, including many activities of daily living and greater defiance of parental instruction. Indeed, children's resistance to parental authority is often interpreted as a healthy form of emotional expression and an indication of developmental growth. While parents are by no means regarded as having lost all authority at home, contemporary advice does depict an overall flattening of household hierarchies, with an egalitarian ideal of family relationships largely replacing an older, patriarchal model of authority. Children have therefore gained greater autonomy over their everyday lives and behaviors in their homes.

Children have also gained autonomy as private, emotional agents. Since the 1960s, parenting advice has focused intensely on children's emotional development by telling parents that expression of emotion is a vital building block of children's self-development. Good parenting practice includes not only parental awareness of and sensitivity to children's emotions but also teaching children to recognize and express themselves using emotional vocabularies. Children's development of this emotional competence is understood to be critical to their self-esteem, which has been regarded since the 1980s as the chief indicator of both children's present well-being and their future success. Thus, as our cultural conception of personhood has come to be rooted ever more in the inner emotional life of individuals, children have gained cultural visibility as emotional agents, and their formation of selfhood through emotional competence has taken center stage in parenting advice. Indeed, popular advice upholds successful individuation and emotional autonomy as necessary common bases for morality and interpersonal connection.

While children have gained private autonomy as emotional agents within their families, they have simultaneously become very restricted in their recognition as social actors outside families. Since the 1980s, children's movements in public have become significantly constrained, and children have become more dependent upon parents to accompany and transport them from place to place. Parents have been told that children and adolescents must be adequately supervised at all times, which has had particularly dramatic effects on how children spend their free time and engage in peer relationships. The need for constant adult supervision has also constrained children's opportunities to demonstrate meaningful responsibility and be recognized for their independent contributions. By stressing parents' supervisory role, the boundary line between adult and child is reinforced, and childhood is constructed as a period of dependence, irresponsibility, and incompetence.

THE SOCIAL CONTEXT OF PRIVATIZATION

One possible explanation for the intensified privatization of family life in the twentieth century is changing demographics. Declining birth rates and increased longevity mean that children and parents of minor children make up smaller proportions of our population at any given time, which results in their decreased visibility as social groups. As a defined interest group, parents speak for a relatively small segment of the population; parents no longer form a citizen group that speaks for the interests of the society as a whole. This shift has weakened parents' sense that as a group they can be effective in lobbying for social changes that will benefit families. However, simple demographic changes alone explain neither why family life has been increasingly privatized nor why we conceive of the personal autonomy expected of children in primarily private ways. After all, everyone spends a portion of life as a child, and many people spend a portion of their adulthoods in active parenting roles. These facts could provide a basis for greater recognition of these as more publicly valued statuses, but they have not.

Throughout my analysis I have pointed toward various broader social and cultural changes that help to explain the continued privatization of parenting and childhood. Although no single variable explains the cultural shift in how we conceive of autonomy for parents and children, I have highlighted as especially important the influential rise of a therapeutic worldview that advocates individual self-fulfillment and induces sentimentalization of family life. This therapeutic worldview largely depends upon a new body of professional and popular psychological knowledge that arose in the twentieth century. However, the therapeutic ethos that has come to dominate American cultural understandings of the self is interdependent with several other significant cultural and economic changes of the contemporary era, which have also helped to shape our cultural understanding of childhood and the practice of parenting today. These include the successful claims of women to public recognition and greater autonomy, the transformation of capitalism in the post-industrial era, and a pervasive sense of risk and anxiety that characterizes our stage of late modernity.

The Rise of the Therapeutic

The rapid growth in the twentieth century of a therapeutic worldview influenced by psychological understandings of personhood had dramatic effects on both family life and the image of childhood.[2] With its focus on the inner life of the individual, this therapeutic ethos casts the self as a primarily emotional entity. Emphasizing self-discovery and self-fulfillment, the therapeutic ethos also makes claims for the rights of individuals to make autonomous choices about the intimate relationships that they deem important to their personal happiness. Thus, this was instrumental in legitimating more varied and flexible family forms as the individual began to take cultural precedence over a more rigid understanding of the nuclear family unit. Within the family, the developmental psychological view became the principal lens through which children are examined, resulting in arguments for their greater autonomy over their behavior and expression of feelings. In the 1980s, Zelizer suggested that the overwhelming entrance of mothers into the paid work force might help to influence a return to childhood usefulness.[3] However, since the 1980s we have seen instead a growing emphasis on children's emotional competence rather than their practical competence, further sentimentalizing and privatizing the "priceless child." And because the work of parenting is framed by this image of children's practical incompetence and dependence, the boundary line between "active" parents of minor children and all other adults (most of whom are also parents) is intensified. For example, the continued emotional and financial support that parents may provide for adult children does not fit the dominant definition of parenting. This reinforces the image of parents (of minor children) as a special interest group and discourages the involvement of many other adults in public advocacy for better social support for families.

Greater Autonomy for Women

Drawing considerable strength from the burgeoning therapeutic ethos, the women's movement in the 1970s was successful in gaining greater recognition for women as public actors. Women's successful assertion of the right to make their own private choices over family patterns of work and care has weakened the recognition of parenting roles as carrying public significance. The breadwinner-homemaker ideal of family life that held sway in American culture for much of the twentieth century insisted on well-marked, gendered boundaries between the private sphere of home and family and the public sphere of government and economy. Although this ideal hinged on the necessity of mother's private activity in the "haven" of home, in articulating a rationale for the complementary but separate spheres the model also institutionalized mothering as a public role and civic obligation. With the dissolution of this model, families have gained the freedom to construct roles of care and work apart from narrowly prescribed gender roles. At the same time, though, parenting has increasingly become regarded as an individual, private choice and as an activity that (most) parents perform during their nonworking hours. Taken together, these demographic and social changes mean that twenty-first-century parenting is largely regarded as a private role, obscuring both the contributions parents make to the public good and the social necessity of better public support for parents.

Although feminist scholarship and practice has had considerable success in degendering the distinction between domestic and public life, this line of demarcation has remained very age-based; children occupy the private space of family, and adults occupy the public realms of economy, polity, and civic sociability.[4] It is important to note that this is not the only way of theoretically conceptualizing the dichotomy of public and private in modern life. Social theorist Jeff Weintraub points out that feminist scholars' treatment of the public as a residual category encompassing everything nondomestic has effectively obscured theoretical public-private distinctions both between public polity and the market economy, on the one hand, and between the political and the civic, on the other hand. He notes that in the Marxist-feminist formulation used in analyses of the separate spheres of work and home, "the market economy has migrated from the heart of the 'private sector' to the heart of the 'public realm.'" In addition, in many feminist analyses, "while the family has been rescued from theoretical invisibility, the end result is that the civic 'public realm' is blanked out."[5] The feminist conceptualization of the private-public dichotomy has, however, carried significant weight in contemporary scholarship on the family and has therefore had a dramatic effect on shaping children's experience today. In a sense, then, by successfully claiming recognition as public actors in the economic and political realms, women effectively left children as the only group who occupied the private realm exclusively, further intensifying the degree to which the family, now an infantilized sphere, was conceived as private.

Post-Industrial Capitalism

Before the therapeutic cultural ethos arose in the twentieth century, capitalism had already succeeded in bringing about the institutional separation between work and home that has characterized the modern era. The transformation of capitalist production from an industrial to a postindustrial base has both complicated and intensified this separation of spheres. Furthermore, there is a strong affinity between contemporary postindustrial capitalism and a therapeutic culture that sees personhood in primarily psychological terms. The rapid pace of technological changes in a postindustrial economy means that work skills must be constantly updated or grow obsolete. Therefore, in preparing children for future employment, it is not the acquisition of particular skills that is emphasized but rather the establishment of a self-confident and resilient personality through sustained attention to building children's self-esteem. Moreover, contemporary capitalism is heavily dependent upon a consumer culture that encourages individualized self-creation and self-expression.

When the transition to an industrial economy in the late nineteenth and early twentieth centuries required a literate population of workers, compulsory elementary education in the "3 Rs" constituted job training. In the early twenty-first century, although workers need to be literate and adept in quantitative reasoning, the ability to read, write, and add are no longer sufficient job skills for middle-class occupations. Because of the extended period of education and training needed for middle-class and professional employment, adolescence is protracted, with some children remaining in school and financially dependent on parents well into their twenties or beyond. This causes an overwhelming emphasis on the socialization of children as "becomings" but away from their abilities as "beings" who contribute to productive work.[6] In addition, the increasing necessity of college-level education for future financial security in a postindustrial era has meant that in the race to help their children succeed, parents adopted the parenting style that Lareau terms "concerted cultivation," which is characterized by high levels of intensive parental involvement with children and a near-constant round of enrichment activities.[7] A number of insightful sociological analyses of children's activities have highlighted the role they play in fostering middle-class cultural capital and reproducing class inequalities.[8] These scholarly arguments often both reflect and reinforce the widespread cultural emphasis that sees children's leisure activities as a form of consumption or passive socialization rather than a form of public social engagement. Therefore, the extended period of education and dependence required by contemporary capitalism delays the recognition of children as social actors who might be autonomously responsible for contributions of public significance.

Furthermore, with its rapid pace of technological change, our postindustrial knowledge economy demands constant updating of technical skills. The emphasis on children's successful emotional self-development is therefore linked to the growing necessity of a set of "soft skills," such as creative thinking and problem-solving, which are widely deemed necessary to middle-class work success in the new era of what Richard Sennett calls "flexible capitalism."[9] Long-term success over a person's work career has less to do with the particular demands of any given job and more to do with this portable set of skills that they can adapt to ever-changing technical requirements. Chief among these soft skills are personality traits and social skills like positive self-esteem, confidence, resilience, and cooperativeness. Sennett explains the new work requirements of capitalism:

> An organization in which the contents are constantly shifting requires the mobile capacity to solve problems; getting deeply involved in any one problem would be dysfunctional, since projects end as abruptly as they begin. The problem analyzer who can move on, whose product is possibility, seems more attuned to the instabilities which rule the global marketplace. The social skill required by a flexible organization is the ability to work well with others in short-lived teams, others you won't have the time to know well. Whenever the team dissolves and you enter a new group, the problem you have to solve is getting down to business as quickly as possible with these new teammates. "I can work with anyone" is the social formula for potential ability. It won't matter who the other person is; in fast-changing firms it can't matter. Your skill likes in cooperating, whatever the circumstances.[10]

Preparing children for future employment, then, has come to focus more and more on the positive self-concept that parents hope will see their children through both a lengthy educational career as well as the likely need to reskill several times over the course of a working career. Therefore, the development of self-esteem has become a chief task of childhood in addition to the fulfillment of the educational prerequisites of primary and secondary education. Increasingly, positive self-concept has come to include the necessity of social and emotional skills—such as empathy—that are required to work effectively with others in rapidly changing groups and circumstances. Although working conditions in contemporary capitalism call for cooperation among individuals, the self who can most efficiently cooperate with others in these circumstances is self-contained; that is, a successful self enjoys a great deal of private autonomy and requires less public recognition as a participant in more collective forms of action.

Postindustrial capitalism is also highly interdependent with a thera-peutic understanding of selfhood in its dependence upon consumption for economic growth. No longer dependent upon production alone, contemporary capitalism requires high levels of consumer demand and individual consumption to sustain its economic vigor.[11] Given the instability of work and the decreased possibility for building a durable identity around vocation, social identity has come to be rooted more and more in the individual choices and self-expression made possible through consumption.[12] During the twentieth century, the children's industry and market researchers increasingly regarded children as desirable consumers. These industries have promoted a view of children that especially highlights children's autonomy as self-expressive consumers.[13] As Daniel Cook has argued, the social identity of consumers, based on highly individuated forms of autonomy, is critical to our cultural understandings of personhood.[14] Therefore, the demands of mature post-industrial capitalism sustain the therapeutic emphasis on privatized freedoms that is promoted by psychological literature in general and by popular parenting magazines in particular.

Pervasive Risk

Finally, parenting at the end of the twentieth century and start of the twenty-first has been significantly altered by the widespread sense of risk and anxiety that characterizes late modernity.[15] In the 1980s and 1990s, highly sensationalized incidents of child victimization such as stranger abductions, day care abuses, and school shootings heightened parents' awareness of the dangers posed to their children by strangers and in public places. Since September 11, 2001, generalized anxiety about risk has become the "new normal" for the latest generation of parents and children. Fears of innocent children's victimization combine with fears of victimization by rebellious or delinquent children to discourage children's independent use of public space.[16] The continued and increased privatization of family life is both a symptom and a cause of these fears: because they perceive the world outside the family as risky for children, parents keep their children close to home and under close supervision. Conversely, because of the retreat into private space of home, public space becomes more thoroughly an adult space, which is therefore perceived as more risky for children. In the past generation, concern about child victims has brought public attention to the fact that children are also victimized at home. Although increased public attention to child victimization within families and new child protection measures have lowered victimization rates, they have also heightened parental mistrust of state bureaucracies.[17]

The effect of the pervasive sense of risk and mistrust is to further individualize parents' responsibility for children's safety, which has resulted in considerable constraints for children's ability to participate as social actors outside the family.

WHY THE DISCOURSE OF
PARENTING MATTERS

The parenting advice in popular magazines is one kind of "barometer" of cultural trends that affect families. Popular advice in magazines both reflects and helps to shape deeper cultural ideals of personal autonomy and social authority, as revealed in how parents and children are portrayed as having or developing individual autonomy. Although advice is not completely representative of real-world parenting practices, it contributes to a discourse of parenting—in Michel Foucault's words, a set of "practices that systematically form the objects of which they speak."[18] Thus, whether parents adopt, adapt, or resist the advice presented by popular media, the advice available to parents helps to discursively shape both childhood and parenting. Parenting advice occurs within and is shaped by a social context, yet advice also contributes to the way that social context continues its existence.

Asking specifically how this advice reflects changes in our cultural understanding of autonomy, I have presented a historical analysis showing a shift in the balance between public and private forms of autonomy for parents and for children that has taken place throughout the last century. While both parents and children have gained greater personal autonomy within the private realm of the family, the continued and intensified privatization of family roles has left both groups considerably constrained as public actors. I have argued that this trade-off between public and private forms of autonomy indicates both an increasing privatization of the family and an increasingly individualized and privatized understanding of the self. This trend toward privatization is supported by our contemporary cultural and economic contexts. In particular, the therapeutic cultural ethos and the demands of postindustrial capitalism have shaped the meaning of the contemporary self and the kinds of autonomy available to that self.

Childrearing demands and expectations do not exist in a vacuum. Instead, they are part of the interconnecting changes in social institutions and culture that constitute our historical era. Therefore, in understanding the effects of social and cultural changes within families, we should also consider the effects of these changes on our broader cultural conceptions of the nature of personal autonomy and social authority. We need a better understanding of the increasing bifurcation of authority between the individual and the state and its implications for other social institutions. Moreover, we need ways of conceptualizing and practicing autonomy that recapture more meaningful forms of collective and public participation in addition to private forms of self-expression—for both children and adults.

Appendix A: Sampling and Coding Procedures for Magazine Texts

---

Parents, first published in 1926, is the longest-running popular magazine targeted to American parents and is currently the best-selling magazine in its category, with a circulation of 2.2 million copies (Audit Bureau of Circulations 2009). Although the magazine has been continuously published since 1926, it has been published under seven different titles: *Children: The Magazine for Parents* (1926–1929), *Children: The Parents' Magazine* (1929), *The Parents' Magazine* (1929–1965), *Parents' Magazine and Better Homemaking* (1966–1969), *Parents' Magazine and Better Family Living* (1969–1977), *Parents' Magazine* (1977–1978), and *Parents* (1979–present). For simplicity, I refer to it uniformly as *Parents* in the text, although bibliographic entries reflect the historical variations in the magazine's title. Currently published by Meredith Corporation, *Parents* claims a readership of 15.3 million adults, with a median age of 33.8 and a median household income of $59,616 (Meredith Corporation 2009).

Analysis of *Parents* is based on a systematic random sample of thirty-four issues covering the years 1929 to 2006. I sampled two issues per year at five-year intervals beginning in 1926; from these years, I sampled the March and September issues, based on the use of a random numbers table for selection of months. (Because a full year was not published in 1926 and owing to limited availability of the earliest issues of the magazine, the March and September issues from 1929—the first year available in the Boston Public Library collection—were used in place of 1926.) From this sample of issues, all advice columns were analyzed. Advice columns have varied some over time, but I consistently found between three and six monthly advice columns in the magazine—some of these are Q&A columns in which reader-submitted questions are answered by "experts" (such as physicians, psychologists, or etiquette guides); some are lay advice columns in which readers offer practical suggestions, answers to published questions, or examples of how they solved their own problems (examples include "Everyday Problems," "Pointers for Parents," and "It Worked for Me"). In addition to advice columns, I read all editorial items and selected for analysis all items that included advice on child development, discipline, parenting methods, and family relationships. For example, although columns offering only recipes were not selected, articles about teaching table manners or the role of meals in family life, such as "The Many Meanings of Food" (1976) and "Don't Make Your Child a Fussy Eater" (Russoto 1956) were selected for analysis. Similarly, features on back-to-school fashion that simply described clothing styles were not selected, but articles such as "Clashing over Clothes: 'You're Going to Wear That?!'" (Elkind 1991) were included for analysis. This yielded a data set of 390 texts, in which I treat each column or article as a single text.

Sample 2: *Good Housekeeping*

Good Housekeeping is a general interest women's magazine with a current circulation of 4.6 million (Audit Bureau of Circulations 2010). Its publisher, Hearst Communications, claims 5.33 adult readers per copy, yielding a total readership of approximately 24.5 million. During its 125-year history, *Good Housekeeping*'s editorial coverage has varied, but has always included content on parenthood and children, and currently 38.4 percent of its readers have one or more children living in their household. The magazine currently devotes 3.3 percent of editorial content specifically to parenthood and children, but another 14.9 percent of editorial content devoted to health and self-help also frequently includes discussion of children and parenting roles (Hearst Communications 2010).

The sample from *Good Housekeeping* consisted of two issues per year at five-year intervals, beginning in 1911 and ending in 2006. Again using a random numbers table I sampled the May and November issues. From these issues, I purposively selected all articles and advice columns relating to children and parenting roles. Because *Good Housekeeping* is a more general interest women's magazine, only a portion of each issue's texts related to childrearing; however, between three and six texts per issue were suitable for analysis, yielding a total sample of ninety texts.

SAMPLE 3: OTHER POPULAR MAGAZINES

In order to broaden the analysis, I drew a third, purposive and thematic sample of articles from a wider variety of magazines. Using the Readers' Guide Retrospective and Academic Search Complete databases to search popular magazines published between 1911 and 2009, I searched for articles tagged with several existing database subject categories relating to children and childrearing. By limiting the search results to include only cover stories and excluding articles from the two magazines already sampled, I collected a total of eighty-five texts from various magazines: major news titles such as *Newsweek, Time,* and *US News and World Report;* mainstream women's interest magazines such as *Better Homes and Gardens, Redbook,* and *Ladies' Home Journal;* and a variety of niche magazines reaching smaller markets, such as *Working Woman, Essence, Christianity Today,* and *National Parent-Child.*

CODING PROCEDURES

In coding texts, I followed procedures based on the grounded theory method described by Strauss and Corbin (Strauss and Corbin 1998). With an initial interest in the ways that parents' and children's autonomy might be expressed in the texts, I allowed a set of categories to emerge from the data. By beginning with open coding of a selection of texts from each decade sampled, I identified broad thematic categories relating to the expertise of advice-givers, parental childrearing decisions, parental authority over children, and children's autonomy. As I continued coding additional texts, these broader themes were refined into finer categories and codes. Once a complete coding scheme was developed, I coded all remaining texts, and the texts that were initially used for open coding were recoded with the final code system. After coding all texts, analysis proceeded with comparisons within and between categories and across time. The objective of this analysis was not to count the number of times each code appeared; rather, I sought to understand qualitatively the meanings of different forms of autonomy and agency depicted for parents and children and how these have changed over time. Coding and analysis of all texts was assisted by the use of MAXQDA 2007, a qualitative analysis software package.

APPENDIX B: INTERVIEW METHODS AND SUMMARY DESCRIPTION OF RESPONDENTS

I used a snowball sampling technique to select interview respondents. Beginning with contacts who work in three school systems in a suburban area in the northeastern United States, I asked for referrals to parents who might participate in interviews. I followed up the resulting interviews by asking respondents for referrals to other parents they know who might be willing to participate. Because the interviews resulting from the initial school contacts included very few working-class respondents, I then sought additional working-class respondents using my own personal networks, again enlarging the number of contacts using snowball sampling. This sampling technique resulted in interviews with twenty-two mothers and eight fathers, for a total of thirty interviews.

All respondents filled out a short survey of demographic information. The interviews themselves were semistructured with open-ended questions asking how parents make decisions about childrearing, where parents seek and how they use childrearing advice, what kinds of social support they have for parenting, what differences they perceive in their own upbringing and how they are raising their children, how they think about children's independence, and what challenges they face as parents. Interviews lasted between forty-nine and ninety-seven minutes, with most interviews lasting slightly more than one hour. I thanked respondents for their participation with a twenty-dollar gift certificate. All interviews were recorded and later transcribed verbatim for analysis. In analyzing the transcripts, I used the coding categories that emerged from the textual analysis of magazines (see Appendix A). Coding and analysis of interviews was assisted by the use of MAXQDA 2007.

In order to investigate how parenting concerns change as children grow, I included parents with children of varying ages. All of the respondents have at least one child between the ages of two and sixteen living at home. Because most respondents have more than one child (most have two or three children), their children inclusively range in age from seven weeks to twenty-four years. Eighteen respondents are middle-class, and twelve are working-class. I defined respondents as middle-class if they have a bachelor's degree and if either they or their spouse work in a profession that requires high-level educational certification or holds significant managerial authority over others. Middle-class respondents include attorneys, medical professionals, teachers, information technology specialists, and corporate analysts. I defined respondents as working-class if either they or their spouse is employed in a position that does not require high-level educational certification and has little or no managerial authority. All working-class respondents had completed high school, and three had taken some college courses but did not hold degrees. They include mechanics, custodians, hairdressers, day care workers, and low-level white-collar workers. With one exception, the middle-class families own the homes they live in; half of the working-class families own homes, and the other half rent. Most of the respondents are married; four are single mothers. Nineteen respondents are white; eleven are racial/ethnic minorities (seven black, three Hispanic, one Asian-American). Seventeen respondents are Protestant, six are Catholic, three are Jewish, and four claim no religious affiliation. The respondents range in age from thirty to fifty-seven, with a median age of forty-one. Of the mothers interviewed, half (eleven) work full-time in paid employment. Seven of the mothers interviewed are stay-at-home mothers, and another four describe themselves as the primary parent but work part-time in paid employment. Of the fathers interviewed, seven work full-time and one works part-time in paid employment. Six of the fathers I interviewed described themselves as equally sharing parenting decisions and tasks with their wives; two said that although they are involved with their children, their wife is the primary parent responsible for childrearing decisions.

Two significant limitations of the interview data are the relatively small sample size and the oversampling of white, middle-class women. The women sampled do, however, resemble the market demographics for *Parents* and *Good Housekeeping*, the two magazines that make up the largest bulk of the data used in the textual analysis.

Notes

Introduction

1. All interview respondents' names are pseudonyms.
2. In this book, I have chosen to write about *parents* and *parenting advice*, rather than *mothers* and *mothering*. Obviously, the discourse of parenting has been, throughout the twentieth century, a highly gendered discourse, with much mainstream advice directed primarily at mothers. Furthermore, changes in women's roles and the degree of autonomy experienced by women during the twentieth century have figured largely in shaping their responses to parenting advice. Although the largely gendered nature of both childrearing and childrearing advice is undeniable, I have chosen to describe *parenting* and *parenting advice*, rather than *mothering* or *mothering advice* for two reasons. First, although my sample includes advice from several women's magazines, the largest proportion of the advice I have analyzed comes from *Parents* magazine, which addresses itself toward both fathers and mothers. Although it is probably clear to anyone who picks up a copy of *Parents* and thumbs through it that both editors and advertisers assume a mostly female readership, the magazine has always included editorial features that were deemed to be of interest to fathers, and lay advice has been offered to and by fathers throughout the magazine's history. Moreover, there has been a decided shift toward androgynous parenting roles in the advice offered in popular magazines during the last thirty years. Second, I believe—and so do many of the parents I interviewed—that we need to think and talk about the work of parenting as belonging to both men and women. Discourses, after all, are not fixed but instead are sites for the contestation of meaning. See Sara Mills, *Discourse* (New York: Routledge, 2004). My word choices alone do not erase decades of power imbalances between men and women as parents; nor are they intended to obscure the work of mothers, who still perform the lion's share of care for minor children; see Anita Garey and Terry Arendell, "Children, Work, and Family: Some Thoughts on 'Mother Blame,'" in *Working Families: The Transformation of the American Home*, ed. Hertz and Marshall (Berkeley: University of California Press, 2001). Recognizing that my words do, however, make up a piece of the discourse of parenting that shapes our future social context, I have opted to refer to parents inclusively, except where the data itself is gender-specific.
3. Markella B. Rutherford, "Authority, Autonomy, and Ambivalence: Moral Choice in Twentieth-Century Commencement Speeches." *Sociological Forum* 19 (2004):583–609.
4. For a full description of sampling and coding procedures for the textual analysis, see Appendix A.

5. Rima D. Apple, *Perfect Motherhood: Science and Childrearing in America* (New Brunswick, N.J.: Rutgers University Press, 2006); Barbara Ehrenreich and Deirdre English, *For Her Own Good: Two Centuries of the Experts' Advice to Women* (Garden City, N.Y.: Anchor, 2005); Julia Grant, *Raising Baby by the Book: The Education of American Mothers* (New Haven, Conn.: Yale University Press, 1998); Christina Hardyment, *Dream Babies: Childcare Advice from John Locke to Gina Ford* (London: Francis Lincoln, 2007); Ann Hulbert, *Raising America: Experts, Parents, and a Century of Advice About Children* (New York: Vintage Books, 2003); A. Sanson and S. Wise, "Children and Parenting: The Past Hundred Years," *Family Matters* 60 (2001):1–13; Peter N. Stearns, *Anxious Parents: A History of Modern Childrearing in America* (New York: New York University Press, 2003).
6. Nancy Walker, *Shaping our Mothers' World: American Women's Magazines* (Jackson: University Press of Mississippi, 2000).
7. On the socioeconomic and racial characteristics of magazine audiences, also see K. Alison Clarke-Stewart, "Popular Primers for Parents," *American Psychologist* 33 (1978):359–369; Grant, *Raising Baby by the Book*, 78.
8. On the limitations of using advice literature as a measure of parental behavior, see Jay Mechling, "Advice to Historians on Advice to Mothers," *Journal of Social History* 9 (1975):44–63. For arguments supporting the claim that trends in advice reflect and shape cultural ideals, see Linda Quirke, "'Keeping Young Minds Sharp': Children's Cognitive Stimulation and the Rise of Parenting Magazines, 1959–2003," *Canadian Review of Sociology* 43 (2006): 387–406, and Sharon Hays, *The Cultural Contradictions of Motherhood* (New Haven: Yale University Press, 1996).
9. Eva Illouz, *Cold Intimacies: The Making of Emotional Capitalism* (Malden, Mass.: Polity, 2007), 10.
10. I initially conducted interviews in order to contextualize how parents negotiate their own autonomy vis-à-vis experts, professionals, and childrearing trends through various forms of advice. Even though this is a relatively small sample, the interviews complement the textual analysis, and the respondents offer helpful perspectives on how parents make sense of and use parenting advice, including books and magazines. In addition, I found that the parents I interviewed were eager to talk about other substantive issues that are central to my argument, such as the importance of self-esteem, the necessity of close supervision, and concerns about children's exposure to mass media. Therefore, I have cited their responses throughout the book to further illuminate the analysis of advice texts.
11. For a full description of interview sampling procedures and a summary description of respondents, see Appendix B.
12. Max Weber, *Economy and Society: An Outline of Interpretive Sociology* (Berkeley: University of California Press, 1978).
13. Georg Simmel, *On Individuality and Social Forms: Selected Writings* (Chicago: University of Chicago Press, 1971); Ferdinand Tönnies, *Community and Civil Society* (New York: Cambridge University Press, 2001).
14. Emile Durkheim, *The Division of Labor in Society* (New York: The Free Press, 1984).
15. Sharon Hays, "Structure and Agency and the Sticky Problem of Culture," *Sociological Theory* 12 (1994):57–72.

16. Mustafa Emirbayer and Ann Mische, "What is Agency?" *American Journal of Sociology* 103 (1998):962–1023.
17. Stephan Fuchs, "Agency (and Intention)," in *Blackwell Encyclopedia of Sociology,* ed. Ritzer. Blackwell Reference Online <http://www.blackwellreference.com/>, 2007).
18. For introductions to the sociology of childhood by leading thinkers in the new paradigm, see Sarane Spence Boocock and Kimberly Ann Scott, *Kids in Context: The Sociological Study of Children and Childhoods* (Lanham, Md.: Rowman & Littlefield, 2005); William A. Corsaro, *The Sociology of Childhood* (Thousand Oaks, Calif.: Pine Forge, 1997); Allison James and Alan Prout, *Constructing and Reconstructing Childhood: Contemporary Issues in the Sociological Study of Childhood* (Washington, D.C.: Taylor & Francis, 1997); Berry Mayall, *Towards a Sociology for Childhood: Thinking from Children's Lives* (Philadelphia: Open University Press, 2002); Barrie Thorne, *Gender Play: Boys and Girls in School* (New Brunswick, N.J.: Rutgers University Press, 1993).
19. James and Prout, *Constructing and Reconstructing Childhood.*
20. William A. Corsaro, *"We're Friends, Right?": Inside Kids' Cultures* (Washington, D.C.: Joseph Henry Press, 2003); Marjorie Faulstich Orellana, "The Work Kids Do: Mexican and Central American Immigrant Children's Contributions to Households and Schools in California," *Harvard Educational Review* 71 (2001):366–389; Allison J. Pugh, *Longing and Belonging: Parents, Children, and Consumer Culture* (Berkeley: University of California Press, 2009); Thorne, *Gender Play.* See also Heather Beth Johnson, *Children and Youth Speak for Themselves* (Bingley, UK: Emerald, 2010).
21. Leon Kuczynski et al., "Psychology's Child Meets Sociology's Child: Agency, Influence and Power in Parent-Child Relationships," in *Through the Eyes of the Child: Revisioning Children as Active Agents of Family Life,* ed. Shehan (Stamford, Conn.: JAI Press, 1999).
22. Allison James and Alan Prout, "Hierarchy, Boundary and Agency: Toward a Theoretical Perspective on Childhood," *Sociological Studies of Children* 7 (1995):77–99.

CHAPTER 1   TAKE IT WITH A GRAIN OF SALT

1. Weber, *Economy and Society.*
2. Zygmunt Bauman, *Legislators and Interpreters: On Modernity, Post-modernity and Intellectuals* (Ithaca, N.Y.: Cornell University Press, 1987).
3. Bauman, *Legislators and Interpreters,* 4.
4. Ehrenreich and English, *For Her Own Good*; Julia Wrigley, "Do Young Children Need Intellectual Stimulation? Experts' Advice to Parents, 1900–1985," *History of Education Quarterly* 29 (1989):41–75.
5. Annette K. Vance Dorey, *Better Baby Contests: The Scientific Quest for Perfect Childhood Health in the Early Twentieth Century* (Jefferson, N.C.: McFarland and Company, 1999); Hardyment, *Dream Babies.*
6. Ehrenreich and English, *For Her Own Good.* Emily D. Cahan, "Toward a Socially Relevant Science: Notes on the History of Child Development Research," in *When Science Encounters the Child: Education, Parenting, and Child Welfare in the 20th Century,* ed. Beatty, Cahan, and Grant (New York: Teachers College Press, 2006).

7. Apple, *Perfect Motherhood*, 7.

8. Hulbert, *Raising America*.

9. Grant, *Raising Baby by the Book*; Markella B. Rutherford and Selina Gallo-Cruz, "Selling the Ideal Birth: Rationalization and Re-enchantment in the Marketing of Maternity Care," in *Patients, Consumers and Civil Society*, ed. Chambre and Goldner (Bingley, UK: Emerald, 2008).

10. Nancy Schrom Dye, "Medicalization of Birth," in *The American Way of Birth*, ed. Eakins (Philadelphia: Temple University Press, 1986); Richard W. Wertz and Dorothy C. Wertz, *Lying In: A History of Childbirth in America* (New Haven, Conn.: Yale University Press, 1989).

11. Ehrenreich and English, *For Her Own Good*.

12. Wertz and Wertz, *Lying In*.

13. Rutherford and Gallo-Cruz, "Selling the Ideal Birth."

14. Apple, *Perfect Motherhood*.

15. Molly Ladd-Taylor, *Raising a Baby the Government Way: Mothers' Letters to the Children's Bureau, 1915–1932* (New Brunswick, N.J.: Rutgers University Press, 1986); Apple, *Perfect Motherhood*.

16. Apple, *Perfect Motherhood*.

17. Stephen Woolworth, "When Physicians and Psychologists Parted Ways: Professional Turf Wars in Child Study and Special Education, 1910–1920," in *When Science Encounters the Child: Education, Parenting, and Child Welfare in 20th-Century America*, ed. Beatty, Cahan and Grant (New York: Teachers College Press, 2006).

18. Apple, *Perfect Motherhood*, 158.

19. Barbara Beatty, et al., *When Science Encounters the Child* (New York: Teachers College Press, 2006); Cahan, "Toward a Socially Relevant Science"; Diana Selig, "The Whole Child: Social Science and Race at the White House Conference of 1930," in *When Science Encounters the Child*, ed. Beatty, Cahan and Grant; Andre Turmel, *A Historical Sociology of Childhood: Developmental Thinking, Categorization and Graphic Visualization* (Cambridge: Cambridge University Press, 2008); Woolworth, "When Physicians and Psychologists Parted Ways."

20. Hardyment, *Dream Babies*; Quirke, "Keeping Young Minds Sharp"; Cathy Urwin and Elaine Sharland, "From Bodies to Minds in Childcare Literature: Advice to Parents in Interwar Britain," in *In the Name of the Child: Health and Welfare, 1880–1940*, ed. Cooter (New York: Routledge, 1992); Wrigley, "Do Young Children Need Intellectual Stimulation?"

21. Beatty, et al., *When Science Encounters the Child*; Cahan, "Toward a Socially Relevant Science."

22. Apple, *Perfect Motherhood*; Hardyment, *Dream Babies*; Hays, *Cultural Contradictions*; Hulbert, *Raising America*.

23. Ehrenreich and English, *For Her Own Good*, 221.

24. Grant, *Raising Baby by the Book*, 139. Also see Rima D. Apple, "'Training' the Baby: Mothers' Responses to Advice Literature in the First Half of the Twentieth Century," in *When Science Encounters the Child*, ed. Beatty, Cahan and Grant.

25. Emily K. Abel, "Correspondence Between Julia C. Lathrop, Chief of the Children's Bureau, and a Working-Class Woman, 1914–1915," *Journal of Women's History* 5 (1993):79–88; Ladd-Taylor, *Raising a Baby*.

26. Cahan, "Toward a Socially Relevant Science."

27. Hardyment, *Dream Babies*.
28. Benjamin Spock, *The Common Sense Book of Baby and Child Care* (New York: Duell, Sloan and Pearce, 1946).
29. Nancy Pottishman Weiss, "Mother, the Invention of Necessity: Dr. Benjamin Spock's Baby and Child Care," *American Quarterly* 29 (1977):519–546.
30. Tinka Engel, "Do You Have Grandmother Problems?" *The Parents' Magazine* 31:3 (1956), 42–43, 70–73.
31. Weiss, "Mother, the Invention of Necessity."
32. "Childhood & Teenage Problems," *The Parents' Magazine* 21:3 (1946).
33. "Childhood/Teenage Problems," *The Parents' Magazine* 11:3 (1936), 28–29.
34. Helen Champlin, "The Question of Punishment," *The Parents' Magazine* 6:3 (1931), 22–23, 68.
35. Abel, "Correspondence"; Ladd-Taylor, *Raising a Baby*; Weiss, "Mother, the Invention of Necessity."
36. Ladd-Taylor, *Raising a Baby*.
37. Evelyn Mellon, "Why Won't They Be Neat?" *The Parents' Magazine* 21:3 (1946), 45, 83–86.
38. In *Parents*, these columns have seen a succession of titles, beginning with "Parental Problems" in the 1930s, which was changed to "Childhood and Teenage Problems" in the 1940s and 1950s. In the 1960s and 1970s, the title was "Family Clinic." In the 1980s and 1990s, reader advice columns were supplanted by various Q&A columns in which experts offer answers to questions sent in by parents. Since the mid-1990s, *Parents* has brought back the reader advice column (in addition to expert Q&A) with the titles "Parents to Parents" and "It Worked For Me." Regardless of the title, the format has been nearly identical.
39. "Parental Problems and Ways to Meet Them," *The Parents' Magazine* 6:3 (1931), 40.
40. "Family Clinic," *Parents' Magazine and Better Family Living* 46:9 (1971), 28–29.
41. "It Worked for Me!" *Parents* 71:3 (1996), 17.
42. Engel, "Do You Have Grandmother Problems?"
43. "Love and Marriage," *Parents* 66:3 (1991), 46–47.
44. Wertz and Wertz, *Lying In*.
45. Apple, *Perfect Motherhood*; Rutherford and Gallo-Cruz, "Selling the Ideal Birth."
46. Anthony Giddens, *Runaway World: How Globalization is Reshaping our Lives* (New York: Routledge, 2003), 31.
47. Ron Taffel, "5 Secrets of Good Parents" *Parents* 73:7 (1998), 108–112.
48. In addition to discipline methods and child safety, the state's authority over children also places certain limits on parental autonomy with regard to both education and financial support. For example, truancy regulations hold parents legally responsible for ensuring that children attend school, and parents who wish to educate their children at home are subject to state approval and supervision. Mitchell L. Stevens, *Kingdom of Children: Culture and Controversy in the Homeschooling Movement* (Princeton, N.J.: Princeton University Press, 2001). The state has also become increasingly willing to intervene in certain parents' decisions regarding financial support to their children, as in "deadbeat dad" laws that enforce the collection of child support from noncustodial parents. State intervention in such matters has never been evenly distributed, and

indeed, mothers who seek government support are required to provide paternity information and seek child support payments, even in cases when they might regard fathers' involvement as unsafe or detrimental to their children. Sharon Hays, *Flat Broke with Children: Women in the Age of Welfare Reform* (New York: Oxford University Press, 2003).

49. Joel Best, *Threatened Children: Rhetoric and Concern about Child-Victims* (Chicago: University of Chicago Press, 1990); Murray Levine and Adeline Levine, *Helping Children: A Social History* (New York: Oxford University Press, 1992); John E. B. Myers, *Child Protection in America: Past, Present, and Future* (New York: Oxford University Press, 2006); Judith Sealander, *The Failed Century of the Child: Governing America's Young in the Twentieth Century* (New York: Cambridge University Press, 2003).

50. David Finkelhor and Lisa Jones, "Why Have Child Maltreatment and Child Victimization Declined?" *Journal of Social Issues* 62 (2006):685–716.

51. Robert H. Bradley, et al., "The Home Environments of Children in the United States Part I: Variations by Age, Ethnicity, and Poverty Status" *Child Development* 72 (2001):1844–1867; Gene H. Brody and Douglas L. Flor, "Maternal Resources, Parenting Practices, and Child Competence in Rural, Single-Parent African American Families" *Child Development* 69 (1998): 803–816; Randal D. Day, et al., "Predicting Spanking of Younger and Older Children by Mothers and Fathers" *Journal of Marriage and the Family* 60 (1998):79–94; Clifton P. Flynn, "Regional Differences in Attitudes Toward Corporal Punishment," *Journal of Marriage and the Family* 56 (1994):314–324; Clifton P. Flynn, "To Spank or Not To Spank: The Effect of Situation and Age of Child on Support for Corporal Punishment," *Journal of Family Violence* 13 (1998):21–37; Rex Forehand and Beth A. Kotchick, "Cultural Diversity: A Wake-up Call for Parent Training," *Behavior Therapy* 27 (1996):187–206; Jean Giles-Sims, et al., "Child, Maternal, and Family Characteristics Associated with Spanking," *Family Relations* 44 (1995):170–176; Philip J. Greven, *Spare the Child: The Religious Roots of Punishment and the Psychological Impact of Physical Abuse* (New York: Random House, 1991); Shirley A. Hill and Joey Sprague, "Parenting in Black and White Families: The Interaction of Gender with Race and Class," *Gender and Society* 13 (1999):480–502; Michelle L. Kelley, et al., "Determinants of Disciplinary Practices in Low-Income Black Mothers," *Child Development* 63 (1992):573–582; Beth A. Kotchick and Rex Forehand, "Putting Parenting in Perspective: A Discussion of the Contextual Factors that Shape Parenting Practices," *Journal of Child and Family Studies* 11 (2002):255–269; Marie Ferguson Peters, "Parenting of Young Children in Black Families," in *Black Families*, ed. McAdoo (Thousand Oaks, Calif.: Sage, 2007); Murray A. Straus and Julie H. Stewart, "Corporal Punishment by American Parents: National Data on Prevalence, Chronicity, Severity, and Duration, in Relation to Child and Family Characteristics," *Clinical Child & Family Psychology Review* 2 (1999):55–70.

52. Rolock and Testa (2005) write that between 1990 and 1999 in Illinois reported incidents of suspected child abuse and neglect were three times more likely to involve African American children than white children and that the likelihood of reports involving African American children outstrips the average rate of substantiation. Nancy Rolock and Mark F. Testa, "Indicated Child Abuse and Neglect Reports: Is the Investigation Process Racially Biased?" in *Race Matters in Child Welfare: The Overrepresentation of African American*

Children in the System, ed. Derezotes, Poertner and Testa (Washington, D.C.: CWLA Press, 2005).

53. Flynn (1994) notes that there is widespread support for spanking in American culture but that the regional culture of the Northeast—where these interviews were conducted—is distinctive. In the Northeast, attitudes toward corporal punishment are markedly less favorable than in other regions, and "Northeastern whites had less favorable attitudes toward corporal punishment than any other group" (321). Flynn, "Regional Differences."

54. Most readers will be familiar with cases involving parents whose religious beliefs prohibit medical interventions, for example, Jehovah's Witnesses or Christian Scientists. See, for example, Larry May, "Challenging Medical Authority: The Refusal of Treatment by Christian Scientists," *The Hastings Center Report* 25 (1995):15–21. Other cases exist, however, in which religion is not an issue but authority comes into dispute. One prominent example from the 1990s was when the Texas Bureau of Child Protective Services assumed custody of Edward and Michele Wernecke's four children because the Werneckes objected to the radiation treatment recommended by doctors to treat their daughter, Katie, for Hodgkin's disease. Ralph Blumenthal, "Girl With Cancer Reunites With Family as State Gives Up Custody," *The New York Times*. November 4, 1995, A16.

55. Hays, *Cultural Contradictions*; Henriette Marshall, "The Social Construction of Motherhood: An Analysis of Childcare and Parenting Manuals," in *Motherhood: Meanings, Practices and Ideologies*, ed. Pheonix, Woollett and Lloyd (London: Sage, 1991); Liana C. Sayer, et al., "Are Parents Investing Less in Children? Trends in Mothers' and Fathers' Time with Children," *American Journal of Sociology* 110 (2004):1–43; Viviana A. Zelizer, *Pricing the Priceless Child: The Changing Social Value of Children* (New York: Basic Books, 1985).

56. Although we might expect that working-class parents have denser social networks than middle-class parents, within my small sample there was similar variation in my perception of the social network density among both middle-class and working-class families; the density depended in both groups upon geographic mobility, degree of religious involvement, family size, and the degree of closeness respondents expressed with their family of origin and extended kin group. On class differences in network density, see Mark S. Granovetter, "The Strength of Weak Ties," *American Journal of Sociology* 78 (1973):1360–1380.

57. Originally conceived by Heidi Murkoff, Arlene Eisenberg, and Sandee Hathaway, the Workman Publishing Company's *What to Expect* series includes *What to Expect When You're Expecting* (4th ed., 2008, by Heidi Murkoff and Sharon Mazel), *What to Expect the First Year* (2nd ed., 1996, by Heidi Murkoff, Arlene Eisenberg, and Sandee Hathaway), and *What to Expect the Toddler Years* (2nd ed., 1996, by Arlene Eisenberg). Little, Brown anchored The Sears Parenting Library with *The Baby Book: Everything You Need to Know About Your Baby from Birth to Age Two*, by William Sears, M.D. and Martha Sears, R.N. This library also includes numerous other titles, such as *The Pregnancy Book, The Birth Book, The Breastfeeding Book, The Baby Sleep Book, The Fussy Baby Book, The Attachment Parenting Book, The Vaccine Book,* and *The Discipline Book*.

58. Bauman, *Legislators and Interpreters*.

CHAPTER 2   SEEN AND HEARD

1. W. A. McKeever, "First Lesson of Obedience," *Good Housekeeping* 53:9 (1911), 342–344.
2. James Vaughn, "How to Get Obedience," *The Parents' Magazine* 4:9 (1929), 16–20.
3. Garry C. Meyers, "The Livable Lovable Child," *Children: The Parents' Magazine* 4:3 (1929), 23–24.
4. McKeever, "First Lesson of Obedience."
5. Elizabeth Wyckoff, "Obedience the Vanishing Virtue," *Children: The Parents' Magazine* 4:3 (1929), 28.
6. McKeever, "First Lesson of Obedience."
7. Alexander Black, "Every Family Needs a Traffic Cop," *Children, The Parents Magazine* March(1929), 19.
8. McKeever, "First Lesson of Obedience."
9. Vaughn, "How to Get Obedience."
10. Wyckoff, "Obedience the Vanishing Virtue."
11. Champlin, "The Question of Punishment."
12. Evelyn Emig Mellon, "What to do When Your Baby Cries," *The Parents' Magazine* 11:9 (1936), 24–25, 81.
13. George R. Pratt, "Nervous Breakdowns . . . A Teenage Danger," *The Parents' Magazine* 6:3 (1931), 14–15, 50–51.
14. J. Allan Hicks, "Don't Nag About Manners," *The Parents' Magazine* 6:9 (1931), 20, 38.
15. G. H. Preston, "Fit Your Child for Living," *The Parents' Magazine* 4:9 (1929), 18, 62–64.
16. McKeever, "First Lesson of Obedience."
17. "Everyday Problems," *The Parents' Magazine* 4:9 (1929), 34–35.
18. "Parental Problems and Ways to Meet Them."
19. Champlin, "The Question of Punishment."
20. Ibid.
21. Anna W. M. Wolf, "New Ways for Mothers," *Parents* March:(1941), 18–19.
22. L. Emmett Holt, "The Problem Eater," *Good Housekeeping* 196:11 (1956), 34–37; Josephine Kenyon, "Fussy Eaters," *Good Housekeeping* 186:5 (1946), 65–69; Carmen Russoto, "Don't Make Your Child a Fussy Eater," *The Parents' Magazine* 31:9 (1956), 52, 64.
23. Kenyon, "Fussy Eaters."
24. Holt, "The Problem Eater."
25. Kenyon, "Fussy Eaters."
26. Holt, "The Problem Eater."
27. Russoto, "Don't Make Your Child a Fussy Eater."
28. L. Emmett Holt, "The Obese Child," *Good Housekeeping* 191:11 (1951), 48–50.
29. "What I Learned from my First Child," *Good Housekeeping* 211:11 (1971), 114–118.
30. "My Husband Was a Terrible Father," *Good Housekeeping* 221:5 (1981), 36–40.
31. David Elkind, "Sense and Nonsense about Preschools," *Parents' Magazine and Better Family Living* 46:9 (1971).
32. Kenyon, "Fussy Eaters."
33. Gary Cross, *The Cute and the Cool: Wondrous Innocence and Modern American Children's Culture* (New York: Oxford University Press, 2004); Gary Cross,

"Wondrous Innocence: Print Advertising and the Origins of Permissive Child Rearing in the US," *Journal of Consumer Culture* 4 (2004):183–201.

34. "The Many Meanings of Food," *Parents' Magazine and Better Family Living* 51:3 (1976), 48, 56–58.

35. Morris A. Wessel, "New Mothers Want to Know," *Parents' Magazine and Better Family Living* 51:3 (1976), 24–25, 28–29.

36. "Q&A," *Parents* 66:9 (1991), 34–49.

37. Annette Lareau, *Unequal Childhoods: Class, Race, and Family Life* (Berkeley: University of California Press, 2003).

38. Tamara Eberlein, "Taming Preschool Anger," *Parents* 81:3 (2006), 153–154.

39. Margaret K. Nelson and Rebecca Schutz, "Day Care Differences and the Reproduction of Social Class," *Journal of Contemporary Ethnography* 36 (2007):281–317.

40. Robert Brooks, "Can-Do Kids," *Parents* 76:3 (2001), 134–139.

41. David Elkind, "Clashing over Clothes," *Parents* 66:9 (1991), 199.

42. Karen Levine, "Big Kid Discipline," *Parents* 76:9 (2001), 137–138.

43. Lareau, *Unequal Childhoods*; Nelson and Schutz, "Day Care Differences."

44. Lareau, *Unequal Childhoods*.

45. Duane F. Alwin, "From Obedience to Autonomy: Changes in Traits Desired in Children, 1924–1978," *Public Opinion Quarterly* 52 (1988):33–52; Day et al., "Predicting Spanking"; Giles-Sims et al., "Child, Maternal, and Family Characteristics Associated with Spanking"; Straus and Stewart, "Corporal Punishment."

46. Benjamin Spock, "Bringing Up Children in an Age of Disenchantment," *Redbook* 126:2 (1966), 20.

CHAPTER 3   KEEPING TABS ON KIDS

1. Mayer Hillman et al., *One False Move . . . : A Study of Children's Independent Mobility* (London: Policy Studies Institute, 1990); Sylvia Parusel and Arlene Tigar McLaren, "Cars before Kids: Automobility and the Illusion of School Traffic Safety," *Canadian Review of Sociology* 47 (2010):129–147.

2. Spencer Cahill, "Childhood and Public Life: Reaffirming Biographical Divisions," *Social Problems* 37 (1990):390–402; Gill Valentine, "Children Should Be Seen and Not Heard: The Production and Transgression of Adults' Public Space," *Urban Geography* 17 (1996):205–220.

3. Sarah L. Martin et al., "National Prevalence and Correlates of Walking and Bicycling to School," *American Journal of Preventive Medicine* 33 (2007):98–105; Noreen C. McDonald, "Active Transportation to School: Trends Among US Schoolchildren, 1969–2001," *American Journal of Preventive Medicine* 32 (2007):509–516.

4. Laurie F. Beck and Arlene I. Greenspan, "Special Report from the CDC: Why Don't More Children Walk to School?" *Journal of Safety Research* 39 (2008):449–452; McDonald, "Active Transportation to School." For discussion of school traffic safety programs, see Parusel and McLaren, "Cars before Kids."

5. Adeline Foster, "Get Them Off to a Happy Start," *The Parents' Magazine* 31:9 (1956), 56, 122.

6. On the rise of child victimization discourses in the 1980s and 1990s, see Best, *Threatened Children*; Frank Furedi, *Paranoid Parenting: Why Ignoring the Experts*

May Be Best for Your Child (Chicago: Chicago Review Press, 2002); Sue Scott et al., "Swings and Roundabouts: Risk Anxiety and the Everyday Worlds of Children," *Sociology* 32 (1998):689–705. A recent popular book tackled questions of parental risk assessment and children's independent mobility head-on: Lenore Skenazy, *Free-Range Kids: Giving our Children the Freedom We Had Without Going Nuts with Worry* (San Francisco: Jossey Bass, 2009). Little scholarly sociological attention has been paid to changes in children's independent mobility in the United States. For sociological work discussing the effects of automobile dependence on children and parents in Canada, see Parusel and McLaren, "Cars before Kids." For recent geographic studies of children's mobility in neighborhoods in the United States, see Kim Susan Blakely, "Parents' Conceptions of Social Dangers to Children in the Urban Environment," *Children's Environments* 11 (1994):16–25, and James C. Spilsbury, "'We Don't Really Get to Go Out in the Front Yard'—Children's Home Range and Neighborhood Violence," *Children's Geographies* 3 (2005): 79–99. Geographers have paid somewhat more attention to charting changes in children's mobility in Europe, Australia, and New Zealand—see, for example, Hillman et al., *One False Move*; Gill Valentine, "'Oh Yes I Can.' 'Oh No You Can't': Children and Parents' Understandings of Kids' Competence to Negotiate Public Space Safely," *Antipode* 29 (1997):65–89; Gill Valentine, *Public Space and the Culture of Childhood* (Burlington, Vt.: Ashgate, 2004); Gill Valentine and John McKendrick, "Children's Outdoor Play: Exploring Parental Concerns about Children's Safety and the Changing Nature of Childhood," *Geoforum* 28 (1997):219–235; Jenny Veitch et al., "Children's Perceptions of the Use of Public Open Spaces for Active Free-play," *Children's Geographies* 5 (2007):409–422, and Damian Collins et al., "'Mind That Child': Childhood, Traffic and Walking in Automobilized Space," in Conley and McLaren, ed., *Car Troubles: Critical Studies of Automobility and Auto-Mobility* (Ashgate, 2009).

7. Nancy Gibbs et al., "Can These Parents Be Saved?," *Time* 174 (2009), 52–57.
8. Leslie G. Pfaff, "Stop School Anxiety!" *Parents* 81:3 (2006), 166.
9. "Q&A," *Parents* 61:9 (1986), 39–46.
10. "Family Clinic."
11. "Childhood and Teenage Problems," *Parents* March (1946), emphasis added.
12. "When a Child is Missing," *Good Housekeeping* 191:5 (1951), 51.
13. Ibid., emphasis added.
14. "Teaching Children to Handle Emergencies," *Good Housekeeping* 206:11 (1966), 188.
15. Phyllis J. Orcate, "Dangers from Strangers," *The Parents' Magazine* 36:9 (1961), 87, 170–172.
16. "What I Learned from my First Child."
17. Joel Best, "Rhetoric in Claims-Making: Constructing the Missing Children Problem," *Social Problems* 34 (1987):101–121; Best, *Threatened Children*.
18. Cahill, "Childhood and Public Life: Reaffirming Biographical Divisions."
19. Margaret K. Nelson, "Watching Children: Describing the Use of Baby Monitors on Epinions.com," *Journal of Family Issues* 29 (2008):516–538.
20. Eileen Franklin, "A Secret Too Terrible to Remember," *Good Housekeeping* 231:11 (1991), 82–86.
21. Hagar Schrer, "Are You a Good Mother?" *Good Housekeeping* 246:5 (2006), 76–79.

22. Valentine (1997) also found in her study of parents in the UK that parental "peer pressure" sometimes caused parents to enforce tighter restrictions on their children than they truly believed were necessary, in order to fit into local parenting customs (p. 73). Valentine, "'Oh Yes I Can.'"

23. Hillman et al., *One False Move*; Parusel and McLaren, "Cars before Kids." Parents are also charged with individualized responsibility for ensuring that their children do not become a danger to others—Collins and Kearns (2001) point out that youth curfews are "as much about enforcing a particular notion of 'parental responsibility' as controlling young people themselves" (389). Damian C. A. Collins and Robin A. Kearns, "Under Curfew and Under Seige? Legal Geographies of Young People," *Geoforum* 32 (2001):389–403.

24. Frank F. Furstenberg, "How Families Manage Risk and Opportunity in Dangerous Neighborhoods," in *Sociology and the Public Agenda*, ed. Wilson (Newbury Park, Calif.: Sage, 1993); Deborah J. Jones et al., "Mothers' Perceptions of Neighborhood Violence and Mother-reported Monitoring of African American Children: An Examination of the Moderating Role of Perceived Support," *Behavior Therapy* 36 (2005):25–34; Susie D. Lamborn et al., "Ethnicity and Community Context as Moderators of the Relations between Family Decision Making and Adolescent Adjustment," *Child Development* 67 (1996):283–301.

25. Rachel Pain, "Gender, Race, Age and Fear in the City," *Urban Studies* 38 (2001):899–913.

26. Blakely, "Parents' Conceptions of Social Dangers"; Belinda Brown et al., "Gender Differences in Children's Pathways to Independent Mobility," *Children's Geographies* 6 (2008):385–401; Cindi Katz, "Growing Girls/Closing Circles: Limits on the Spaces of Knowing in Rural Sudan and US Cities," in *Full Circles: Geographies of Women over the Life Course*, ed. Katz and Monk (London:Routledge, 1993); Spilsbury, "'We Don't Really Get To Go Out in the Front yard'"; Valentine, *Public Space and the Culture of Childhood*.

27. Blakely, "Parents' Conceptions of Social Dangers."

28. Lareau, *Unequal Childhoods*; Valentine, *Public Space and the Culture of Childhood*.

29. Furstenberg, "How Families Manage Risk and Opportunity in Dangerous Neighborhoods"; Cindi Katz, "Disintegrating Developments: Global Economic Restructuring and the Eroding Ecologies of Youth," in *Cool Places: Geographies of Youth Cultures*, ed. Skelton and Valentine (New York: Routledge, 1998); Pugh, *Longing and Belonging*; Spilsbury, "'We Don't Really Get To Go Out in the Front Yard'"; Robert M. Vanderbeck and James H. Jr. Johnson, "'That's the Only Place Where You Can Hang Out': Urban Young People and the Space of the Mall," *Urban Geography* 21 (2000):5–25.

30. Cahill, "Childhood and Public Life"; Collins and Kearns, "Under Curfew and Under Seige?"; Valentine, "Children Should Be Seen and Not Heard."

31. Hillman et al., *One False Move*, found a similar generational lag of two and a half years in a study of when children gain licenses to cross the street, walk alone to school, and use public transportation in England.

32. "Teaching Children to Handle Emergencies."

33. As Sheller points out, the need to chauffeur children means that cars are part of the emotional connection through which parents express and demonstrate love and care. Mimi Sheller, "Automotive Emotions: Feeling the Car," *Theory, Culture, & Society* 21 (2004):221–242.

34. Richard Lerner and Charyl Omen, "Keeping Tabs without being a Nag," *Parents* 71:9 (1996), 111–112.
35. Donna Christiano, "Disciplining in Public," *Parents* 76:3 (2001), 112–117.
36. James Comer, "Parents Can Be Embarrassing," *Parents* 56:9 (1981), 108.
37. Dan Kiley, "But Mom, Everyone Else Does It!" *Good Housekeeping* 221:5 (1981), 133–138.
38. James Comer, "Keeping Tabs on Your Kids," *Parents* 66:9 (1991),197.
39. Anita Bartholomew, "Keeping a Child's Spirit Alive," *Good Housekeeping* 236:5 (1996), 28.
40. Comer, "Keeping Tabs on Your Kids."
41. "Behavior Q&A," *Parents* 81:3 (2006), 42–43.
42. On the conversion of unstructured play time into adult-directed activities, see also Howard P. Chudacoff, *Children at Play: An American History* (New York: New York University Press, 2007), and Lareau, *Unequal Childhoods*.
43. Thorne, *Gender Play*.
44. Lareau, *Unequal Childhoods*; Nelson and Schutz, "Day Care Differences and the Reproduction of Social Class."
45. Murray Milner, Jr., *Freaks, Geeks, and Cool Kids: American Teenagers, Schools, and the Culture of Consumption* (New York: Routledge, 2004).
46. M. P. Baumgartner, *The Moral Order of a Suburb* (New York: Oxford University Press, 1988); Donald J. Black, *The Social Structure of Right and Wrong* (San Diego: Academic Press, 1998).
47. Spilsbury, "'We Don't Really Get To Go Out in the Front Yard'"; Vanderbeck and Johnson, "'That's the Only Place Where You Can Hang Out.'"
48. Demie Kurz, "'I Trust Them but I Don't Trust Them': Issues and Dilemmas in Monitoring Teenagers," in *Who's Watching?: Daily Practices of Surveillance among Contemporary Families*, ed. Nelson and Garey (Nashville, Tenn.: Vanderbilt University Press, 2009).
49. Barbara K. Hofer et al., "The Electronic Tether: Communication and Parental Monitoring during the College Years," in *Who's Watching?*, ed. Nelson and Garey.
50. C. S. Littledale, "What to Do about the Comics," *The Parents' Magazine* 16:3 (1941), 26–27.
51. "Childhood/Teenage Problems."
52. Diane Halles, "Too Sexy, Too Soon?" *Parents* 76:3 (2001), 92–96.
53. Daniel Okrent et al., "Raising Kids Online," *Time* 153 (1999), 38.
54. Schrer, "Are You a Good Mother?"
55. Okrent, et al., "Raising Kids Online."
56. Halles, "Too Sexy, Too Soon?"; Harry Hanauer, "Teenagers and Credit Cards," *Good Housekeeping* 221:11 (1981), 141–146; Okrent et al., "Raising Kids Online,"
57. In his excellent history of American childhood, Steven Mintz also argues that children are both getting older and getting younger. Steven Mintz, *Huck's Raft: A History of American Childhood* (Cambridge, Mass.: Belknap Press, 2004).
58. Valentine, "Children Should Be Seen and Not Heard."

CHAPTER 4   MIXED MESSAGES ABOUT RESPONSIBILITY

1. Zelizer, *Pricing the Priceless Child*.
2. Jack Harrison Pollack, "Girl Dropouts," *Parents' Magazine and Better Homemaking* 41:9 (1966), 91, 113–115.

3. Miri Song, *Helping Out: Children's Labor in Ethnic Businesses* (Philadelphia: Temple University Press, 1999).
4. Orellana, "The Work Kids Do."
5. Lisa Dodson and Jillian Dickert, "Girls' Family Labor in Low-Income Households: A Decade of Qualitative Research," *Journal of Marriage and the Family* 66 (2004):318–332.
6. Pavla Miller, "Useful and Priceless Children in Contemporary Welfare States," *Social Politics* 12 (2005):13.
7. Jens Qvortrup, "From Useful to Useful: The Historical Continuity of Children's Constructive Participation," *Sociological Studies of Children* 7 (1995):49–76.
8. Zelizer, *Pricing the Priceless Child.*
9. Alice Fox Pitts, "Make it the Best Year Ever," *The Parents' Magazine* 4:9 (1929), 15, 44–47.
10. James D. Kirkpatrick, "A Child of Divorce," *The Parents' Magazine* 21:9 (1946), 26.
11. "Parental Problems and Ways to Meet Them."
12. "Childhood/Teenage Problems."
13. "Parental Problems and Ways to Meet Them."
14. "Childhood/Teenage Problems."
15. Marion Ellison Faegre, "First Steps Toward Self-Reliance," *Ladies' Home Journal* 50(1933), 31.
16. Blanche Halbert, "Every Boy Needs Tools," *The Parents' Magazine* 4:9 (1929), 24, 53–54.
17. "When They Are Eight," *The Parents' Magazine* 16:3 (1946), 41, 79–80.
18. "Teaching Children about Money," *Good Housekeeping* 206:5 (1966), 176. For an excellent discussion of the problem posed by children's money and the "culturally invented boundary between wage and allowance," see Zelizer, 97–112.
19. Zelizer, *Pricing the Priceless Child.*
20. Joyce Brothers, "Fit the Chore to the Child," *Good Housekeeping* 206:11 (1966), 56–59, 61.
21. Ibid.
22. "Love and Marriage," *Parents* 56:3 (1981), 20–21.
23. Brooks, "Can-Do Kids"; Joan Leonard, "Raising Responsible Kids" *Parents* 71:3 (1996), 79–82. Rick Epstein, "Whose Chore Is It, Anyway?" *Parents* 71:3 (1996), 85–86; Peg Tyre et al., "The Power of No," *Newsweek* 144 (2004), 42–51.
24. This idealized portrayal is in contrast to numerous studies of children's actual household work, which show that tasks are still somewhat gender differentiated and that girls perform more household work than boys. See Dodson and Dickert, "Girls' Family Labor in Low-Income Households"; Constance T. Gager et al., "The Effects of Family Characteristics and Time Use on Teenagers' Household Labor," *Journal of Marriage and the Family* 61 (1999):982–994; Beth Manke et al., "The Three Corners of Domestic Labor: Mothers,' Fathers,' and Children's Weekday and Weekend Housework," *Journal of Marriage and the Family* 56 (1994):657–668; Vanessa R. Wight et al., "The Time Use of Teenagers," *Social Science Research* 38 (2009):792–809. The finding that girls spend more time in household labor than boys is one of the few commonalities in crosscultural comparison of children's time use. Reed W. Larson and Suman Verma, "How Children and Adolescents Spend

Time across the World: Work, Play, and Developmental Opportunities," *Psychological Bulletin* 125 (1999):701–736.

25. Leonard, "Raising Responsible Kids."

26. Ibid.; Tyre et al., "The Power of No."

27. Beth Levine, "Is Your Marriage Missing Action," *Parents* 76:9 (2001), 143–147.

28. Zelizer, *Pricing the Priceless Child*, 212.

29. Viviana A. Zelizer, "The Priceless Child Revisited," in *Studies in Modern Childhood: Society, Agency and Culture,* ed. Qvortrup (London: Palgrave, 2005).

30. Tyre et al., "The Power of No."

31. Charmin Kerr Stein, "Your Child Can Be Tidy and Like It," *The Parents' Magazine* 31:3 (1956), 38–39, 120–122.

32. Miller, "Useful and Priceless Children in Contemporary Welfare States."

33. Anne Solberg, "Negotiating Childhood: Changing Constructions of Age for Norwegian Children," in *Constructing and Reconstructing Childhood: Contemporary Issues in the Sociological Study of Childhood,* ed. James and Prout (London: Falmer Press, 1997), 142. On the intersection of women's studies and childhood studies, also see Barrie Thorne, "Re-Visioning Women and Social Change: Where are the Children?" *Gender and Society* 1 (1987):85–109; Ann Oakley, "Women and Children First and Last: Parallels and Differences between Children's and Women's Studies," in *Children's Childhoods: Observed and Experienced,* ed. Mayall (London: Falmer Press, 1994); and Leena Alanen, "Gender and Generation: Feminism and the 'Child Question,'" in *Childhood Matters,* ed. Qvortrup et al. (Aldershot, UK: Avebury, 1994).

34. Dodson and Dickert, "Girls' Family Labor in Low-Income Households"; Gager et al., "The Effects of Family Characteristics and Time Use on Teenagers' Household Labor"; Sandra L. Hofferth and John F. Sandberg, "How American Children Spend their Time," *Journal of Marriage and the Family* 63 (2001):295–308; Manke et al., "The Three Corners of Domestic Labor"; Virginia Morrow, "Invisible Children?: Toward a Reconceptualization of Childhood Dependency and Responsibility," *Sociological Studies of Children* 7 (1995):207–230; Virginia Morrow, "Responsible Children and Children's Responsibilities? Sibling Caretaking and Babysitting by School-age Children," in *Responsibility, Law, and the Family,* ed. Jo Bridgeman, Heather Keating, and Craig Lind (Burlington, Vt.: Ashgate, 2008); Orellana, "The Work Kids Do"; Wight et al., "The Time Use of Teenagers"; Zelizer, "The Priceless Child Revisited."

35. Miller, "Useful and Priceless Children in Contemporary Welfare States."

36. Dodson and Dickert, "Girls' Family Labor in Low-Income Households"; Hofferth and Sandberg, "How American Children Spend Their Time"; Wight et al., "The Time Use of Teenagers."

37. Morrow, "Responsible Children and Children's Responsibilities," 108.

38. Morrow, "Invisible Children?," 224.

39. Quirke, "Keeping Young Minds Sharp"; Wrigley, "Do Young Children Need Intellectual Stimulation?"

40. Hilary Levey, "Pageant Princesses and Math Whizzes: Understanding Children's Activities as a Form of Children's Work," *Childhood* 16 (2009):195–212; Qvortrup, "From Useful to Useful"; Zelizer, "The Priceless Child Revisited."

41. Nancy Seid, "Be an A+ Parent," *Parents* 76:9 (2001), 201–203.

42. Although there is widespread belief that homework contributes to academic success, the actual connection between homework and educational outcomes is a much-studied but poorly understood issue. See, for example, Harris Cooper et al., "Relationships among Attitudes about Homework, Amount of Homework Assigned and Completed, and Student Achievement," *Journal of Educational Psychology* 90 (1998):70–83.

43. "Back to School from A to Z," *Parents* 81:3 (2006), 162–164; Roberta Israeloff, "When Your Child Acts Up at School," *Parents* 71:3 (1996). 66–69.

44. "When Your Child Acts Up at School."

45. "School Days," *Parents* 61:9 (1986), 58–60.

46. Walecia Konrad, "More Tests = More Anxiety," *Good Housekeeping* 246:11 (2006), 109–112.

47. Lareau, *Unequal Childhoods*.

48. Douglas Kleiber and Gwynn Powell, "Historical Change in Leisure Activities during After-School Hours," in *Organized Activities as Contexts of Development: Extracurricular Activities, After-School and Community Programs*, ed. Mahoney, Larson and Eccles (Mahwah, N.J.: Lawrence Erlbaum Associates, 2005).

49. Elliott A. Medrich et al., *The Serious Business of Growing Up: A Study of Children's Lives Outside of School* (Berkeley: University of California Press, 1982).

50. "Q&A," *Parents* 56:9 (1981), 12–14.

51. "Behavior Q&A" (2006).

52. Patricia A. Adler and Peter Adler, "Social Reproduction and the Corporate Other: The Institutionalization of Afterschool Activities," *The Sociological Quarterly* 35 (1994):309–328; Tiffani Chin and Meredith Phillips, "Social Reproduction and Child-Rearing Practices: Social Class, Children's Agency, and the Summer Activity Gap," *Sociology of Education* 77 (2004):185–210; Jason Kaufman and Jay Gabler, "Cultural Capital and the Extracurricular Activities of Girls and Boys in the College Attainment Process," *Poetics* 32 (2004):145–168; Lareau, *Unequal Childhoods*; Hilary Levey, "Outside Class: A Historical Analysis of American Children's Competitive Activities," in *Childhood in American Society*, ed. Sternheimer (Boston: Allyn & Bacon, 2010).

53. Adler and Adler, "Social Reproduction and the Corporate Other."

54. Levey, "Pageant Princesses and Math Whizzes," 210.

55. Lauren Picker, "And Now, the Hard Part," *Newsweek* 145 (2005), 46–50.

56. Tyre et al., "The Power of No."

57. Kiley, "But Mom, Everyone Else Does It!"

58. Rebecca Shahmoon, "Happily Ever Afterschool," *Parents* 66:9 (1991), 195.

59. On the pressure for children to specialize early in sports, see Adler and Adler, "Social Reproduction and the Corporate Other" and Hilary Levey, "Trophies, Triumphs, and Tears: Children's Experiences with Competitive Activities," in Johnson, ed., *Children and Youth Speak for Themselves: Sociological Studies of Children and Youth*, Volume 13 (Bingley, UK: Emerald, 2010).

60. Francis Roberts, "Start School Right," *Parents* 56:9 (1981), 106.

61. Peg Rosen, "How to Raise a Really Good Kid," *Parents* 81:3 (2006).

62. Bonnie B. Morris, "The Dawdler Dilemma," *Parents* 71:9 (1996), 66–69.

63. Annette Lareau and Elliot B. Weininger, "Time, Work, and Family Life: Reconceptualizing Gendered Time Patterns through the Case of Children's Organized Activities," *Sociological Forum* 23 (2008):419–454.

64. William H. Burnham, "Cultivating a Wholesome Personality," *The Parents' Magazine* 6:9 (1931), 13, 42–43.
65. "Childhood and Teenage Problems," *The Parents' Magazine* 21:3 (1946).
66. Stanley Feingold, "Raise Good Citizens," *The Parents' Magazine* 26:9 (1951), 58.
67. W. Howard Pillsbury, "Our Schools Prepare for Tomorrow," *The Parents' Magazine* 16:9 (1941), 14.
68. Terrel H. Bell, "Teaching the Basics at Home," *Parents' Magazine and Better Family Living* 51:3 (1976), 37–38, 64.
69. Feingold, "Raise Good Citizens."
70. H. C. Tate, "What Kind of High School?" *The Parents' Magazine* 21:9 (1946), 45, 124.
71. Ruth Brecher and Edward Brecher, "You Can Trust your Town's Teens," *The Parents' Magazine* 36:3 (1961), 54–55, 111–113.
72. Ibid.
73. "Great Projects for Teens without Summer Work," *Good Housekeeping* 211:5 (1971), 190.
74. Leonard, "Raising Responsible Kids."
75. Ron Taffel, "The Me! Me! Me! Generation," *Parents* 76:3 (2001), 104–109.
76. Jenny Friedman, "Charity Begins at Home," *Parents* 71:3 (1996), 89–93.
77. On declining civic participation and community trust, see Robert D. Putnam, *Bowling Alone: The Collapse and Revival of American Community* (New York: Simon & Schuster, 2000).

CHAPTER 5   PSYCHOLOGY'S CHILD

1. Urwin and Sharland, "From Bodies to Minds."
2. The influence of psychoanalytic perspectives is evident in scholarly literature beginning in the 1920s. See Diana Baumrind, "Effects of Authoritative Parental Control on Child Behavior" *Child Development* 37 (1966):887. Here, however, I refer to its popularization for a lay audience, which was fully evident by the 1940s and 1950s.
3. Beatty et al., *When Science Encounters the Child*.
4. Eva Illouz, *Oprah Winfrey and the Glamour of Misery: An Essay on Popular Culture* (New York: Columbia University Press, 2003).
5. Joel Pfister, "Glamorizing the Psychological: The Politics of the Performances of Modern Psychological Identities," in *Inventing the Psychological*.
6. Joan David, "Behavior Clinic for Normal Children," *The Parents' Magazine* 26:9 (1951), 186–196, emphasis added.
7. Dorothy Barclay, "Care of Infant's Emotions," *New York Times*, June 29, 1952, SM 24.
8. Illouz, *Saving the Modern Soul*.
9. Illouz, *Oprah Winfrey and the Glamour of Misery*; Illouz, *Cold Intimacies*.
10. Nancy Schnog, "On Inventing the Psychological," in *Inventing the Psychological*.
11. Cahan, "Toward a Socially Relevant Science."
12. John Demos, "Oedipus and America: Historical Perspectives on the Reception of Psychoanalysis in the United States," in *Inventing the Psychological*, ed. Pfister and Schnog; Illouz, *Saving the Modern Soul*.

13. Daniel Thomas Cook, *The Commodification of Childhood: The Children's Clothing Industry and the Rise of the Child Consumer* (Durham, N.C.: Duke University Press, 2004).

14. Roberta Israeloff, "What It Feels Like to Be . . . Two," *Parents* September (1991), 84–90.

15. "Should My Child Go To Private School?" *Parents' Magazine and Better Homemaking* 41:9 (1966), 64–65, 140–141.

16. Cecelia M. Dobrish, "Can Values Really Be Learned at School?" *Parents' Magazine and Better Family Living* 46:9 (1971), 44, 66–68.

17. Bernice Weissbourd, "Help Your Child Feel Great," *Parents* 61:3 (1986), 174, emphasis added.

18. Comer, "Parents Can Be Embarrassing."

19. Burnham, "Cultivating a Wholesome Personality."

20. Pratt, "Nervous Breakdowns . . . A Teenage Danger."

21. Faegre, "First Steps Toward Self-Reliance."

22. Katherine T. Williams, "So Much to Learn Before Six," *The Parents' Magazine* 26:3 (1951), 32–33, 56–57.

23. Mellon, "Why Won't They Be Neat."

24. Meyers, "The Livable Lovable Child."

25. O. Spurgeon English, "Father's Changing Role," *The Parents' Magazine* 26:9 (1951), 44–45, 153–155.

26. "Childhood and Teenage Problems," *The Parents' Magazine* 26:9 (1951), 52–53.

27. How much children are praised, and for which actions, varies by class culture. See Nelson and Schutz, "Day Care Differences and the Reproduction of Social Class."

28. English, "Father's Changing Role."

29. Arthur Fleming, "Don't Turn Your Back on Troubled Teens," *Good Housekeeping* 201:11 (1961), 44–48.

30. Sidney Blau, "Help Your Child Like Himself," *Parents' Magazine and Better Homemaking* 38:12 (1963), 37–38, 62–63; Vivian S. Sherman, "What Injures a Child's Self-Esteem?" *PTA Magazine* 61:3 (1967), 23–25.

31. "Mother's Girl," *Good Housekeeping* 206:11 (1966), 74–81; Stephen Birnbaum, "My Teenage Daughter was an Alcoholic," *Good Housekeeping* 226:5 (1986), 28–30; Swanee Hunt, "I Couldn't Reach My Daughter . . . ," *Good Housekeeping* 236:11 (1996), 100–105; "I Couldn't Control My Teenage Daughter . . . ," *Good Housekeeping* 226:11 (1986), 38–41; "My Husband Was a Terrible Father"; "Our Son was Failing in School," *Good Housekeeping* 172:5 (1971), 16.

32. "I Couldn't Control My Teenage Daughter."

33. "Our Son was Failing in School."

34. Hunt, "I Couldn't Reach My Daughter."

35. Brooks, "Can-Do Kids"; David Elkind, "Boosting Self-Esteem" *Parents* 66:3 (1991), 195; Jane Marks, "Joshua, Cara & Anne: Raising a Child Who's Different," *Parents* 61:9 (1986), 90–92, 172–176; Rosen, "How to Raise a Really Good Kid"; Weissbourd, "Help Your Child Feel Great."

36. For example, Israeloff, "What It Feels Like to Be . . . Two"; Susan S. Mirrell, "Playing Favorites," *Parents* 71:9 (1996), 116–118; Laura Nathanson, "The Case Against Baby Fat," *Parents* 71:9 (1996), 45–48.

37. Taffel, "The Me! Me! Me! Generation."

38. Joyce Brothers, "Ask Dr. Joyce Brothers," *Good Housekeeping* 216:11 (1976), 90–93.
39. Bell, "Teaching the Basics at Home."
40. William Sloan and Daphne West, "Don't Rush Your Kids into Organized Sports," *Parents' Magazine and Better Homemaking* 41:9 (1966), 79, 88.
41. Joyce Brothers, "Fit the Chore to the Child," *Good Housekeeping* 11 (1966), 56–59, 61.
42. Meg Schneider, "Raising Your Child's Social IQ," *Good Housekeeping* 236:5 (1996), 83–85.
43. Illouz, *Cold Intimacies*. What Illouz terms emotional competence is also called "emotional intelligence" or "EQ" in contemporary popular psychology.
44. Vera L. Connolly, "Let's Look at the Home," *Good Housekeeping* 166:11 (1926), 24–25, 264, 266, 269–270, 273–274, 276.
45. LaBerta A. Hattwick, "The Young Child Needs Companionship," *The Parents' Magazine* 16:9 (1941), 24–25, 96–97, emphasis added.
46. Constance Foster, "Are You Old Enough to Stay Married?" *Parents' Magazine* (Dec. 1947): 25, 148–153. Quoted in Francesca M. Cancian and Steven L. Gordon, "Changing Emotion Norms in Marriage: Love and Anger in U.S. Women's Magazines Since 1900," *Gender & Society* 2 (1988):308–342, 319.
47. Cancian and Gordon, "Changing Emotion Norms."
48. "Behavior Q&A," *Parents* 76:9 (2001), 36–37.
49. Schneider, "Raising Your Child's Social IQ."
50. Eberlein, "Taming Preschool Anger."
51. Ann Murphy, "Behavior Q&A," *76* March (2001), 61.
52. Schneider, "Raising Your Child's Social IQ."
53. The growing emphasis on children's emotional awareness may also help to explain the recent prevalence of diagnoses of autism spectrum disorders, such as Asperger's syndrome. The greater emotional competence required of children today may place individuals with Asperger's at a greater disadvantage than used to be the case, making their challenges with social and emotional processes more obvious than they would have been in past social contexts.
54. Schneider, "Raising Your Child's Social IQ."
55. Anne Cassidy, "Beginner Manners," *Parents* 71:3 (1996), 113–114; Christiano, "Disciplining in Public"; Stanley Greenspan, "From Savage to Sweetheart," *Parents* 71:9 (1996), 93–94; Rosen, "How to Raise a Really Good Kid."
56. Kiley, "But Mom, Everyone Else Does It!"
57. Joan Costello, "The Golden Rule," *Parents* 56:9 (1981), 104.
58. Rosen, "How to Raise a Really Good Kid."
59. Illouz, *Saving the Modern Soul*.
60. Ibid., 83.
61. Josephine Kenyon, "Discipline," *Good Housekeeping* 166:11 (1926), 98. See also Josephine Kenyon, *Healthy Babies are Happy Babies: A Complete Handbook for Modern Mothers* (Boston: Little, Brown, & Co., 1938).
62. Ari Brown and Denise Fields, "The 20 Commandments of Toddler Discipline," *Parents* 81:9 (2006), 46–51.
63. Konrad, "More Tests = More Anxiety."
64. Salvatore Gentile and Joan Leonard, "Mom's Weekend Off," *Good Housekeeping* 231:5 (1991), 62–65.
65. Schrer, "Are You a Good Mother?"
66. Illouz, *Saving the Modern Soul*.

67. Lawrence Kutner, "Ask the Expert," *Parents* 71:3 (1996), 72, 76–77.
68. "I Couldn't Control My Teenage Daughter."
69. Illouz, *Saving the Modern Soul*, 93.
70. Ibid., 89.
71. Conflict Research Consortium, quoted in ibid., 92.
72. Elizabeth Hartley-Brewer, "Tune In to Your Child," *Scholastic Parent & Child* 14 (2006), 59–60.
73. Murphy, "Behavior Q&A."
74. Peggy Post, "Behavior Q&A," *Parents* 81:9 (2006), 52.
75. Konrad, "More Tests = More Anxiety."
76. James Comer, "Puberty, Petulance, and Silence," *Parents* 56:3 (1981), 111.
77. Illouz, *Saving the Modern Soul*, 92.
78. Brooks, "Can-Do Kids."
79. Illouz, *Saving the Modern Soul*, 105.
80. Weissbourd, "Help Your Child Feel Great," emphasis added.
81. Best, *Threatened Children*; Stevi Jackson and Sue Scott, "Risk Anxiety and the Social Construction of Childhood," in *Risk and Sociocultural Theory: New Directions and Perspectives*, ed. Lupton (New York: Cambridge University Press, 1999); Morrow, "Invisible Children?"

CHAPTER 6   CONCLUSION

1. Bauman, *Legislators and Interpreters*; Giddens, *Runaway World*.
2. For excellent overviews of the historical rise of psychology and therapeutic culture, see Ellen Herman, *The Romance of American Psychology: Political Culture in the Age of Experts* (Berkeley: University of California Press, 1995); Joel Pfister and Nancy Schnog, *Inventing the Psychological*, and Illouz, *Saving the Modern Soul*. For essays showing the range of cultural effects of the therapeutic beyond the family, see Jonathan Imber, *Therapeutic Culture: Triumph and Defeat* (New Brunswick, N.J.:Transaction, 2004).
3. Zelizer, *Pricing the Priceless Child*.
4. Since the late 1980s, a number of feminist scholars have begun to address the effects of feminist scholarship on the cultural construction of children. See in particular Thorne, "Re-Visioning Women and Social Change: Where are the Children?" and Oakley, "Women and Children First and Last."
5. Weintraub, "The Theory and Politics of the Public/Private Distinction."
6. The distinction between "becomings" and "beings" is from James and Prout, "Hierarchy, Boundary and Agency."
7. Lareau, *Unequal Childhoods*.
8. Adler and Adler, "Social Reproduction and the Corporate Other"; Kaufman and Gabler, "Cultural Capital and Extracurricular Activities"; Lareau, *Unequal Childhoods*.
9. Richard Sennett, *The Corrosion of Character: The Personal Consequences of Work in the New Capitalism* (New York: W. W. Norton, 1998).
10. Richard Sennett, *The Culture of the New Capitalism* (New Haven: Yale University Press, 2006).
11. John Kenneth Galbraith, *The Affluent Society* (Boston: Houghton Mifflin, 1998).
12. Zygmunt Bauman, "From the Work Ethic to the Aesthetic of Consumption," in *The Bauman Reader*, ed. Beilharz (Malden, Mass.: Blackwell, 2001).

13. Daniel Thomas Cook, "The Other 'Child Study': Figuring Children as Consumers in Market Research, 1910s–1990s," *The Sociological Quarterly* 41 (2000):487–507; Cook, *The Commodification of Childhood*.

14. Daniel Thomas Cook, "Agency, Children's Consumer Culture and the Fetal Subject: Historical Trajectories, Contemporary Connections," *Consumption, Markets and Culture* 6 (2003):115–132.

15. Ulrich Beck, *Risk Society: Towards a New Modernity* (London: Sage Publications, 1992); Giddens, *Runaway World*; Stearns, *Anxious Parents*.

16. Best, *Threatened Children*; Joel Best, "Troubling Children: Children and Social Problems," in Best, ed., *Troubling Children: Studies of Children and Social Problems* (New York: Aldine de Gruyter, 1994); Cahill, "Childhood and Public Life"; Valentine, "Children Should Be Seen and Not Heard."

17. Finkelhor and Jones, "Why Have Child Maltreatment and Child Victimization Declined?"

18. Michel Foucault, *The Archaeology of Knowledge* (1972), quoted in Mills, *Discourse*, 15.

BIBLIOGRAPHY

Abel, E. K. 1993. Correspondence between Julia C. Lathrop, chief of the Children's Bureau, and a working-class woman, 1914–1915. *Journal of Women's History* 5:79–88.

Adler, P. A., and P. Adler. 1994. Social reproduction and the corporate other: The institutionalization of afterschool activities. *The Sociological Quarterly* 35: 309–328.

Alanen, L. 1994. Gender and generation: Feminism and the "child question." In *Childhood matters*, edited by J. Qvortrup, M. Bardy, G. Sgritta, and H. Wintersberger, 27–42. Aldershot, UK: Avebury.

Alwin, D. F. 1988. From obedience to autonomy: Changes in traits desired in children, 1924–1978. *Public Opinion Quarterly* 52:33–52.

Apple, R. D. 2006. *Perfect motherhood: Science and childrearing in America.* New Brunswick, N.J.: Rutgers University Press.

———. 2006. "Training" the baby: Mothers' responses to advice literature in the first half of the twentieth century. In *When science encounters the child*, edited by Beatty, Cahan, and Grant, 195–214. New York: Teachers College Press.

Audit Bureau of Circulations. 2009. *Parents.* Schaumburg, Ill.

———. 2010. *Good Housekeeping.* Schaumburg, Ill.

Back to school from A to Z. 2006. *Parents* 81:3, 162–164.

Barclay, D. 1952. Care of infant's emotions. *New York Times,* June 29, 1952, SM 24.

Bartholomew, A. 1996. Keeping a child's spirit alive. *Good Housekeeping* 236:5, 28.

Bauman, Z. 1987. *Legislators and interpreters: On modernity, post-modernity and intellectuals.* Ithaca, N.Y.: Cornell University Press.

Bauman, Z. 2001. From the work ethic to the aesthetic of consumption. In *The Bauman reader*, edited by P. Beilharz, 311–333. Malden, Mass.: Blackwell.

Baumgartner, M. P. 1988. *The moral order of a suburb.* New York: Oxford University Press.

Baumrind, D. 1966. Effects of authoritative parental control on child behavior. *Child Development* 37:887–907.

Beatty, B., E. D. Cahan, and J. Grant, eds. 2006. *When science encounters the child: Education, parenting, and child welfare in 20th-century America.* New York: Teachers College Press.

Beck, L. F., and A. I. Greenspan. 2008. Special report from the CDC: Why don't more children walk to school? *Journal of Safety Research* 39:449–452.

Beck, U. 1992. *Risk society: Towards a new modernity.* London: Sage Publications.

Behavior Q&A. 2001. *Parents* 76:9, 36–37.

―――. 2006. *Parents* 81:3, 42–43.

Bell, T. H. 1976. Teaching the basics at home. *Parents' Magazine and Better Family Living* 51:3, 37–38, 64.

Best, J. 1987. Rhetoric in claims-making: Constructing the missing children problem. *Social Problems* 34:101–121.

―――. 1990. *Threatened children: Rhetoric and concern about child-victims.* Chicago: University of Chicago Press.

―――. 1994. Troubling children: Children and social problems. In *Troubling children: Studies of children and social problems*, edited by J. Best, 3–19. New York: Aldine de Gruyter.

Birnbaum, S. 1986. My teenage daughter was an alcoholic. *Good Housekeeping* 226:5, 28–30.

Black, A. 1929. Every family needs a traffic cop. *Children, The Parents Magazine* 4:3, 19.

Black, D. J. 1998. *The social structure of right and wrong.* San Diego: Academic Press.

Blakely, K. S. 1994. Parents' conceptions of social dangers to children in the urban environment. *Children's Environments* 11:16–25.

Blau, S. 1963. Help your child like himself. *Parents' Magazine and Better Homemaking* 38:12, 37–38, 62–63.

Blumenthal, R. 2005. Girl with cancer reunites with family as state gives up custody. *New York Times*, November 4, 1995, A16.

Boocock, S. S., and K. A. Scott. 2005. *Kids in context: The sociological study of children and childhoods.* Lanham, Md.: Rowman & Littlefield.

Bradley, R. H., R. F. Corwyn, H. P. McAdoo, and C. G. Coll. 2001. The home environments of children in the United States. Part I: Variations by age, ethnicity, and poverty status. *Child Development* 72:1844–1867.

Brecher, R., and E. Brecher. 1961. You can trust your town's teens. *The Parents' Magazine* 36:3, 54–55, 111–113.

Brody, G. H., and D. L. Flor. 1998. Maternal resources, parenting practices, and child competence in rural, single-parent African American families. *Child Development* 69:803–816.

Brooks, R. 2001. Can-do kids. *Parents* 76:3, 134–139.

Brothers, J. 1966. Fit the chore to the child. *Good Housekeeping* 206:11, 56–59, 61.

―――. 1976. Ask Dr. Joyce Brothers. *Good Housekeeping* 216:11, 90–93.

Brown, A., and D. Fields. 2006. The 20 commandments of toddler discipline. *Parents* 81:9, 46–51.

Brown, B., R. Mackett, Y. Gong, K. Kitazawa, and J. Paskins. 2008. Gender differences in children's pathways to independent mobility. *Children's Geographies* 6:385–401.

Burnham, W. H. 1931. Cultivating a wholesome personality. *The Parents' Magazine* 6:9, 13, 42–43.

Cahan, E. D. 2006. Toward a socially relevant science: Notes on the history of child development research. In *When science encounters the child*, edited by Beatty, Cahan, and Grant, 16–34. New York: Teachers College Press.

Cahill, S. 1990. Childhood and public life: Reaffirming biographical divisions. *Social Problems* 37:390–402.

Cancian, F. M., and S. L. Gordon. 1988. Changing emotion norms in marriage: Love and anger in U.S. women's magazines since 1900. *Gender & Society* 2:308–342.

Cassidy, A. 1996. Beginner manners. *Parents* 71:3, 113–114.

Champlin, H. 1931. The question of punishment. *The Parents' Magazine* 6:3, 22–23, 68.

Childhood/teenage problems. 1936. *The Parents' Magazine* 11:3, 28–29.

———. 1946. *The Parents' Magazine* 21:3.

———. 1951. *The Parents' Magazine* 26:9, 52–53.

Chin, T., and M. Phillips. 2004. Social reproduction and child-rearing practices: Social class, children's agency, and the summer activity gap. *Sociology of Education* 77:185–210.

Christiano, D. 2001. Disciplining in public. *Parents* 76:3, 112–117.

Chudacoff, H. P. 2007. *Children at play: An American history.* New York: New York University Press.

Clarke-Stewart, K. A. 1978. Popular primers for parents. *American Psychologist* 33:359–369.

Collins, D., C. and R. Kearns. 2009. "Mind that child": Childhood, traffic and walking in automobilized space." In *Car troubles: Critical studies of automobility and auto-mobility,* edited by J. Conley and A. T. McLaren, 127–143. Burlington, Vt.: Ashgate.

Collins, D. C. A., and R. A. Kearns. 2001. Under curfew and under seige? Legal geographies of young people." *Geoforum* 32:389–403.

Comer, J. 1981. Parents can be embarrassing. *Parents* 56:9, 108.

———. 1981. Puberty, petulance, and silence. *Parents* 56:3, 111.

———. 1991. Keeping tabs on your kids. *Parents* 66:9, 197.

Connolly, V. L. 1926. Let's look at the home. *Good Housekeeping* 166:11, 24–25, 264, 266, 269–270, 273–274, 276.

Cook, D. T. 2000. The other "child study": Figuring children as consumers in market research, 1910s–1990s. *The Sociological Quarterly* 41:487–507.

———. 2003. Agency, children's consumer culture and the fetal subject: Historical trajectories, contemporary connections. *Consumption, Markets and Culture* 6:115–132.

———. 2004. *The commodification of childhood: The children's clothing industry and the rise of the child consumer.* Durham, N.C.: Duke University Press.

Cooper, H., J. J. Lindsay, B. Nye, and S. Greathouse. 1998. Relationships among attitudes about homework, amount of homework assigned and completed, and student achievement. *Journal of Educational Psychology* 90:70–83.

Corsaro, W. A. 1997. *The sociology of childhood.* Thousand Oaks, Calif.: Pine Forge.

———. 2003. *"We're friends, right?": Inside kids' cultures.* Washington, D.C.: Joseph Henry Press.

Costello, J. 1981. The golden rule. *Parents* 56:9, 104.

Cross, G. 2004. *The cute and the cool: Wondrous innocence and modern American children's culture.* New York: Oxford University Press.

———. 2004. Wondrous innocence: Print advertising and the origins of permissive child rearing in the US. *Journal of Consumer Culture* 4:183–201.

David, J. 1951. Behavior clinic for normal children. *The Parents' Magazine* 26:9, 186–196.

Day, R. D., G. W. Peterson, and C. McCracken. 1998. Predicting spanking of younger and older children by mothers and fathers. *Journal of Marriage and the Family* 60:79–94.

Demos, J. 1997. Oedipus and America: Historical perspectives on the reception of psychoanalysis in the United States. In *Inventing the psychological: Toward a cultural history of emotional life in America*, edited by Pfister and Schnog, 63–78. New Haven, Conn.: Yale University Press.

Dobrish, C. M. 1971. Can values really be learned at school?" *Parents' Magazine and Better Family Living* 46:9, 44, 66–68.

Dodson, L., and J. Dickert. 2004. Girls' family labor in low-income households: A decade of qualitative research." *Journal of Marriage and the Family* 66: 318–332.

Dorey, A.K.V. 1999. *Better baby contests: The scientific quest for perfect childhood health in the early twentieth century.* Jefferson, N.C.: McFarland and Company.

Durkheim, E. 1984. *The division of labor in society.* New York: The Free Press.

Dye, N. S. 1986. Medicalization of birth. In *The American way of birth*, edited by P. S. Eakins, 21–46. Philadelphia: Temple University Press.

Eberlein, T. 2006. Taming preschool anger. *Parents* 81:3, 153–154.

Ehrenreich, B., and D. English. 2005. *For her own good: Two centuries of the experts' advice to women.* Garden City, N.Y.: Anchor.

Elkind, D. 1971. Sense and nonsense about preschools. *Parents' Magazine and Better Family Living* 46:9.

———. 1991. Boosting self-esteem. *Parents* 66:3, 195.

———. 1991. Clashing over clothes. *Parents* 66:9, 199.

Emirbayer, M., and A. Mische. 1998. What is agency? *American Journal of Sociology* 103:962–1023.

Engel, T. 1956. Do you have grandmother problems? *The Parents' Magazine* 31:3, 42–43, 70–73.

English, O. S. 1951. Father's changing role. *The Parents' Magazine* 26:9, 44–45, 153–155.

Epstein, R. 1996. Whose chore is it, anyway? *Parents* 71:3, 85–86.

Everyday problems. 1929. *The Parents' Magazine* 4:9, 34–35.

Faegre, M. E. 1933. First steps toward self-reliance. *Ladies' Home Journal* 50:31.

Family clinic. 1971. *Parents' Magazine and Better Family Living* 46:9, 28–29.

Feingold, S. 1951. Raise good citizens. *The Parents' Magazine* 26:9, 58.

Finkelhor, D., and L. Jones. 2006. Why have child maltreatment and child victimization declined? *Journal of Social Issues* 62:685–716.

Flynn, C. P. 1994. Regional differences in attitudes toward corporal punishment. *Journal of Marriage and the Family* 56:314–324.

———. 1998. To spank or not to spank: The effect of situation and age of child on support for corporal punishment. *Journal of Family Violence* 13:21–37.

Forehand, R., and B. A. Kotchick. 1996. Cultural diversity: A wake-up call for parent training. *Behavior Therapy* 27:187–206.

Foster, A. 1956. Get them off to a happy start. *The Parents' Magazine* 31:9, 56, 122.

Franklin, E. 1991. A secret too terrible to remember. *Good Housekeeping* 231:11, 82–86.

Friedman, J. 1996. Charity begins at home. *Parents* 71:3, 89–93.

Fuchs, S. 2007. Agency (and intention). In Blackwell Encyclopedia of Sociology, ed. G. Ritzer. Blackwell Reference Online. http://www.blackwellreference .com/.

Furedi, F. 2002. *Paranoid parenting: Why ignoring the experts may be best for your child.* Chicago: Chicago Review Press.

Furstenberg, F. F. 1993. How families manage risk and opportunity in dangerous neighborhoods. In *Sociology and the public agenda*, edited by W. J. Wilson, 231–258. Newbury Park, Calif.: Sage.

Gager, C. T., T. M. Cooney, and K. T. Call. 1999. The effects of family characteristics and time use on teenagers' household labor. *Journal of Marriage and the Family* 61:982–994.

Galbraith, J. K. 1998. *The affluent society.* Boston: Houghton Mifflin.

Garey, A., and T. Arendell. 2001. Children, work, and family: Some thoughts on "mother blame." In *Working families: The transformation of the American home*, edited by R. Hertz and N. Marshall, 293–303. Berkeley: University of California Press.

Gentile, S. and Leonard, J. 1991. Mom's weekend off. *Good Housekeeping* 231:5, 62–65.

Gibbs, N., K. Ball, A. Silver, E. Dias, and S. Yan. 2009. Can these parents be saved? *Time* 174:52–57.

Giddens, A. 2003. *Runaway world: How globalization is reshaping our lives.* New York: Routledge.

Giles-Sims, J., M. A. Straus, and D. B. Sugarman. 1995. Child, maternal, and family characteristics associated with spanking. *Family Relations* 44:170–176.

Granovetter, M. S. 1973. The strength of weak ties. *American Journal of Sociology* 78:1360–1380.

Grant, J. 1998. *Raising baby by the book: The education of American mothers.* New Haven, Conn.: Yale University Press.

Great projects for teens without summer work. 1971. *Good Housekeeping* 211: 5, 190.

Greenspan, S. 1996. From savage to sweetheart. *Parents* 71:9, 93–94.

Greven, P. J. 1991. *Spare the child: The religious roots of punishment and the psychological impact of physical abuse.* New York: Random House.

Halbert, B. 1929. Every boy needs tools. *The Parents' Magazine* 4:9, 24, 53–24.

Halles, D. 2001. Too sexy, too soon? *Parents* 76:3, 92–96.

Hanauer, H. 1981. Teenagers and credit cards. *Good Housekeeping* 221:11, 141–146.

Hardyment, C. 2007. *Dream babies: Childcare advice from John Locke to Gina Ford.* London: Francis Lincoln.

Hartley-Brewer, E. 2006. Tune in to your child. *Scholastic Parent & Child* 14:59–60.

Hattwick, L. A. 1941. The young child needs companionship. *The Parents' Magazine* 16:9, 24–25, 96–97.

Hays, S. 1994. Structure and agency and the sticky problem of culture. *Sociological Theory* 12:57–72.

———. 1996. *The cultural contradictions of motherhood*. New Haven: Yale University Press.

———. 2003. *Flat broke with children: Women in the age of welfare reform*. New York: Oxford University Press.

Hearst Communications, Inc. 2010. Good Housekeeping media kit. http://www.ghmediakit.com

Herman, E. 1995. *The romance of American psychology: Political culture in the age of experts*. Berkeley: University of California Press.

Hicks, J. A. 1931. Don't nag about manners. *The Parents' Magazine* 6:9, 20, 38.

Hill, S. A., and J. Sprague. 1999. Parenting in black and white families: The interaction of gender with race and class. *Gender and Society* 13:480–502.

Hillman, M., J. Adams, and J. Whitelegg. 1990. *One false move . . . : A study of children's independent mobility*. London: Policy Studies Institute.

Hofer, B. K., C. Souder, E. K. Kennedy, N. Fullman, and K. Hurd. 2009. The electronic tether: Communication and parental monitoring during the college years. In *Who's watching?: Daily practices of surveillance among contemporary families*, edited by M. K. Nelson and A. I. Garey, 277–294. Nashville: Vanderbilt University Press.

Hofferth, S. L., and J. F. Sandberg. 2001. How American children spend their time. *Journal of Marriage and the Family* 63:295–308.

Holt, L. E. 1951. The obese child. *Good Housekeeping* 191:11, 48–50.

———. 1956. The problem eater. *Good Housekeeping* 196:11, 34–37.

Hulbert, A. 2003. *Raising America: Experts, parents, and a century of advice about children*. New York: Vintage Books.

Hunt, S. 1996. I couldn't reach my daughter. *Good Housekeeping* 236:11, 100–105.

I couldn't control my teenage daughter. 1986. *Good Housekeeping* 226:11, 38–41.

Illouz, E. 2003. *Oprah Winfrey and the glamour of misery: An essay on popular culture*. New York: Columbia University Press.

———. 2007. *Cold intimacies: The making of emotional capitalism*. Malden, Mass.: Polity.

———. 2008. *Saving the modern soul: Therapy, emotions, and the culture of self-help*. Berkeley: University of California Press.

Imber, J., ed. 2004. *Therapeutic culture: Triumph and defeat*. New Brunswick, N.J.: Transaction.

Israeloff, R. 1991. What it feels like to be . . . two. *Parents* September, 84–90.

———. 1996. When your child acts up at school. *Parents* 71:3, 66–69.

It worked for me! 1996. *Parents* 71:3, 17.

Jackson, S., and S. Scott. 1999. Risk anxiety and the social construction of childhood. In *Risk and sociocultural theory: New directions and perspectives*, edited by D. Lupton, 86–107. New York: Cambridge University Press.

James, A., and A. Prout. 1995. Hierarchy, boundary and agency: Toward a theoretical perspective on childhood. *Sociological Studies of Children* 7:77–99.

———, ed. 1997. *Constructing and reconstructing childhood: Contemporary issues in the sociological study of childhood*. Washington, D.C.: Taylor & Francis.

Johnson, H. B., ed. 2010. *Children and youth speak for themselves*. Bingley, UK: Emerald.

Jones, D. J., R. Forehand, C. O'Connell, L. Armistead, and G. Brody. 2005. Mothers' perceptions of neighborhood violence and mother-reported monitoring of African American children: An examination of the moderating role of perceived support. *Behavior Therapy* 36:25–34.

Katz, C. 1993. Growing girls/closing circles: Limits on the spaces of knowing in rural Sudan and US cities. In *Full circles: Geographies of women over the life course*, edited by C. Katz and J. Monk. London: Routledge.

———. 1998. Disintegrating developments: Global economic restructuring and the eroding ecologies of youth. In *Cool places: Geographies of youth cultures*, edited by T. Skelton and G. Valentine, 130–144. New York: Routledge.

Kaufman, J., and J. Gabler. 2004. Cultural capital and the extracurricular activities of girls and boys in the college attainment process. *Poetics* 32:145–168.

Kelley, M. L., T. G. Power, and D. D. Wimbush. 1992. Determinants of disciplinary practices in low-income black mothers. *Child Development* 63:573–582.

Kenyon, J. 1926. Discipline. *Good Housekeeping* 166:11, 98.

———. 1938. *Healthy babies are happy babies: A complete handbook for modern mothers*. Boston: Little, Brown & Co.

———. 1946. Fussy eaters. *Good Housekeeping* 186:5, 65–69.

Kiley, D. 1981. "But mom, everyone else does it!" *Good Housekeeping* 221:5, 133–138.

Kirkpatrick, J. D. 1946. A child of divorce. *The Parents' Magazine* 21:9, 26.

Kleiber, D., and G. Powell. 2005. Historical change in leisure activities during after-school hours. In *Organized activities as contexts of development: Extracurricular activities, after-school and community programs*, edited by J. L. Mahoney, R. W. Larson, and J. S. Eccles, 23–44. Mahwah, N.J.: Lawrence Erlbaum Associates.

Konrad, W. 2006. More tests = more anxiety. *Good Housekeeping* 246:11, 109–112.

Kotchick, B. A., and R. Forehand. 2002. Putting parenting in perspective: A discussion of the contextual factors that shape parenting practices. *Journal of Child and Family Studies* 11:255–269.

Kuczynski, L., L. Harach, and S. C. Bernardini. 1999. Psychology's child meets sociology's child: Agency, influence and power in parent-child relationships. In *Through the eyes of the child: Revisioning children as active agents of family life*, edited by C. L. Shehan, 21–52. Stamford, Conn.: JAI Press.

Kurz, D. 2009. "I trust them but I don't trust them": Issues and dilemmas in monitoring teenagers. In *Who's watching?: Daily practices of surveillance among contemporary families*, edited by M. K. Nelson and A. I. Garey, 260–276. Nashville: Vanderbilt University Press.

Kutner, L. 1996. Ask the expert. *Parents* 71:3, 72, 76–77.

Ladd-Taylor, M., ed. 1986. *Raising a baby the government way: Mothers' letters to the Children's Bureau, 1915–1932*. New Brunswick, N.J.: Rutgers University Press.

Lamborn, S. D., S. M. Dornbusch, and L. Steinberg. 1996. Ethnicity and community context as moderators of the relations between family decision making and adolescent adjustment. *Child Development* 67:283–301.

Lareau, A. 2003. *Unequal childhoods: Class, race, and family life*. Berkeley: University of California Press.

Lareau, A., and E. B. Weininger. 2008. Time, work, and family life: Reconceptualizing gendered time patterns through the case of children's organized activities. *Sociological Forum* 23:419–454.

Larson, R. W., and S. Verma. 1999. How children and adolescents spend time across the world: Work, play, and developmental opportunities. *Psychological Bulletin* 125:701–736.

Leonard, J. 1996. Raising responsible kids. *Parents* 71:3, 79–82.

Lerner, R., and C. Omen. 1996. Keeping tabs without being a nag. *Parents* 71:9, 111–112.

Levey, H. 2009. Pageant princesses and math whizzes: Understanding children's activities as a form of children's work. *Childhood* 16:195–212.

———. 2010. Outside class: A historical analysis of American children's competitive activities. In *Childhood in American Society*, edited by K. Sternheimer, 342–354. Boston: Allyn & Bacon.

———. 2010. Trophies, triumphs, and tears: Children's experiences with competitive activities. In *Children and youth speak for themselves: Sociological studies of children and youth*, edited by H. B. Johnson, 319–349. Volume 13. Bingley, UK: Emerald.

Levine, B. 2001. Is your marriage missing action? *Parents* 76:9, 143–147.

Levine, K. 2001. Big kid discipline. *Parents* 76:9, 137–138.

Levine, M., and A. Levine. 1992. *Helping children: A social history*. New York: Oxford Univerisity Press.

Littledale, C. S. 1941. What to do about the comics. *The Parents' Magazine* 16:3, 26–27.

Love and marriage. 1981. *Parents* 56:3, 20–21.

———. 1991. *Parents* 66:3, 46–47.

Manke, B., B. L. Seery, A. C. Crouter, and S. M. McHale. 1994. The three corners of domestic labor: Mothers', fathers', and children's weekday and weekend housework. *Journal of Marriage and the Family* 56:657–668.

The many meanings of food. 1976. *Parents' Magazine and Better Family Living* 51:3, 48, 56–58.

Marks, J. 1986. Joshua, Cara, & Anne: Raising a child who's different. *Parents* 61:9, 90–92,172–176.

Marshall, H. 1991. The social construction of motherhood: An analysis of childcare and parenting manuals. In *Motherhood: Meanings, practices and ideologies*, edited by A. Pheonix, A. Woollett, and E. Lloyd, 66–85. London: Sage.

Martin, S. L., S. M. Lee, and R. Lowry. 2007. National prevalence and correlates of walking and bicycling to school. *American Journal of Preventive Medicine* 33:98–105.

May, L. 1995. Challenging medical authority: The refusal of treatment by Christian Scientists. *The Hastings Center Report* 25:15–21.

Mayall, B. 2002. *Towards a sociology for childhood: Thinking from children's lives*. Philadelphia: Open University Press.

McDonald, N. C. 2007. Active transportation to school: Trends among US schoolchildren, 1969–2001. *American Journal of Preventive Medicine* 32:509–516.

McKeever, W. A. 1911. First lesson of obedience. *Good Housekeeping* 53:9, 342–344.

Mechling, J. 1975. Advice to historians on advice to mothers. *Journal of Social History* 9:44–63.

Medrich, E. A., J. A. Roizen, V. Rubin, and S. Buckley. 1982. *The serious business of growing up: A study of children's lives outside of school.* Berkeley: University of California Press.

Mellon, E. 1936. What to do when your baby cries. *The Parents' Magazine* 11:9, 24–25, 81.

———. 1946. Why won't they be neat? *The Parents' Magazine* 21:3, 45, 83–86.

Meredith Corporation. 2009. Parents media kit. http://www.meredith.com/mediakit/parents

Meyers, G. C. 1929. The livable lovable child. *Children: The Parents' Magazine* 4:3, 23–24.

Miller, P. 2005. Useful and priceless children in contemporary welfare states. *Social Politics* 12:3–41.

Mills, S. 2004. *Discourse.* New York: Routledge.

Milner, M., Jr. 2004. *Freaks, geeks, and cool kids: American teenagers, schools, and the culture of consumption.* New York: Routledge.

Mintz, S. 2004. *Huck's raft: A history of American childhood.* Cambridge, Mass.: Belknap Press.

Mirrell, S. S. 1996. Playing favorites. *Parents* 71:9, 116–118.

Morris, B. B. 1996. The dawdler dilemma. *Parents* 71:9, 66–69.

Morrow, V. 1995. Invisible children?: Toward a reconceptualization of childhood dependency and responsibility. *Sociological Studies of Children* 7:207–230.

———. 2008. "Responsible children and children's responsibilities? Sibling caretaking and babysitting by school-age children." In *Responsibility, law, and the family,* edited by J. Bridgeman, H. Keating, and C. Lind, 105–123. Burlington, Vt.: Ashgate.

Mother's girl. 1966. *Good Housekeeping* 206:11, 74–81.

Murphy, A. 2001. Behavior Q&A. *Parents* 76:3, 61.

My husband was a terrible father. 1981. *Good Housekeeping* 221:5, 36–40.

Myers, J. E. B. 2006. *Child protection in America: Past, present, and future.* New York: Oxford University Press.

Nathanson, L. 1996. The case against baby fat. *Parents* 71:9, 45–48.

Nelson, M. K. 2008. Watching children: Describing the use of baby monitors on Epinions.com. *Journal of Family Issues* 29:516–538.

Nelson, M. K., and R. Schutz. 2007. Day care differences and the reproduction of social class. *Journal of Contemporary Ethnography* 36:281–317.

Oakley, A. 1994. Women and children first and last: Parallels and differences between children's and women's studies. In *Children's childhoods: Observed and experienced,* edited by B. Mayall, 15–20. London: Falmer Press.

Okrent, D., M. M. Buechner, N. Christian, W. Cole, M. Sieger, N. Harbert, M. Krantz, and E. Marshall. 1999. Raising kids online. *Time* 153:38.

Orcate, P. J. 1961. Dangers from strangers. *The Parents' Magazine* 36:9, 87, 170–172.

Orellana, M. F. 2001. The work kids do: Mexican and Central American immigrant children's contributions to households and schools in California. *Harvard Educational Review* 71:366–389.

Our son was failing in school. 1971. *Good Housekeeping* 172:5, 16.

Pain, R. 2001. Gender, race, age and fear in the city. *Urban Studies* 38:899–913.

Parental problems and ways to meet them. 1931. *The Parents' Magazine* 6:3, 40.

———. 1931. *The Parents' Magazine* 6:9, 36.

Parusel, S., and A. T. McLaren. 2010. Cars before kids: Automobility and the illusion of school traffic safety. *Canadian Review of Sociology* 47:129–147.

Peters, M. F. 2007. Parenting of young children in black families. In *Black families*, edited by H. P. McAdoo, 203–218. Thousand Oaks, Calif.: Sage.

Pfaff, L. G. 2006. Stop school anxiety! *Parents* 81:3, 166.

Pfister, J. 1997. Glamorizing the psychological: The politics of the performances of modern psychological identities. In *Inventing the psychological*, edited by J. Pfister and N. Schnog, 167–213. New Haven: Yale University Press.

Pfister, J., and N. Schnog, ed. 1997. *Inventing the psychological: Toward a cultural history of emotional life in America*. New Haven: Yale University Press.

Picker, L. 2005. And now, the hard part. *Newsweek* 145:46–50.

Pillsbury, W. H. 1941. Our schools prepare for tomorrow. *The Parents' Magazine* 16:9, 14.

Pitts, A. F. 1929. Make it the best year ever. *The Parents' Magazine* 4:9, 15, 44–47.

Pollack, J. H. 1966. Girl dropouts. *Parents' Magazine and Better Homemaking* 41:9, 91, 113–115.

Post, P. 2006. Behavior Q&A. *Parents* 81:9, 52.

Pratt, G. R. 1931. Nervous breakdowns . . . a teenage danger. *The Parents' Magazine* 6:3, 14–15, 50–51.

Preston, G. H. 1929. Fit your child for living. *The Parents' Magazine* 4:9, 18, 62–64.

Pugh, A. J. 2009. *Longing and belonging: Parents, children, and consumer culture*. Berkeley: University of California Press.

Putnam, R. D. 2000. *Bowling alone: The collapse and revival of American community*. New York: Simon & Schuster.

Q&A. 1981. *Parents* 56:9, 12–14.

———. 1986. *Parents* 61:9, 39–46.

———. 1991. *Parents* 66:9, 34–49.

Quirke, L. 2006. "Keeping young minds sharp": Children's cognitive stimulation and the rise of parenting magazines, 1959–2003. *Canadian Review of Sociology* 43:387–406.

Qvortrup, J. 1995. From useful to useful: The historical continuity of children's constructive participation. *Sociological Studies of Children* 7:49–76.

Roberts, F. 1981. Start school right. *Parents* 56:9, 106.

Rolock, N., and M. F. Testa. 2005. Indicated child abuse and neglect reports: Is the investigation process racially biased? In *Race matters in child welfare: The overrepresentation of African American children in the system*, edited by D. M. Derezotes, J. Poertner, and M. F. Testa, 119–130. Washington, D.C.: CWLA Press,

Rosen, P. 2006. How to raise a really good kid. *Parents* 81:3, 126–128, 196–197.

Russoto, C. 1956. Don't make your child a fussy eater. *The Parents' Magazine* 31:9, 52, 64.

Rutherford, M. B. 2004. Authority, autonomy, and ambivalence: Moral choice in twentieth-century commencement speeches. *Sociological Forum* 19:583–609.

———. 2004. Sacralization of a secular ideal: The ascendancy of choice in ceremonial discourse. Ph.D. diss., University of Virginia.

Rutherford, M. B., and S. Gallo-Cruz. 2008. Selling the ideal birth: Rationalization and re-enchantment in the marketing of maternity care. In *Patients, consumers and civil society*, edited by S. M. Chambre and M. Goldner, 75–98. Bingley, UK: Emerald.

Sanson, A., and S. Wise. 2001. Children and parenting: The past hundred years. *Family Matters* 60:1–13.

Sayer, L. C., S. M. Bianchi, and J. P. Robinson. 2004. Are parents investing less in children? Trends in mothers' and fathers' time with children. *American Journal of Sociology* 110:1–43.

Schneider, M. 1996. Raising your child's social IQ. Good Housekeeping 236:5, 83–85.

Schnog, N. 1997. On inventing the psychological. In *Inventing the psychological*, edited by J. Pfister and N. Schnog, 3–16.

School days. 1986. *Parents* 61:9, 58–60.

Schrer, H. 2006. "Are you a good mother? *Good Housekeeping* 246:5, 76–79.

Scott, S., S. Jackson, and K. Backett-Milburn. 1998. Swings and roundabouts: Risk anxiety and the everyday worlds of children. *Sociology* 32:689–705.

Sealander, J. 2003. *The failed century of the child: Governing America's young in the twentieth century.* New York: Cambridge University Press.

Seid, N. 2001. Be an A+ parent. *Parents* 76:9, 201–203.

Selig, D. 2006. The whole child: Social science and race at the White House conference of 1930. In *When science encounters the child*, edited by Beatty, Cahan, and Grant, 136–156. New York: Teachers College Press.

Sennett, R. 1998. *The corrosion of character: The personal consequences of work in the new capitalism.* New York: W. W. Norton.

———. 2006. *The culture of the new capitalism.* New Haven: Yale University Press.

Shahmoon, R. 1991. Happily ever afterschool. *Parents* 66:9, 195.

Sheller, M. 2004. Automotive emotions: Feeling the car. *Theory, Culture, & Society* 21:221–242.

Sherman, V. S. 1967. What injures a child's self-esteem? *PTA Magazine* 61:3, 23–25.

Should my child go to private school? 1966. *Parents' Magazine and Better Homemaking* 41:9, 64–65, 140–141.

Simmel, G. 1971. *On individuality and social forms: Selected writings.* Chicago: University of Chicago Press.

Skenazy, L. 2009. *Free-range kids: Giving our children the freedom we had without going nuts with worry.* San Francisco: Jossey Bass.

Sloan, W., and D. West. 1966. Don't rush your kids into organized sports. *Parents' Magazine and Better Homemaking* 41:9, 79, 88.

Solberg, A. 1997. Negotiating childhood: Changing constructions of age for Norwegian children. In *Hierarchy, boundary, and agency*, edited by James and Prout, 126–144. Washington, D.C.: Taylor and Francis.

Song, M. 1999. *Helping out: Children's labor in ethnic businesses.* Philadelphia: Temple University Press.

Spilsbury, J. C. 2005. "We don't really get to go out in the front yard": Children's home range and neighborhood violence. *Children's Geographies* 3:79–99.

Spock, B. 1946. *The common sense book of baby and child care.* New York: Duell, Sloan and Pearce.

———. 1966. Bringing up children in an age of disenchantment. *Redbook* 126: 2, 20.

Stearns, P. N. 2003. *Anxious parents: A history of modern childrearing in America.* New York: New York University Press.

Stein, C. K. 1956. Your child can be tidy and like it. *The Parents' Magazine* 31:3, 38–39, 120–122.

Stevens, M. L. 2001. *Kingdom of children: Culture and controversy in the homeschooling movement.* Princeton: Princeton University Press.

Straus, M. A., and J. H. Stewart. 1999. Corporal punishment by American parents: National data on prevalence, chronicity, severity, and duration, in relation to child and family characteristics. *Clinical Child & Family Psychology Review* 2:55–70.

Strauss, A., and J. Corbin. 1998. *Basics of qualitative research: Techniques and procedures for developing grounded theory.* Thousand Oaks, Calif.: Sage.

Taffel, R. 1998. 5 secrets of good parents. *Parents* 73:7, 108–112.

———. 2001. The Me! Me! Me! Generation. *Parents* 76:3, 104–109.

Tate, H. C. 1946. What kind of high school? *The Parents' Magazine* 21:9, 45, 124.

Teaching children about money. 1966. *Good Housekeeping* 206:5, 176.

Teaching children to handle emergencies. 1966. *Good Housekeeping* 206:11, 188.

Thorne, B. 1987. Re-visioning women and social change: Where are the children? *Gender and Society* 1:85–109.

———. 1993. *Gender play: Boys and girls in school.* New Brunswick, N.J.: Rutgers University Press.

Tönnies, F. 2001. *Community and civil society.* New York: Cambridge University Press.

Turmel, A. 2008. *A historical sociology of childhood: Developmental thinking, categorization and graphic visualization.* Cambridge: Cambridge University Press.

Tyre, P., J. Scelfo, B. Kantrowitz, C. Skipp, V. Juarez, C. Sulmers, A. Markels, M. Nelson, and J. Sieder. 2004. The power of no. *Newsweek* 144:42–51.

Urwin, C., and E. Sharland. 1992. From bodies to minds in childcare literature: Advice to parents in interwar Britain. In *In the name of the child: Health and welfare, 1880–1940,* edited by R. Cooter. New York: Routledge,

Valentine, G. 1996. Children should be seen and not heard: The production and transgression of adults' public space. *Urban Geography* 17:205–220.

———. 1997. "Oh yes I can." "Oh no you can't": Children and parents' understandings of kids' competence to negotiate public space safely. *Antipode* 29:65–89.

———. 2004. *Public space and the culture of childhood.* Burlington, Vt.: Ashgate.

Valentine, G., and J. McKendrick. 1997. Children's outdoor play: Exploring parental concerns about children's safety and the changing nature of childhood. *Geoforum* 28:219–235.

Vanderbeck, R. M., and J. H. J. Johnson. 2000. "That's the only place where you can hang out": Urban young people and the space of the mall. *Urban Geography* 21:5–25.

Vaughn, J. 1929. How to get obedience. *The Parents' Magazine* 4:9, 16–20.

Veitch, J., J. Salmon, and K. Ball. 2007. Children's perceptions of the use of public open spaces for active free-play. *Children's Geographies* 5:409–422.

Walker, N. 2000. *Shaping our mothers' world: American women's magazines.* Jackson: University Press of Mississippi.

Weber, M. 1946. *From Max Weber: Essays in sociology.* New York: Oxford University Press.

———. 1978. *Economy and society: An outline of interpretive sociology.* Berkeley: University of California Press.

Weintraub, J. The theory and politics of the public/private distinction. In *Public and private in thought and practice: Perspectives on a grand dichotomy,* edited by J. Weintraub and K. Kumar, 1–42. Chicago: University of Chicago Press.

Weiss, N. P. 1977. Mother, the invention of necessity: Dr. Benjamin Spock's baby and child care. *American Quarterly* 29:519–546.

Weissbourd, B. 1986. Help your child feel great. *Parents* 61:3, 174.

Wertz, R. W., and D. C. Wertz. 1989. *Lying in: A history of childbirth in America.* New Haven, Conn.: Yale University Press.

Wessel, M. A. 1976. New mothers want to know. *Parents' Magazine and Better Family Living* 51:3, 24–25, 28–29.

What I learned from my first child. 1971. *Good Housekeeping* 211:11, 114–118.

When a child is missing. 1951. *Good Housekeeping* 191:5, 51.

When they are eight. 1946. *The Parents' Magazine* 16:3, 41, 79–80.

Wight, V. R., J. Price, S. M. Bianchi, and B. R. Hunt. 2009. The time use of teenagers. *Social Science Research* 38:792–809.

Williams, K. T. 1951. So much to learn before six. *The Parents' Magazine* 26:3, 32–33, 56–57.

Wolf, A. W. M. 1941. New ways for mothers. *Parents* 11:3, 18–19.

Woolworth, S. 2006. When physicians and psychologists parted ways: Professional turf wars in child study and special education, 1910–1920. In *When science encounters the child,* edited by Beatty, Cahan, and Grant, 96–115. New York: Teachers College Press.

Wrigley, J. 1989. Do young children need intellectual stimulation? Experts' advice to parents, 1900–1985. *History of Education Quarterly* 29:41–75.

Wyckoff, E. 1929. Obedience, the vanishing virtue. *Children: The Parents' Magazine* 4:3, 28.

Zelizer, V. A. 1985. *Pricing the priceless child: The changing social value of children.* New York: Basic Books.

———. 2005. The priceless child revisited. In *Studies in modern childhood: Society, agency and culture,* edited by J. Qvortrup, 184–200. London: Palgrave.

Index

abuse, 26, 27, 159, 173n52. *See also* corporal punishment; spanking
academic advice, 6
academic success, 183n42; college and, 109–110, 157. *See also* education; school
accomplishments of children, 118, 126–130, 133
active listening, 139, 143–145
Adler, Patricia, 109, 131
Adler, Peter, 109, 131
adolescents, 54, 157; behaviorism and, 41; chores and, 93, 98; community involvement of, 114, 117; defiance of, 52; emotional control of, 144–145; emotional development advice about, 32, 125, 126; empathy for, 145; mobility of, 71, 75, 117; supervision of, 28, 78–79, 117, 119, 153. *See also* older children; teens
adult children, 155
adult spaces, 159. *See also* public spaces
advice, 16, 28–36; academic, 6; back-to-school, 62–64, 93, 103; contradictory, 4, 25; experts and, 10, 13–14, 22–25, 29, 39, 150; gender and, 35–36; infant care and, 30–31; on Internet, 29, 32–33, 36; interpersonal, 29, 31–32; magazines and, 31–32, 36–38; marriage, 134; medical, 6, 15, 21; older children and, 31–32; one-size-fits-all, 23–24,

36–37, 150–151; printed, 29; range of, 28–29; religious books and, 34–35; sleep and, 30–31; social class and, 34–36; teens and, 23, 32–33; television and, 35. *See also* authority/authorities; lay advice; magazines
African American families, 26, 173n52. *See also* race; white families
age, 78–79; chores and, 98; feminist literature and, 100, 155–156; of growing up, 85–87; mobility autonomy and, 75–76, 85–86; power and, 140; of respondents, 168; usefulness and, 101
age-grading of developmental stages, 123–125
age-integrated play, 78–79
agency, 7, 8–10; changing meanings of, 149, 165; children's responsibility and, 101–102; defiance as natural expression of, 51, 101; education and, 105; emotional, 120, 121, 123–126, 137, 141, 144, 147; freedom of expression and, 53, 57, 120, 134, 139–140, 152; of mothers to interpret advice, 18. *See also* autonomy
allowances, 96
American Medical Association, 16
American Pediatric Society, 16
Ames, Louise Bates, 124

About the Author

Markella Rutherford is an assistant professor of sociology at Wellesley College in Massachusetts.

CPSIA information can be obtained at www.ICGtesting.com
Printed in the USA
266412BV00002B/3/P